Reason in Law

Reason in Law

FIFTH EDITION

Lief H. Carter J.D., Ph.D.
The Colorado College

An imprint of Addison Wesley Longman, Inc.

New York • Reading, Massachusetts • Menlo Park, California • Harlow, England
Don Mills, Ontario • Sydney • Mexico City • Madrid • Amsterdam

Executive Editor: Pam Gordon
Acquisitions Editor: Peter Glovin
Associate Editor: Jessica Bayne
Marketing Manager: Suzanne Daghlian
Project Coordination and Text Design: Electronic Publishing Services Inc., NYC
Cover Designer: John Callahan
Cover Photo: PhotoDisc, Inc.
Full Service Production Manager: Valerie L. Zaborski
Manufacturing Manager: Hilda Koparanian
Electronic Page Makeup: Electronic Publishing Services Inc., NYC
Printer and Binder: Maple-Vail Book Manufacturing Group
Cover Printer: Coral Graphic Services, Inc.

For permission to use copyrighted material, grateful acknowledgment is made to the copyright holders on p. 187, which are hereby made part of this copyright page.

Library of Congress Cataloging-in-Publication Data
Reason in Law, Fifth Edition
Carter, Lief H.
    Reason in law / Lief H. Carter, — 5th ed.
        p.   cm
    Includes index.
    ISBN 0-321-01111-2
    1. Law—United States—Methodology.   2. Law—United States—
Interpretation and construction.   3. Law and politics.   I. Title.
KF380.C325   1997   97-35721
349.73'01--dc21   CIP

ISBN 0-321-01111-2

12345678910—MA—00999897

For Nancy, always

Contents

Preface

The Fifth Edition of this book takes it into its third decade. With so much experience, both mine with more than a thousand students and that of literally dozens of outside reviewers, the time may have come to say here more directly than before what this book is and does.

First, *Reason in Law* makes a strong and distinctive argument. Like legal argument itself, it stakes out a position and invites readers to accept and criticize it. For those academics who care about labels, my argument is "postmodern." Reality does not lie around "out there" waiting to be discovered. We construct reality through the languages we use to talk about our experiences and our relationships. We continuously construct our legal reality as we talk about the law. People in all sorts of situations talk about law in all sorts of ways. Legal reasoning, one of many such ways, describes the way that lawyers and judges talk "publicly" and formally about the law. It is not the "correct" way, or even necessarily the best way, to talk about the law. However, legal reasoning is the way that those with official legal authority talk about law. Hence legal reasoning describes a particularly powerful set of legal realities. In the liberal democracy we inhabit, those of us who don't hold legal power nevertheless retain the civic right and duty to decide whether we accept the realities that official law talk creates. This book seeks to give readers the tools for doing that job.

Second, while its theme is postmodern, this book makes what appears just now to be rather an old-fashioned demand. Readers must actually read this book, slowly and carefully, and learn—memorize!—its main assertions, chapter-by-chapter. As a college teacher in the age of high-speed information bits and bites, I'm acutely aware that reading no longer plays the central role it once did in the process of self-education. I'm sure that people across history have mastered many wisdoms without reading about them. I'm constantly amazed at the wisdom of expert basketball and hockey players! But to master law, one cannot avoid old-fashioned reading. This is because, unlike the "body language" of basketball or the intuitive processes of mastering computer programs, formal law speaks through written texts, and legal realities exist only to the extent that people read these texts and understand them.

Finally, this book falls into no specific academic or curricular category. Law is political, and so this book is about politics. But law, and hence this book, also wrestles with philosophical and ethical and scientific and sociological questions—indeed with just about every question imaginable. I think of this book as offering its own small version of a liberal arts education. Many students over the years have come to me at the end of my legal reasoning course to say that, for the first time, they felt they were actually getting the college education they had imagined when they came to college from high school. More than a few students, having gone on to law school, have written or appeared at my office door to announce that they learned more about law in this book than they did in three years of law school. So please read this book carefully, and with an open, and expectant, and critical mind.

As with the prior editions, I have been blessed in preparing this edition by the probing and most helpful comments of outside reviewers: Robert A. Carp, The University of Houston; Michael McCann, University of Washington; Lee S. Weinberg, University of Pittsburgh; O'Linnel Finley, Sr., University of Alabama; Susan Adair Dwyer-Shick, Pacific Lutheran University; Peter Lehman, University of Southern Maine; Nancy Sanders, University of South Florida, Christopher Markwood, University of Central Oklahoma; Drew Lanier, University of North Texas. I've made many clarifications and changes based on their suggestions. While I know I'll never get this book "right," these reviewers have certainly helped make it better. To those named here and those I've thanked by name in prior editions, and to all the unnamed friends and strangers whose work and play nourish and educate me, go my deepest thanks.

Manitou Springs, Colorado
March 22, 1997

About the Author

Lief Carter grew up in the Seattle area in the age of "innocent" Rock 'n Roll (the 1950s). He earned his A.B. from Harvard College (1962) and his law degree from Harvard Law School (1965). The Vietnam War ended his career as a legal practitioner just as it started. He served in the Peace Corps (Bolivia) as an alternative form of service in 1966–1967 and then returned to graduate school at the University of California, Berkeley, where he earned his Ph.D. in political science (1972). His dissertation received the Corwin Award of the American Political Science Association. He taught at the University of Georgia from 1973 until 1995, when he became the McHugh Family Distinguished Professor at the Colorado College. In addition to Reason in Law, he has published books on criminal prosecution, administrative law, and theories of constitutional interpretation. His most recent publication, an article in Law and Social Inquiry titled "Supreme Fictions," reviews the ways in which judicial opinions can and cannot fairly be called "fictional." He currently lives in Manitou Springs, Colorado.

CHAPTER 1

What Legal Reasoning Is, and Why It Matters

I have grown to see that the [legal] process in its highest reaches is not discovery, but creation.
—BENJAMIN N. CARDOZO

They ain't nuthin' until I calls 'em.
—ATTRIBUTED TO UMPIRE BILL KLEM

AN OVERVIEW OF LAW AND POLITICS

Readers who use this book to explore legal reasoning for the first time deserve some signposts at the start of their journey, for this book does not take some roads you might expect it to travel. First, this is not a "prelaw" book. I have not written it to teach people how to be lawyers, how to pass law school admissions tests or bar exams, or how to get rich. Second, this book does not exhaustively review all the scholarship on its subject, much of which is technical and geared toward a professional audience of jurisprudents. Instead, underneath this exploration of legal reasoning lies a study of politics and power. Legal reasoning serves simultaneously as the velvet glove covering the fist of judicial power and as the sincerest expression of our ideals of justice and of community.[1]

---

[1] "Community" can mean many different things, depending on the context in which people use this (or any) word. We can speak of a community of Madonna fans and of Kevin Bacon fans. For my purposes here, community means the physical space that courts rule. California courts, for example, speak on matters of California law to the community of everyone in California, including prisoners, infants, and illegal aliens, because the California courts have power over all of them. Federal courts speak to the community of all people in the United States.

1

Because readers need to know what legal reasoning is in order to see clearly its political significance, I leave my main analysis of the political character of law and legal reasoning until the end of the book. But readers should know now that the legal reasoning road goes there. "Politics" refers to those things people do in communities in order to minimize threats to their well-being. Political behavior sometimes tries to conserve what is and sometimes tries to change what is. People who thrive because their communities support them tend to do political things that preserve their communities. When people do not experience community support, they either give up or do political things to try to change their community.

Law does both of these things. By the end of the book you will have encountered many examples of legal actions that preserve communities and legal actions that change them. Both legal outcomes and legal methods can affect the quality of communities. When people believe that judges cynically manipulate legal language to reach partisan and self-interested political ends, faith in fairness and equity ebbs, motives for social cooperation falter, and communal life becomes more nasty and brutish. The sense of injustice can cause explosive social damage, as the reaction in Los Angeles to the Rodney King verdict in early 1992 suggests. And when the *New York Times* on its front page quotes conservative judges appearing to lay their political ideologies aside in favor of principles of legal reasoning, in the 1992 *Casey* decision reaffirming a woman's right to choose whether to have an abortion, our trust in the virtue of those who govern may increase.[2]

Thus for good political reasons judges debate issues of legal reasoning because they take legal reasoning seriously. It is the way judges exert power. The opinions in the abortion case (*Casey*) defended both the preservation of the woman's right to choose *and* methods of legal reasoning. The dominant coalition justified the result by defending the practice of following questionable precedents for the sake of legal stability and integrity. Robert Bork, however, shot back, on a *New York Times* "op ed" page, that "adherence has never been important in constitutional cases, since only the Court can correct its past constitutional mistakes. . . . 'Institution integrity,' turns out to mean the Court must not overturn a wrong decision if there is angry opposition to it."[3]

Judges, much more than other politicians, take legal reasoning seriously, for it is their language for preserving their authority and trustworthiness.[4] The late Richard John Neuhaus once wrote:

> [T]he law calls life to account. That is to say, the law possesses authority. Without such authority the law is merely a bundle of rules backed up by force; with such authority the law is a power we are bound to acknowledge.[5]

Legal reasoning is a language through which we can debate the rightness and wrongness of what our community is and what we want it to become. Both the best and

---

[2]"Three Who Spoke as One," *New York Times*, June 30, 1992, p. A1.

[3]"Again, a Struggle for the Soul of the Court," July 8, 1992, p. A13.

[4]Thirty years ago academics thought and taught about law "not as a body of rules to be learned, but as man's chief means of political and social control." Charles Howard and Robert Summers, *Law: Its Nature, Function, and Limits* (Englewood Cliffs: Prentice-Hall, 1965), p. iii. Today's metaphors for exploring law are very different. We instinctively resist the technocratic and mechanistic implications of "social control."

[5]"Law and the Rightness (and Wrongness) of Things," (22 *Worldview* 40 (1979).

worst elements of politics pervade all elements of law. We return to this theme at the end of the book.

Many paths connect law and politics. The politics of selecting judges routinely screens out certain marginal voices and interests from the legal process. Protecting either personal or group interests via the legal process costs so much money that the law does not consistently hear the voices of the poor. The law favors those who know from experience how to manipulate the system—landlords, corporate managers, and experienced felons, perhaps—against their more naive or inexperienced opponents. The adversary system, where British and American courts (but not continental courts) leave the task of presenting facts and shaping arguments up to the contending parties, can screen out important social issues. The "rich and famous"—O. J. Simpson, Michael Jackson, and William Kennedy Smith, to name a few recent examples—seem frequently to escape the "clutches" of the law.

These and many more political issues can and do fill many worthy books on legal politics. However, to avoid confusion or frustrated expectations, let me alert students here that legal reasoning, the subject matter of *this* book, does not address these questions directly. We are looking at one part of a much larger picture: Judges, and usually appellate judges, give reasons explaining why they reach a decision, why they conclude that one side should win and the other lose. When we examine judges' legal reasoning, we ask questions like these: Do we trust the integrity of the decision? Do we trust that judges have used their power with integrity? These questions differ from questions about whether we, if we were in their shoes, would decide the same way. If you don't see this distinction clearly now, I hope you will by the end of the book, which is at its deepest level a book about political morality. We know we can't always have it our way, and having it our way isn't always just.[6]

So this book at bottom explores this classic political question: By what standards can we say that someone with whom we disagree nevertheless argues with integrity? Other good books describe what law is; this book explores what law ought to be.

A DEFINITION OF LAW

Law is a language, not simply a collection of rules. What distinguishes law from other ways of making sense of life? Lawyers and judges attempt to prevent and solve other people's problems, but so do physicians, priests, professors, and plumbers. "Problem solving" therefore defines too much. Lawyers and judges work with certain kinds of problems, problems that can lead to conflicts, even physical fights, among people. It is the *kind* of problem with which judges and lawyers work that helps define law.

Contrary to the impression that television drama gives, with its emphasis on courtroom battles, most lawyers generally practice "preventive law." They help people discover ways to reduce their taxes or write valid wills and contracts. They study complex insurance policies and bank loan agreements. Such efforts reduce the probability of

---

[6]For example, Matthew Poncelet made callow excuses for his brutal killing in the 1996 film *Dead Man Walking*.

conflict. Most lawyers usually play a planning role. They help people create their own "private laws," laws governing their personal affairs and no more.

But, of course, some conflicts start anyway. Why? Sometimes they start because a lawyer did the planning and preventing poorly or because the client did not follow a lawyer's good advice. Sometimes lawyers cannot find in rules of law a safe plan with which to prevent a conflict. Many conflicts, however, such as the auto collision, the dispute with a neighbor over a property line, or the angry firing of an employee, begin without lawyers. Then people may call them in after the fact, not for an ounce of prevention but for the pounding of a cure.

If a battle erupts spontaneously, lawyers may find a solution in the rules of law, though once people get angry at each other they may refuse the solution lawyers offer. If a struggle arises, however, and if the lawyers don't find a solution or negotiate a compromise, then either one side gives up or the opponents go to court; they call in the judges to give their solution.

You may now think you have a solid definition of law: Law is the process of preventing or resolving conflicts between people. Lawyers and judges do this; professors, plumbers, and physicians, at least routinely, do not. But parents prevent or resolve conflicts among their children daily. And parents, perhaps exasperated from coping with family fights, may turn to a family counselor to deal with their own conflicts. Many ministers no doubt define one of their goals as reducing conflict. Lawyers, then, aren't the only people who try to resolve conflicts.

Law, like the priesthood and professional counseling, encounters an immense variety of problems. Law requires the ability to see specifics and to avoid premature generalizing and jumping to conclusions. So do good counseling, good "ministration," and good parenting. But what distinguishes the conflict solving of lawyers and judges from the conflict solving of parents, counselors, or ministers? Consider these three cases. What makes them distinctively *legal* problems?

- A Massachusetts supermarket chain's order of a carload of cantaloupe from Arizona arrives two weeks late and partially rotten. The supermarket chain refuses to take delivery of the melons and refuses to pay for them. Did the seller in the contract of sale guarantee their safe arrival? Did the delay cause the decay, or had some spore infected the melons before shipment? Did the railroad act negligently in causing the delay, thus making it liable for the loss? Should the supermarket chain try to recover the profit it didn't make because it had no melons to sell, and if so, from whom? Do any regulations made by the Department of Agriculture or the Interstate Commerce Commission speak to the problem?[7]
- A young man, entranced by the thought of flying, steals a Cessna from an airstrip in Rhode Island and manages to survive a landing in a Connecticut corn patch. He is prosecuted under the National Motor Vehicle Theft Act, which prohibits transportation "in interstate or foreign commerce [of] a motor vehicle, knowing the

---

[7]Real life provides us with a much more complicated version of this case of the rotten cantaloupe. See *L. Gillarde Co. v. Joseph Martinelli and Co., Inc.*, 168 F.2d 276 (1st Cir. 1948) and 169 F.2d 60 (1948, rehearing). The case has introduced two generations of students at Harvard Law School, myself among them, to the complexities of the legal process in Henry M. Hart, Jr., and Albert M. Sacks, *The Legal Process* (Cambridge: Harvard Law School, 1958), pp. 10–75. These materials were published in 1994 in William N. Eskridge, Jr., *The Legal Process: Problems in the Making and Application of Law* (Westbury, Ct.: Foundation Press).

same to have been stolen. . . ." The statute defines motor vehicle to "include an automobile, automobile truck, automobile wagon, motorcycle, or any other self-propelled vehicle not designed for running on rails." Does the pilot's brief flight amount to transportation of the plane "in interstate . . . commerce?" Is an airplane a "vehicle" within the meaning of the act?[8]

• A U.S. president seeks to protect himself while in office against charges of sexual harassment, which allegedly took place prior to his taking office. Does the Constitution protect a sitting president from facing charges that other citizens—including other elected officials like former Senator Robert Packwood—cannot sidestep?[9]

These are legal problems, not counseling or psychological or parental problems, because we define their nature and limits—but not necessarily their solution—in terms of rules that the state, the government, has made. The laws of contract and of negligence help define the problem or the quarrel between the melon seller and the melon buyer. So, as it turns out, do Department of Agriculture shipping regulations for farm produce. Criminal statutes passed by legislatures define, among many concepts, how the government may deal with thieves. The Constitution sets limits on presidential power. Governments have made these rules; they are laws. The process of resolving human conflicts through law begins when one person or several persons decide to take advantage of the fact that the government has made rules to prevent or resolve such conflicts. When people convert a problem into a legal conflict by taking it to court, the court's resolution of the problem has the force of the government behind it. Even in a noncriminal case, if the loser or losers don't pay up, the judge may order jail terms.

The law, then, is a language that lawyers and judges use when they try to prevent or resolve problems—human conflicts—using official rules made by the state as their starting point. To study reason in this process is to study how lawyers and judges justify the choices they inevitably make among alternative legal solutions. For example, legal reasoning studies how they justify saying an airplane is or is not a "vehicle" in the context of the National Motor Vehicle Theft Act. Throughout this book we shall study the legal process by asking the central questions lawyers and judges ask themselves as they do their work: What does the law mean as applied to the problem before me? What different and sometimes contradictory solutions to the problem does the law permit?

Now stop and compare this definition of law and legal reasoning with your own intuitive conception of law, with the definition of the legal process you may have developed from television, movies, and other daily experiences. Do the two overlap? Probably not very much. The average layperson usually thinks of law as trials, and criminal trials at that. But trials, by our definition, are one of the less legal, or "law-filled," parts of the legal process because much of the conflict-settling work of lawyers and judges involves deciding not what law means but what happened. Devotees of the O. J. Simpson affair

---

[8]Cf. *McBoyle v. United States,* 283 U.S. 25 (1931). The letter abbreviations following the names of cases identify the series of books that contains the judicial opinion deciding the case. The first number indicates the volume in the series that contains the opinion, and the second number is the starting page of the opinion. The appendix discusses *McBoyle* further.

[9]See *Jones v. Clinton,* 72 F.3d 1354 (8th Cir. 1996). On May 27, 1997, the U.S. Supreme Court in *Clinton v. Jones,* unanimously concluded that a sitting U.S. president is not immune from lawsuits alleging civil wrongs prior to that president's assuming office. 137 L.Ed.2d 945 (1997).

do not question the law that governed the case. They seek the facts. Trials, like Simpson's criminal and civil trials, are not so much legal reasoning as they are a microscopic kind of historical research: Did the deceased pull a knife on the defendant before the defendant shot him or didn't he? Did that witness really see the defendant run the red light just before the defendant hit the police car? We are confident enough that these historical problems do not require legal reasoning that we often turn the job of solving them over to groups of amateur historians, better known as juries.

Rules do tell juries what facts to seek. Pulling the knife *could* excuse the shooting through the law of self-defense, though if the deceased were a child of three it would almost surely not. Running the red light could establish legal negligence, though it might not if the defendant were driving his car in a funeral procession at the time.

We cannot totally separate law and facts, but the heart of the reasoning part of law, and the subject of this book, lies not in analyzing what happened but in analyzing what facts the rules allow us to seek and what to do with these facts once we "know" them. Turning to the eager flyer, the historical problem we must solve is whether or not that particular defendant at some specified point in the past actually flew someone else's airplane to another state without permission. The legal reasoning problem, on the other hand, requires deciding whether or not we ought to call the plane a "vehicle" in this statute's context.

The illustrative case at the end of this chapter sets out the distinction between trial and appellate decisions. In that case a trial court had decided that a certain Mr. Prochnow was the father of his wife's baby. The facts—which included a suspicious liaison between the wife and another man, the physical separation of the husband and wife except for one encounter eight months before the birth of a full-term baby, and the incompatibility of the husband's blood type with that of the child—seemed to point conclusively in the other direction. Nevertheless, certain official rules of law, as interpreted by the appellate court, seemed to prevent the trial judge from treating all this evidence as conclusive. This case also provides our first full-length example of a court trying (and in my judgment failing) to do legal reasoning well.

A DEFINITION OF LEGAL REASONING

A fundamental political expectation in the United States holds that people who exercise power and authority over others must *justify* how and why they use their power as they do. We expect, both in private and in public life, that people whose decisions directly affect our lives will give reasons why they deserve to hold their power and show how their decisions serve common rather than purely selfish ends. We expect teachers to have and articulate grading standards. We expect elected politicians to respond to the needs of voters. In all such cases we reject the authoritarian notion that power justifies itself, that those with money or political office can therefore do whatever they please. Holding judges responsible for justifying their power may seem obvious to us, but this practice is actually a fairly recent development in Western political philosophy. The alternatives—governing through greater physical strength and brute force, and governing through pure tradition and authoritarian right (as did kings when they proclaimed "divine right" to rule)—may have seemed acceptable theories when people believed that God willed everything. However, religious theories of government, still prevalent in many parts of the world, tend to produce so much religious warfare and bloodshed that liberal philosophers from John Locke forward have tried to substitute reason and justification for force and authority.[10] The most common criticism of Robert Bork's theory of constitutional interpretation—a theory that requires faithful adherence today to the intentions and purposes of the men who originally wrote the Constitution—points out that Bork speaks in the religious language of preliberal authoritarian government. The title of Bork's book—*The Tempting of America: The Political Seduction of the Law*—gives you the idea.[11]

Courts in the United States hold and exercise political power. Judicial outcomes in lawsuits can literally kill and bankrupt people. Courts, as a coequal branch of government, also possess and use power to make law. Whether appellate judges meet or fail to meet our fundamental expectation about the use of judicial power depends on the quality of their legal reasoning. Appellate judges in most nontrivial cases write opinions explaining and thereby justifying the results they reach.[12] Just as elections hold legislators, governors, presidents, and many other politicians accountable, so their opinions hold appellate judges accountable.[13]

Our culture encourages some misunderstanding about legal reasoning. Perhaps because, starting in the Renaissance, a stream of discoveries about the physical world has continuously bombarded Western civilization, we too often assume that legal reasoning is good when it discovers the law's "right answer," the correct legal solution to a problem. The idea that we live under a government of laws, not men, seems based on the assumption that correct legal results exist, like undiscovered planets or subatomic particles, quite independent of man's knowledge.

Of course if law (and science) actually worked that way, a book on legal reasoning would be absurd. To see whether a judge settled a contract dispute correctly, we would study the law of contract. To determine the correctness of the U.S. Supreme Court's 1954 decision banning official public school segregation, we would study the Constitution. In all cases trained lawyers and legal scholars would, like priests in olden days, have special access to correct answers that laypeople—most readers of this book—could not hope to match. The layperson would either defer to the conclusion of the expert or, if they didn't like the legal result, rebel.

Appellate judges do justify their power through the quality of the opinions they write. The quality of their opinions, however, depends on something other than proving that they got the law right. After all, when the law is clear enough that people on opposite sides of a case can agree on what it commands, people usually don't spend the

---

[10]I develop this theme further in the first chapter of *An Introduction to Constitutional Interpretation: Cases in Law and Religion* (White Plains, N.Y.: Longman, 1991).

[11](New York: The Free Press, 1990). See also Bork's *Slouching Towards Gomorrah* (New York: HarperCollins, 1996). Bruce Ackerman's "Robert Bork's Grand Inquisition," 99 *Yale Law Journal* 1419 (1990) dissects Bork's religious rhetoric particularly well.

[12]For an introduction to the legal procedures and terms by which cases reach the appellate level, see the appendix, beginning at p. 181.

[13]All federal judges are appointed for life. Impeachment and removal from office are very rare. The majority of state judges are elected, but election challenges, especially at the appellate level, are also rare. The defeat of California Chief Justice Rose Bird and Associate Justices Cruz Reynoso and Joseph Grodin in November 1986 was an exception. See Henry J. Abraham, *The Judicial Process*, 6th ed. (New York: Oxford University Press, 1993), pp. 21–39.

many thousands of dollars that contesting a case in an appellate court requires. Legal reasoning, in other words, describes what judges do to justify their decision when they *cannot* demonstrate or prove that they have reached the "right answer." As Benjamin Cardozo pointed out the better part of a century ago, appellate judges *create* law. The uncertainties and imperfections in law force judges to choose what the law ought to mean, not merely report on what it does mean.

To persuade us that the law ought to mean what the judge has decided, the judicial opinion ought to persuade us to share the judge's beliefs about four kinds of things:

1. the *case facts* established in the trial and preserved in the record of the evidence produced at the trial;
2. the facts, events, and other conditions that we observe in the world, quite apart from the case at hand, which we call *social background facts;*
3. what the *rules of law,* that is, the official legal texts created by the state, say about cases like this;
4. widely shared moral *values* and social principles.

These four elements are the main building blocks of all legal reasoning. Sometimes judges hide them, but the elements are always there. And thus we arrive at our definition of legal reasoning:

> *Legal reasoning describes how a legal opinion combines the four elements: the facts established at trial, the rules that bear on the case, social background facts, and widely shared values. When a judge reasons well, the opinion harmonizes or "fits together" these four elements.*

This definition, no doubt, seems abstract and fuzzy at first. I hope that by the time you finish this book you will understand my definition and see that it is not simply one professor's theory of law. These four building blocks are so essential to legal reasoning that we should practice learning how to identify and distinguish them in concrete cases. Here, from recent news stories, are brief examples of each of the four.

CASE FACTS EXAMPLE

In a controversial opinion in March 1996, the Supreme Court decided to uphold a Michigan law that allowed Michigan to confiscate the car of one Mr. Bennis, who was arrested for having sex with a prostitute in the car. You might think that if the state has the power to fine or jail Mr. Bennis for this crime, it also has the power to take his car as punishment. The trouble was, Mrs. Bennis co-owned the car. *She* brought the appeal claiming that the law violated her legal interest in the car, and she certainly was not an accessory or a co-conspirator in her husband's crime. But read the opinions for the Court and you discover these telling facts about this case: The car, an 11-year-old Pontiac, had been purchased for $600 and had depreciated since then. Mrs. Bennis was entitled at most, under Michigan law, to only one-half of the proceeds after the sale of the car, minus the costs of selling the car at auction. She lost because, on the facts of her case, she failed to prove that she would get any money at all for her half of the car.[14]

---

[14]*Bennis v. Michigan,* 116 S.Ct. 994 (1996).

SOCIAL BACKGROUND FACTS EXAMPLE

Traci Messinger, the wife of a dermatologist, Gregory Messinger, gave birth via emergency Caesarean section to a baby at 25 weeks into the pregnancy. The baby weighed 1 pound, 11 ounces. Believing that babies born that prematurely are highly likely to suffer brain damage and have less than a 50 percent chance of surviving at all, Dr. Messinger asked the nurses attending the baby to leave the room an hour after the delivery. He then personally unplugged the life-support system: The baby died. In ruling that a criminal prosecution could proceed, the judge considered the social background facts concerning the statistical chances of 25-week babies for survival.[15]

RULES OF LAW EXAMPLE

Mumia Abu-Jamal was sentenced to death for killing a white police officer in Philadelphia. He appealed his death sentence on the ground that, while the jurisdiction in which he was tried was 40 percent black, only two black jurors were selected to sit on his jury. The outcome of his case depended on the meaning of legal rules, in this case, the precedents interpreting the constitutional guarantees to a fair trial provided by the Fifth, Sixth, and Fourteenth Amendments of the Constitution.[16]

VALUES EXAMPLE

In 1996, Larry Don McQuay, a convicted sexual molester of young children, petitioned Texas authorities to grant his request for surgical castration prior to his mandatory release from prison in Texas. McQuay had tried in prison unsuccessfully to castrate himself with a razor. He described himself as "scum of the earth . . . , doomed to eventually rape and then murder my poor little victims . . . ." No clear law in Texas spoke to this issue. The decision depended on a mix of competing values. To name just two: Should anyone have the power to choose to alter themselves in this circumstance? Does the value of the procedure justify the state's paying for the operation?[17]

You can see or imagine how all four building blocks of legal reasoning play some role in each of these cases: *Rules of law* describing premeditation and emotional state of mind would shape the prosecution of Dr. Messinger. So would questions about the *value* of the life of a severely brain-damaged baby. And it is a *social background fact* question of whether castration reliably stops males from sexually assaulting others. But in each of these cases, one of the four legal reasoning elements stands out.

Several immensely important corollaries follow from this definition of legal reasoning. First, legal reasoning does *not* refer to the specific calculations that go on in a judge's

---

[15]"Medical and Legal Quandary in Father's Letting Baby Die," *New York Times,* August 3, 1994, p. A8.

[16]"Pending Execution of Ex-Reporter Divides Black Journalists," *New York Times,* July 17, 1995, p. A7.

[17]"Molester Seeks Castration; Texas Agrees," *New York Times,* April 5, 1996, p. A9. McQuay was released in April without undergoing the procedure. On August 2, 1996, the *Dallas Morning News* reported that McQuay had been rearrested on charges based on an alleged incident in 1989. Presumably the state rearrested him on old charges to sidestep facing the castration issue. Since keeping him in prison will presumably cost much more than the surgical procedure, the case pits the value of retribution against the value of efficiently spending the taxpayers's money.

head. In 1929, U.S. District Judge Joseph Hutcheson confessed that the actual decision-making process revolved around the judicial "hunch."[18] Professor Warren Lehman in 1986 agreed: "What we call the capacity for judgment . . . is an intellectualized account of the capacity for decision making and action, whose nature is not known to us."[19] Legal reasoning justifies the decision but does not explain how the judge arrived at it.[20]

Second, two judges may reach different results in the same case, yet each may reason equally well or badly. Like two excellent debaters, two opposing opinions may still persuade us that each judge has fit together the four elements into a vision of justice that we trust.

Third, to repeat, legal reasoning is ultimately political, not technically legal. Laypeople who read judicial opinions can and should react to them and decide whether the opinion actually persuades them. No one opinion will persuade everyone. Reactions for and against judicial decisions about such volatile issues as abortion inevitably shape the development of law in the future.

Finally, the process by which judges seek to fit the four elements of legal reasoning together inevitably requires them to simplify and distort each element to some degree. Therefore, most opinions will fail to meet the requirements of formal logic. (The Supreme Court's rulings about establishment of religion—which allow churches and church schools many tax advantages yet prohibit the government from providing money to church schools for normal teaching aids—are notoriously incoherent by purely logical standards.) So too, opinions will simplify the moral and empirical issues in them. Simplification and alteration are a fact of life. We always must reshape raw materials if we want to fit them together smoothly.

Thus we return to the point made previously, that law does not provide a technique for generating "right answers." This book's analysis assumes that nothing, including science and technology, can ever be correct in an absolute demonstrable sense. It is a commonplace belief in the philosophy of science today that, as the dust jacket for a noted physics book puts it:

> Physicists do not discover the physical world, they invent *a* physical world—they invent a story that fits as closely as possible the facts they create in their experimental apparatus. In the words of Einstein, "Physical concepts are free creations of the human mind. . . ." Physicists do not always agree on the same theories, or even on the same facts, but they agree on the procedures to be followed in testing theories and establishing facts. . . . The physical world is made up of leptons and quarks because physicists *talk* about the world in terms of leptons and quarks. This is the vocabulary that gives them the power to predict the

---

[18]Joseph C. Hutcheson, Jr., "The Judgment Intuitive: The Function of the 'Hunch' in Judicial Decision," 14 *Cornell Law Quarterly* 274 (1929). Hutcheson defined "hunch" as "a strong intuitive impression that something is about to happen."

[19]Warren Lehman, *How We Make Decisions* (Madison: Institute for Legal Studies of the University of Wisconsin Law School, 1986), p. 12. For an analysis of the subconscious influences on a judge, see Richard Danzig, "Justice Frankfurter's Opinions in the Flag Salute Cases," 36 *Stanford Law Review* 675 (1984).

[20]Not long ago I was fortuitously seated at a dinner with the chief justice of a state supreme court. That court had just issued a decision in a highly politicized case. The guests naturally pressed the judge to explore the reasoning in the case. He freely volunteered that his legal solution to the case came to him in a flash just as he opened the refrigerator door at 2:00 A.M. He was searching for something to eat to ease the insomnia that this perplexing case had caused.

outcome of their experiments. The word *real* is not descriptive. *Real* is an honorific term we bestow on our most cherished beliefs—our most treasured ways of speaking.[21]

For the same reasons, pitches in baseball become balls and strikes, for all practical purposes, because the umpire calls them that way—even when we may see the pitch differently. Just so with judges and lawyers, who agree to follow certain procedures and to use a common vocabulary of legal reasoning but who do not automatically agree on legal outcomes or even on which techniques of legal reasoning to use and when to use them.

THREE WAYS TO CLASSIFY LAW

Formal Categories of Official Legal Texts

The range of legal problems and conflicts is practically infinite, but lawyers and judges will, one way or another, resolve the issues by referring to and reasoning about official legal texts created by the state ("rules of law" or just "legal rules" for short). Despite the endless variety of legal problems, lawyers and judges usually resort to four categories of official texts: *statutes, common law, constitutional law,* and *administrative regulations.*

The easiest category to understand is what we often call "laws"—the *statutes* passed by legislatures. Laypeople tend to think of statutes as the rules that define types of behavior that society wishes to condemn: crimes. However, legislatures enact statutes governing (and sometimes creating!) many problems without enacting criminal statutes—no-fault insurance, income tax rates, social security benefit levels, for example. For our purposes this statutory category also includes the local ordinances passed by the elected bodies of cities and counties.

But there is a problem here: Legislatures do not enact statutes to cover everything. And when lawyers and judges face a problem without a statute, they normally turn to that older set of legal texts called *common law.*

Judges, not legislators, make common law rules, but not by calling together a judicial convention to argue, log-roll, draft, and finally vote on (or bury) proposed laws. Common law rules have emerged through a process introduced in England before the discovery of the New World. The process began essentially because the Crown in England chose to assert national authority by sending judges throughout the country to act, to decide cases, in the name of the Crown. The king did not write rules to govern all judges' decisions. It was because the judges acted in the name of the central government, certainly a shaky government by our standards, that their decisions became law common to all the king's domain. Many common law rules originated in local custom or the minds of the judges themselves.

The process by which these decisions became "law" took a surprisingly long time. In the beginning, the reasons for judicial decisions were murky, and judges applied

---

[21]Bruce Gregory, *Inventing Reality: Physics as Language* (New York: John Wiley and Sons, 1988). And Geoffrey Joseph wrote, "What one finds [in the physical sciences] is a succession of theories, each of which resolutely ignores certain fundamental questions." "Interpretation in the Physical Sciences," 58 *Southern California Law Review* 9 (1985), p. 12.

them inconsistently. But observers of the courts wrote descriptions of the cases, often just the facts and the result, and judges began to look to these descriptions for past examples to guide current judicial action. The formal practice whereby judges write opinions explaining their choices, which other judges in turn treat as legal authority called *precedents,* is only a few hundred years old, but it is a powerful and stabilizing force in legal reasoning today. Precedents, the official legal texts created by courts themselves, will receive much attention in this book because the facts and values embedded in the examples of precedents are fundamental tools of legal reasoning.

Chapters 3 and 4 examine legal reasoning in statutory and common law, and Chapter 5 explores the third category of official legal texts, *constitutional law.* The Constitution of the United States and the 50 state constitutions set out the structure and powers of government. They also place legal limits on the way those who govern can use their power. While statutes (and common law where statutory law is silent) can govern anybody, constitutions govern the government.[22] The U.S. Constitution even governs presidents, although most constitutional cases involve an alleged conflict between the national or state constitutions and a decision made and enforced by lesser public administrators who claim to act under statutory authority.

Administrative regulations—of the Internal Revenue Service, or the San Francisco Zoning Board, or any of the thousands of national, state, and local administrative agencies—make up the fourth category. Executives and nonelected administrators can make rules only when a constitution or a statute gives them the authority to do so. Problems in administrative law can fascinate and perplex as much as any. Because the length of this book and your time have limits, we shall examine reasoning about administrative regulations only indirectly. You should not, however, let this deliberate neglect mislead you into thinking the subject is unimportant. Administrative regulations are shaping law and our lives more and more.[23] The scope of this book is confined to historically more developed official legal texts: *statutes, common law,* and *constitutional law.*

Before concluding this discussion, I want to emphasize this central truth: Judges write opinions explaining their legal choices. They do so when they apply older, judge-made common law rules, and they do so when they choose among alternative possible meanings of statutes, constitutional provisions, and administrative regulations. All these opinions create precedents, guides to help judges in similar future cases make similar kinds of decisions. *Judicial opinions, the official legal texts created by courts, give meaning to all types of official legal texts.*

The Problems That Laws Address

The second way of classifying laws examines the various social objectives that different laws try to achieve. Scholars classify these so-called functions of laws in varying ways. In one common method, examples of the kinds of problems laws attempt to prevent or

---

[22]If I, as a private citizen, don't like a speech of yours and forcibly remove you from your podium, I will probably violate a principle of common or statutory law. And I would violate the value favoring free exchange of ideas. But I will not violate the First Amendment of the Constitution. If I did this to you while working as a government official, such as an FBI agent, however, that could be a constitutional violation.

[23]See Lief Carter and Christine Harrington, *Administrative Law and Politics* (New York: HarperCollins, 1991). The Congress of the United States generally enacts a few hundred statutes per year, but the federal bureaucracy issues three thousand to five thousand rules per year.

resolve are simply listed. Some laws (but only a small fraction of the total) deter crimes by threatening punishments. These same criminal laws also diminish the occurrence of vigilante justice; they allow people outraged by crimes to vent their anger safely on the criminal through the punishments decided by the courts. Other laws, like those regulating the operation of radio and television broadcasters, do not prevent good people from doing bad things or punish bad people in hopes of making them good. Instead, these laws coordinate people with different but equally "good" wants, in this case the competing interests of broadcasters and listeners. Note that the problem here arises from a limited resource, the airwaves, which society must use wisely for its collective advantage.[24]

Some laws promote government itself and keep it financially viable by raising tax revenues. Other laws protect citizens from government. They preserve our freedoms not only to participate in politics but also to transact and enforce private economic agreements. Many laws, like building and sanitation codes, seek to protect our individual health. Others, like laws that prohibit racial discrimination, identify broad objectives for society as a whole.

Superficially, these classifications do seem important and useful. It *is* important to know the legal process helps people trust that essential expectations about life will come true. When this minimum trust collapses, societies quickly slip toward anarchy. Law *does* help people cope with many kinds of problems. But, on closer inspection, how helpful is this classification? Since policy makers in government express their policy choices as rules of law, the list of problems that laws address can become no more than a laundry list of public policies.

More to the point, a judge who knows that rule X protects individual health or that rule Y seeks to raise revenues does not, by that knowledge, move any closer to deciding the case before the court. Indeed, in the typical case, the judge must evaluate a variety of legal rules with many functions—some directly opposing one another—all of which potentially apply to the case.

Thus the first two ways of classifying laws are not entirely satisfactory. In this book therefore we focus less on the sources and functions of law than on the choices judges must make when they decide legal cases and on the manner in which they can make such choices wisely. How can we begin to classify the kinds of choices judges make?

The Choices That Legal Reasoning Confronts

In most cases, judges must reconcile the potential inconsistencies and contradictions among widespread values, the actual words of legal rules and prior judicial opinions, and their own views of the case facts and the social background facts in the cases before them. Judges must make difficult choices such as these:

- Does the case before me call for continued adherence to the historical meaning of legal words? Must I do what the framers of statutory or constitutional language hoped their language would accomplish? How can I discover what they hoped?

---

[24]For example, during the 1996 presidential campaign, third-party candidate Ross Perot brought a legal action to compel television broadcasters to sell him prime time (thus displacing popular commercial shows) so Perot could deliver his message to voters more effectively. Perot lost in court.

When do social, political, and technological changes permit or require a different or revised interpretation?

- Does this case call for judicial deference to the literal meaning of the words themselves? In what circumstances do I decide more wisely by ignoring the actual dictionary definitions of the words in a statute or constitution?
- Does this case obligate me to follow a judicial precedent the wisdom of which I doubt? When am I free to ignore a relevant precedent?

Throughout the following chapters we shall see that choices like these—the choice of change or stability and of literal or flexible interpretation of words and precedents, for example—have no "right answer." Judges inevitably have discretion to decide.

There exists a second reason why judges will continuously create law. The moral values that claim to govern a case collide. Thus, the Constitution contains language protecting the freedom of the press. It also contains language ensuring the fairness of criminal trials. But an unrestrained press can do much to prejudice the fairness of a trial.

In this instance, perhaps judges can do justice by reaching a fair compromise between these interests. A more difficult problem arises not when two interests collide but when two ideas of justice itself collide. One such collision pits *general* justice against *particular* justice. Is it just for bus drivers and train engineers to pull away from the station always exactly on time, even though someone racing down the platform to get home for Christmas will miss it? Is it not true in the long run, to paraphrase the late Professor Zechariah Chafee, that fewer people will miss buses and trains if everyone knows that buses and trains always leave on the dot, that more people will miss if they assume that they can dally and still find the vehicle at the station? While it is often possible to engineer compromises among competing interests, it is often impossible to compromise between different visions of justice itself. Unless she is corrupt or lazy, a judge will *strive* to do justice, but whether she succeeds often remains debatable.

A particularly poignant example of sacrificing particular justice to general justice occurred on June 22, 1992, when the United States Supreme Court struck down the conviction of a white teenager who burned a crudely made cross in the yard of a neighboring African-American family. All nine justices struck down the conviction, which was based on the St. Paul, Minnesota, Bias-Motivated Crime ordinance. The ordinance read in part:

> Whoever places on public or private property a symbol, object, appellation, characterization or graffiti, including, but not limited to, a burning cross or Nazi swastika, which one knows or has reasonable grounds to know arouses anger, alarm, or resentment in others on the basis of race, color, creed, religion, or gender commits disorderly conduct and is guilty of a misdemeanor.

All nine justices condemned the placement of the burning cross. However, Justice Scalia found the ordinance violated First Amendment principles of free expression because it punished some expressions but not others based on the political acceptability of the contents. While Scalia found the ordinance too narrow, other justices found it unconstitutional because it was too broad. Legitimate political expression often arouses alarm or resentment, they reasoned, and this ordinance would punish desirable as well as obnoxious expression.[25] For the sake of both these general principles of justice the injured family lost because the vandal went unpunished.

The ways of making legal choices I describe and advocate here do not make judges or anyone else completely "objective," because legal decisions require choices from among competing values. The problem of general versus particular justice is a good illustration. A value, a preference, or a moral "feeling" is not a concept we can prove to be right or wrong. Those who adopt values that conflict with yours will call you biased, and you may feel the same way about them. A discussion of legal reasoning can stress that some values are better than others, but arguments on both sides will remain. If the argument gets heated, each side will accuse the other of being biased. In the final chapter, we will examine more fully the nature of bias and impartiality in law. If "biases" and "values" are identical psychological feelings or beliefs about right and wrong, then legal reasoning cannot eliminate them, but we will see that judges can act impartially nevertheless. You can guess, from my definition of legal reasoning, that the impartial judge will persuasively harmonize, or coherently fit together, the four elements described in this chapter. I trust that with the next four chapters under your belt, you will follow easily the more complete development of this idea in the final chapter.

Impartiality, however, does not eliminate the tragic element in law. In Martha Nussbaum's great book, *The Fragility of Goodness,* we learn that tragic situations exist whenever circumstances pull people in two inconsistent but equally good directions at once. Imagine yourself having to decide the premature baby case or the hate speech case, above, and you will feel their inherently tragic nature. Nussbaum (and most contemporary moral philosophers) rejects Kant's claim, as Nussbaum puts it, "that objective practical rules be in every situation consistent, forming a harmonious system like a system of true beliefs. . . . It appears that our duties may conflict. But this cannot be so, since the very concepts of duty and practical law rule out inconsistencies." Impartiality requires a judge to persuade us that she has reached the better result. But if a judge fakes reaching a mechanically correct result and denies the tragic choices in a case, she will not persuade us to trust her exercise of power over us. We will know better because we know, from Greek mythology and from our own experiences, that we often cannot do right without doing wrong. Legal reasoning matters because, done well, it helps communities survive and transcend life's tragic side. As Nussbaum writes, "If we were such that we could in a crisis dissociate ourselves from one commitment because it clashed with another, we would be less good."[26]

ILLUSTRATIVE CASE

Each chapter's end gives you a chance to apply some of its materials to an example of legal reasoning. At the end of the opinion I pose questions that will help you identify the four legal reasoning elements in this case.

---

[25]See *R. A. V., Petitioner v. City of St. Paul,* 112 S.Ct. 2538 (1992).

[26]Martha C. Nussbaum, *The Fragility of Goodness: Luck and Ethics in Greek Tragedy and Philosophy* (New York: Cambridge University Press, 1986), pp. 31 and 50.

Prochnow v. Prochnow
Supreme Court of Wisconsin
274 Wisconsin 491 (1957)

A husband appeals from that part of a decree of divorce which adjudged him to be the father of his wife's child and ordered him to pay support money. The actual paternity is the only fact which is in dispute.

Joyce, plaintiff, and Robert, defendant, were married September 2, 1950, and have no children other than the one whose paternity is now in question. In February 1953, Robert began his military service. When he came home on furloughs, which he took frequently in 1953, he found his wife notably lacking in appreciation of his presence. Although he was home on furlough for eight days in October and ten in December, after August 1953, the parties had no sexual intercourse except for one time, to be mentioned later. In Robert's absence Joyce had dates with a man known as Andy, with whom she danced in a tavern and went to a movie, behaving in a manner which the one witness who testified on the subject thought unduly affectionate. This witness also testified that Joyce told her that Robert was dull but that she and Andy had fun. She also said that a few days before Friday, March 12, 1954, Joyce told her she had to see her husband who was then stationed in Texas but must be back to her work in Milwaukee by Monday.

On March 12, 1954, Joyce flew to San Antonio and met Robert there. They spent the night of the 13th in a hotel where they had sex relations. The next day, before returning to Milwaukee, she told him that she did not love him and was going to divorce him. Her complaint, alleging cruel and inhuman treatment as her cause of action, was served on him April 8, 1954. On September 16, 1954, she amended the complaint to include an allegation that she was pregnant by Robert and demanded support money.

The child was born November 21, 1954. Robert's letters to Joyce are in evidence in which he refers to the child as his own. He returned to civilian life February 13, 1955, and on February 18, 1955, answered the amended complaint, among other things denying that he is the father of the child born to Joyce; and he counterclaimed for divorce alleging cruel and inhuman conduct on the part of the wife.

Before trial two blood grouping tests were made of Mr. and Mrs. Prochnow and of the child. The first was not made by court order but was ratified by the courts and accepted in evidence as though so made. This test was conducted in Milwaukee on March 21, 1955. The second was had in Waukesha September 29, 1955, under court order. The experts by whom or under whose supervision the tests were conducted testified that each test eliminated Robert as a possible parent of the child. An obstetrician, called by Robert, testified that it was possible for the parties' conduct on March 13, 1954, to produce the full-term child which Mrs. Prochnow bore the next November 21st. Mrs. Prochnow testified that between December 1953 and May 1954, both inclusive, she had no sexual intercourse with any man but her husband. . . .

BROWN, Justice. The trial judge found the fact to be that Robert is the father of Joyce's child. The question is not whether, on this evidence, we would have so found: we must determine whether that finding constituted reversible error.

Section 328.39 (1) (a), Stats., commands:

Whenever it is established in an action or proceeding that a child was born to a woman while she was the lawful wife of a specified man, any party asserting the illegitimacy of the child in such action or proceeding shall have the burden of proving beyond all reasonable doubt that the husband was not the father of the child. . . .

Ignoring for the moment the evidence of the blood tests and the effect claimed for them, the record shows intercourse between married people at a time appropriate to the conception of this baby. The husband's letters after the child's birth acknowledge it is his own. The wife denies intercourse with any other man during the entire period when she could have conceived this child. Unless we accept the illegitimacy of the baby as a fact while still to be proved, there is no evidence that then, or ever, did she have intercourse with anyone else. The wife's conduct with Andy on the few occasions when the witness saw them together can justly be called indiscreet for a married woman whose husband is absent, but falls far short of indicating adultery. Indeed, appellant did not assert that Andy is the real father but left that to the imagination of the court whose imagination, as it turned out, was not sufficiently lively to draw the inference. Cynics, *among whom on this occasion we must reluctantly number ourselves* [emphasis supplied], might reasonably conclude that Joyce, finding herself pregnant in February or early March, made a hasty excursion to her husband's bed and an equally abrupt withdrawal when her mission was accomplished. The subsequent birth of a full-term child a month sooner than it would usually be expected if caused by this copulation does nothing to dispel uncharitable doubts. But we must acknowledge that a trial judge, less inclined to suspect the worst, might with reason recall that at least as early as the preceding August, Joyce had lost her taste for her husband's embraces. Divorce offered her freedom from them, but magnanimously she might determine to try once more to save the marriage: hence her trip to Texas. But when the night spent in Robert's arms proved no more agreeable than such nights used to be she made up her mind that they could live together no more, frankly told him so and took her departure. The medical testimony concerning the early arrival of the infant does no more than to recognize eight months of gestation as unusual. It admits the possibility that Robert begat the child that night in that San Antonio hotel. Thus, the mother swears the child is Robert's and she knew, in the Biblical sense, no other man. Robert, perforce, acknowledges that it may be his. Everything else depends on such reasonable inferences as one chooses to draw from the other admitted facts and circumstances. And such inferences are for the trier of the fact. Particularly, in view of Sec. 328.39 (1) (a), Stats., supra, we cannot agree with appellant that even with the blood tests left out of consideration, the record here proves beyond a reasonable doubt that Joyce's husband was not the father of her child.

Accordingly we turn to the tests. The expert witnesses agree that the tests excluded Mr. Prochnow from all possibility of this fatherhood. Appellant argues that this testimony is conclusive; that with the tests in evidence Joyce's testimony that she had no union except with her husband is insufficient to support a finding that her husband is the father. . . . But the Wisconsin statute authorizing blood tests in paternity cases pointedly refrains from directing courts to accept them as final even when they exclude the man sought to be held as father. In its material parts it reads:

> Sec. 325.23 *Blood tests in civil actions.* Whenever it shall be relevant in a civil action to determine the parentage or identity of any child, . . . the court . . . may direct any party to the action and the person involved in the controversy to submit to one or more blood tests, to be made by duly qualified physicians. Whenever such test is ordered and made the results thereof shall be receivable in evidence, but only in cases where definite exclusion is established. . . .

This statute does no more than to admit the test and its results in evidence—there to be given weight and credibility in competition with other evidence as the trier of the fact considers it deserves. No doubt in this enactment the legislature recognized that whatever infallibility is accorded to science, scientists and laboratory technicians by whom the tests must be conducted, interpreted, and reported retain the human fallibilities of other witnesses. It had been contended before this that a report on the analysis of blood is a physical fact which controls a finding of fact in opposition to lay testimony on the subject, and the contention was rejected. . . . When the trial judge admitted the Prochnow tests in evidence and weighed them against the testimony of Mrs. Prochnow he went as far in giving effect to them as our statute required him to do. Our opinions say too often that trial courts and juries are the judges of the credibility of witnesses and the weight to be given testimony which conflicts with the testimony of others for us to say that in this case the trial court does not have that function. . . .

The conclusion seems inescapable that the trial court's finding must stand when the blood-test statute does not make the result of the test conclusive but only directs its receipt in evidence there to be weighed, as other evidence is, by the court or jury. We hold, then, that the credibility of witnesses and the weight of all the evidence in this action was for the trial court, and error cannot be predicated upon the court's acceptance of Joyce's testimony as more convincing than that of the expert witnesses.

Judgment affirmed.

WINGERT, Justice (dissenting). With all respect for the views of the majority, Mr. Chief Justice FAIRCHILD, Mr. Justice CURRIE, and the writer must dissent. In our opinion the appellant, Robert Prochnow, sustained the burden placed upon him by Sec. 328.39 (1) (a), Stats., of proving beyond all reasonable doubt that he was not the father of the child born to the plaintiff.

To meet the burden, appellant produced two classes of evidence, (1) testimony of facts and circumstances, other than blood tests, which create grave doubt that appellant is the father, and (2) the evidence of blood tests and their significance, hereinafter discussed. In our opinion the blood test evidence should have been treated as conclusive in the circumstances of this case.

Among the numerous scientific achievements of recent decades is the development of a method by which it can be definitely established in many cases, with complete accuracy, that one of two persons cannot possibly be the parent of the other. The nature and significance of this discovery are summarized by the National Conference of Commissioners on Uniform State Laws, a highly responsible body, in the prefatory note to the Uniform Act on Blood Tests to Determine Paternity, as follows:

> In paternity proceedings, divorce actions and other types of cases in which the legitimacy of a child is in issue, the modern developments of science have made it possible to determine with certainty in a large number of cases that one charged with being the father of a child could not be. Scientific methods may determine that one is not the father of the child by the analysis of blood samples taken from the mother, the child, and the alleged father in many cases, but it cannot be shown that a man is the father of the child. If the negative fact is established it is evident that there is a great miscarriage of justice to permit juries to hold on the basis of oral testimony, passion, or sympathy, that the person charged is the father and is responsible for the support of the child and other incidents of paternity. . . . There is no need for a dispute among the experts, and true experts will not disagree. Every test will show the same results. . . .
>
> [T]his is one of the few cases in which judgment of court may be absolutely right by use of science. In this kind of a situation it seems intolerable for a court to permit an opposite result to be reached when the judgment may scientifically be one of complete accuracy. For a court to permit the establishment of paternity in cases where it is scientifically impossible to arrive at that result would seem to be a great travesty on justice. (Uniform Laws Annotated, 9 Miscellaneous Acts, 1955 Pocket Part, p. 13.)

In the present case the evidence showed without dispute that the pertinent type of tests were made of the blood of the husband, the wife, and the child on two separate occasions by different qualified pathologists, at separate laboratories, and that such tests yielded identical results, as follows:

	3/17/55	9/29/55
	Blood types	
Robert Prochnow (Husband)	AB	AB
Joyce Prochnow (Wife)	O	O
David Prochnow (Child)	O	O

There is no evidence whatever that the persons who made these tests were not fully qualified experts in the field of blood testing, nor that the tests were not made properly, nor that the results were not correctly reported to the court. . . .

Two qualified experts in the field also testified that it is a physical impossibility for a man with type AB blood to be the father of a child with type O blood, and that therefore appellant is not and could not be that father of the child David. Both testified that there are no exceptions to the rule. One stated "There is no difference of opinion regarding these factors amongst the authorities doing this particular work. None whatsoever." The evidence thus summarized was not discredited in any way and stands undisputed in the record. Indeed, there was no attempt to discredit it except by the wife's own self-serving statement that she had not had sexual relations with any other man during the period when the child might have been conceived . . . .

QUESTIONS ABOUT THE CASE

1. This case requires the court to interpret several statutes. Which are they? The case also involves a procedural rule that differentiates the work of appellate courts from that of trial courts. What is that rule?
2. What factual assertions about this dispute did the trial court accept as proved? What factual assertions did it reject?
3. What social background facts are at issue here? What choice did the appellate court have to make about social background facts in order to decide this case?[27]
4. Did not the majority's decision to reject the conclusive proof of the blood tests rest on some value choices? Does the court articulate these choices? If not, what might they have been? Does this decision necessarily depend on a fundamentalist religious conviction that God can always alter nature if He wishes? Or might the court have believed that, in the interest of giving David any father at all, it was best to assign paternity to Robert despite science?
5. Why was the law ambiguous in this case?
6. Do you find that the majority or the dissenting opinion does a better job of legal reasoning? Why?
7. How does this opinion change the law? That is, if the dissent had prevailed in this case, how would the reading of the rules of law at issue in this case change?

FOR FURTHER THOUGHT

1. The baseball umpire adage, "They ain't *nuthin'* until I calls 'em," and our discussion of the way language constructs reality in the world of physics has introduced you to the thorny nature of what things "mean." Sometimes legal cases deal directly with questions of meaning. For example, in 1990 law enforcement officials in Cincinnati, Ohio, prosecuted Dennis Barrie, director of the Contemporary Arts Center, for obscenity and illegally displaying photos of nude children when the center showed selected works of the late photographer Robert Mapplethorpe. The trial jury acquitted

---

[27]*Hint:* Don't discount the social background fact that medical practitioners make mistakes. In 1995 a Harvard School of Public Health research team studying two well-regarded Boston hospitals found 334 errors in drug delivery to patients over a six month period. ("Hundreds of Drug Errors Are Found at Two Hospitals," *New York Times,* July 6, 1995, p. A8.) Does not the possiblity for error help explain why the statute uses the phrase "receivable in evidence"?

the defendants, but it could not help but weigh and resolve the extraordinarily different social values the two sides held.

> Where the prosecution sees a "pornographer," the art experts see "a brilliant artist."
> Where the prosecution sees a photograph of a man urinating into the mouth of
> another man, the art experts see "symmetry" and "classical proportions." Where the
> prosecution talks of "genitalia," the art experts talk of "retrospective" and "inten-
> tionalism."
>
> The conflicting terminology reflects a basic disagreement about the case. The
> defense sees the issue as the freedom of an artist to create whatever he will and the
> freedom of a museum to exhibit it. The prosecution represents those who have
> labored for years to rid Cincinnati of sexually explicit merchandise and material
> because they find it offensive or dangerous, and they regard Mr. Mapplethorpe's
> photos, however blessed by the critical establishment, as no different.[28]

2. Since at least the days of Socrates and Plato, people have wrestled with the question,
   "What is justice?" The philosopher Richard Rorty recently offered a fascinating potential answer to that question. Rorty argued that, in practice, justice is the label we
   attach to whatever we do to protect the community to which we feel primarily loyal.
   If a mother and father, knowing their child is implicated in a serious crime, hide that
   child from the police, then, according to Rorty's thesis, the parents will define hiding
   the child as just. They will not say, "We hide our child from the police, but we know
   it is unjust." They will say, "Our family comes before the community and its need to
   enforce the law. Therefore hiding our child is just." Do you find the Rorty thesis convincing? It certainly would seem to explain why members of cults, like the Branch
   Davidians in Waco, Texas, or the Heaven's Gate cult members, who all committed
   suicide together in 1997, could so easily deny the validity of the legal, political, and
   social worlds around them. The thesis could also explain the anger of Timothy
   McVeigh, reported by many witnesses in his trial in the spring of 1997 for the
   Oklahoma City bombing of the federal building, as well as the anger of all extremist
   groups of right and left at the workings of "the law." If we accept for the sake of
   argument that Rorty has described a powerful reality, at least in our culture, it would
   follow that the task of mainstream law and politics is to encourage people to move
   their loyalties "up and out." We will not achieve the kind of social cooperation that
   complex and highly interdependent modern life requires if people regularly feel loyal
   to small and personal groups at the expense of the community. As you read the rest
   of this book, consider what our legal system would have to do and be to maintain popular loyalty to the larger community and its law, rather than to family or neighborhood
   or church.[29]

---

[28]"Clashes at Obscenity Trial On What an Eye Really Sees," *New York Times,* October 3, 1990, p. A12.
  [29]Rorty presented this position in a paper delivered at the University of Colorado at Colorado Springs
on October 14, 1996.

CHAPTER 2

Change and Stability in Legal Reasoning

The mystery of life is not a problem to be solved, but a reality to be experienced.

—AART VAN DER LEEUW

The first chapter began to narrow this book's scope of inquiry. We do not in this book put ourselves in the shoes of legislators, nor do we examine how elections or lobbying efforts or presidential leadership produce new law. While this book does not explore many important political issues, it does inevitably steer us into political waters in three critical ways.

First, studying legal reasoning shows us that "the law" does not substitute for politics, it *is* politics. Unless the parties agree that "the law" automatically resolves a case (and when this happens they usually don't go to court in the first place), the judge will make and defend choices. That is, the judge will use his or her political power to change people's lives—to send them to jail or the death chamber, to bankrupt them, to humiliate them or vindicate them. Legal reasoning, as the first chapter explained, becomes the language we use for analyzing whether the judge has used this political power fairly and persuasively.

Second, once we learn from studying legal reasoning that the most impartial and fair judges inevitably make political choices when they decide cases, we learn that we must take other questions about legal politics very seriously. Whom we elect as president, for example, will affect the selection of people to sit on the federal courts, and different presidential selections will inevitably make different decisions. This fact does not reflect some monstrous failure to achieve objective, and hence "correct," legal judgments. Legal reasoning can help us distinguish better from worse judgments or distinguish well-reasoned from poorly reasoned opinions. But that is about as far as the human brain can go.[1]

---

[1] For a wide-ranging treatment of why language and logic do not yield objectively "correct" interpretations of the world, see Stanley Fish's essays collected in *There's No Such Thing As Free Speech* (New York: Oxford University Press, 1994). Recent empirical studies of judicial decision making support the approach I take here. See, for example, Jeffrey A. Segal and Harold J. Spaeth, *The Supreme Court and the Attitudinal*

Third, the legal process, with all its political characteristics, is still a distinctive kind of politics. The practices and customs and norms that go with being a U. S. Congressperson or Senator inevitably shape how that kind of politician thinks (and, as Representative Newt Gingrich found out, why major reform of legislative politics is so hard to achieve from within). Judicial and legal thinking differs considerably from legislative thinking, but the practices of law, over time, similarly shape and very much limit the thinking and decisions of people who deal in law terms. Law, like any language practice, limits the horizons of what becomes thinkable within that framework. What counts as good evidence, or an appropriate case to hear, or a recognizable social background fact or legitimate social value, all depend on the tradition of legal practices that make such things thinkable in the first place. So, as you grapple with legal reasoning issues throughout this book, please keep in the back of your mind that you are simultaneously studying the political language by which the law creates and perpetuates its power.[2]

The first section of this chapter explores why legal language does not generate "correct" answers to contested legal questions. The second section asserts that this uncertainty and ambiguity benefits us more than it harms us, at least as a general rule. The third section examines the other side of the uncertainty coin, the general philosophical conditions in which judges should choose legal clarity and stability at the expense of other values. The concluding section reviews some general and inevitable characteristics of law that make it forever changing, never perfected.

UNPREDICTABILITY IN LAW

Reasoning from Words

Cases often go to courts (and particularly appellate courts) because the law does not determine the outcome. Both sides believe they have a chance to win. The legal process is in these cases *unpredictable*. Legal rules are made with words, and we can begin to understand why law is unpredictable by examining the ambiguity of words, the "disorderly conduct of words," as Professor Chafee put it.[3] Sometimes our language fails to give us precise definitions. There is, for example, no way to define the concept of "table" so as to exclude some items we call "benches" and the reverse.[4] More often, words and

---

Model (Cambridge: Cambridge University Press, 1993); Saul Brenner and Harold Spaeth, *Stare Indecisis* (Cambridge: Cambridge University Press, 1995); and Lee Epstein and Jack Knight, *The Choices Judges Make* (Washington, D. C.: Congressional Quarterly Press, 1997).

[2]Stanley Fish's essay, "The Law Wishes to Have a Formal Existence," in *There's No Such Thing As Free Speech*, cited in note 1, pp. 141–179, describes this phenomenon particularly well. I'm particularly grateful to Michael McCann for showing me why specifying this point is so essential to this book's larger argument. For a thorough description of how law helps constitute the hopes and expectations of lay persons outside the judical system, see McCann's *Rights At Work* (Chicago: University of Chicago Press, 1994).

[3]Zechariah Chafee, "The Disorderly Conduct of Words," 41 *Columbia Law Review* 381 (1941). The perfecting of computer enhancement of visual images threatens to make seemingly objective photographs and video records, offered as physical evidence in trials, as uncertain as verbal testimony. The technique, called *morphing*, and seen in movies like *Star Trek VI* and *Terminator II*, can change one image into an imaginary one as realistic as the original.

[4]My thanks to Professor Martin Landau, University of California, Berkeley, for this example. If you don't believe it, try creating this definitional distinction paying attention to coffee tables and tool benches. Furthermore suppose a state enacts a statute exempting from its sales tax all "food and food stuffs." What is "food"? Is chewing gum food? Is coffee? Is beer?

statements that seem clear enough in the abstract may, nevertheless, have different meanings to each of us because we have all had different experiences with the objects or events in the world that the word has come to represent. The experiences of each of us are unique in many respects, so no one word or set of words necessarily means the same thing to all of us. How many parents must reject some names for a new child because, while the mother associates a given name with a friend or hero from the past, the father once knew a villain of the same name?

Words, furthermore, are malleable: People can shape them to suit their own interests. To illustrate, in 1962 Congress, to encourage new business investment, allowed businesspeople up to a 10 percent tax credit for investing in new personal property for their business. Investments like new machinery would qualify, but new buildings and permanent building fixtures would not. In 1982 the Justice Department sued the accounting firm of Ernst and Whinney for using words to disguise real property as personal property. What the accountants called "movable partitions," "equipment accesses," and "decorative fixtures" were in reality doors, manholes, and windows—all real property unqualified for the tax deduction. A "freezer" was in reality an entire refrigerated warehouse, "cedar decoration" was a wood-paneled wall, and "movable partitions—privacy" described toilet stalls.[5]

Words are slippery because their meaning always depends on their context: John Train has developed lists of what he calls "antilogies," words that can have opposite meanings in different contexts.[6] Thus the infinitive "to dust" can refer to removing dust or to laying down dust, as in crop dusting. "To continue" can mean to proceed or to delay a proceeding. "To sanction" both authorizes and condemns. "To buckle" can mean to fasten together or fall apart. Or consider a great old computer joke. The experts had invented a machine that would translate from English to Russian and back. To test it they programmed in the phrase, "The spirit is willing but the flesh is weak," then took the Russian translation and programmed it in to come back in English. Lacking the specific biblical context for the original, the computer did the best it could with the Russian context, but the English retranslation came back, "The vodka is agreeable but the meat is rotten." This sudden confusion of contexts is a primary source of humor, as revealed in the story where the city lawyer asked a witness if "you, too, were shot in the fracas?" He got this answer from a less sophisticated witness: "No, sir, I was shot midway between the fracas and the navel."

The disorderly conduct of words affects legal reasoning most immediately when a judge faces the task of interpreting a statute for the first time, when no judicial precedent interpreting the statute helps the judge to find its meaning. Therefore, we shall refine the problem of disorderly words in Chapter 3, which examines judicial choices in statutory interpretation "in the first instance."

Reasoning from Examples of Precedents

The previous paragraph suggests that precedents help narrow the range of legal choices judges face when they justify a decision. Indeed, precedents do just that, but they never

---

[5]Jim Drinkhall, "Turnabout has IRS Accusing Taxpayers of Gobbledygook," *Wall Street Journal,* November 12, 1982, p. 1.

[6]See "Antilogies," *Harvard Magazine,* November–December 1985, p. 18, and "More Antilogies," *Harvard Magazine,* March–April 1986, p. 17.

provide complete certainty. Reasoning by example also perpetuates a degree of unpredictability in law. To see why, we proceed through six analytical stages.

Stage One: Reasoning by Example in General   Reasoning by example, in its simplest form, means accepting one choice and rejecting another because the past provides an example that the accepted choice somehow "worked." Robert, for example, wants to climb a tree but wonders if its branches will hold. He chooses to attempt the climb because his older sister has just climbed the tree without mishap. Robert reasons by example. His reasoning hardly guarantees success: His older sister may still be skinnier and lighter. Robert may regret a choice based on a bad example, but he still reasons that way. If he falls and survives, he will possess a much better example from which to reason in the future.

The most important characteristic of reasoning by example in any area of life is that no rules tell the decider *how* to decide which facts are similar and which are different. Let us therefore see how this indeterminacy occurs in legal reasoning.

Stage Two: Examples in Law   In law, decisions in prior cases provide examples for legal reasoning. For starters, a precedent contains the analysis and the conclusion reached in an earlier case in which the facts and the legal question(s) resemble the current conflict a judge has to resolve. Even when a statute or a constitutional rule is involved, a judge will look at what other judges have said about the meaning of that rule when they applied it to similar facts and answered similar legal questions. Not only might a judge resolve Chapter 1's case of the rotten cantaloupe in terms of common law precedents of contract, but a judge hearing the cases of the airplane thief or of Bill Clinton's defense in the Paula Jones case would look beyond the National Motor Vehicle Act and the Constitution to see how judges have interpreted these rules or rules like them in earlier precedents.

To understand more fully how precedents create examples we must return to the distinction between law and history. How does a judge know whether facts of a prior case really do resemble those in the case now before the court?

Trials themselves do *not* normally produce precedents. As we have seen, trials seek primarily to find the immediate facts of the dispute, to discover who is lying, whose memory has failed, and who can reliably speak to the truth of the matter. When a jury hears the case, the judge acts as an umpire, making sure the lawyers present the evidence properly to the jury so that it decides the "right" question.[7] Often judges do the jury's job altogether. The law does not allow jury trials in some kinds of cases. When the law does allow jury trials, the parties may elect to go before a judge anyway, perhaps because they feel the issues are too complex for laypeople or perhaps because "bench trials" take less time and cost less money.

Of course, a trial judge must decide the issues of law that the lawyers raise. The conscientious trial judge will explain to the parties orally for the record why and how she

---

[7]The rules of evidence at trials themselves get shaped and reshaped on appeal. One of the most fascinating trial questions that weaves fact-finding and lawmaking together involves the amount of damages the winning party ought or ought not to receive. Injured parties unable to work traditionally have by law recovered their lost wages from the defendant, but only very recently have courts begun to weight the loss of nonmonetary pleasures—hedonic damages—in monetary terms. Ask yourself whether you think a plaintiff who loses the sense of taste and smell from a negligent overdose of anesthesia deserves to recover damages for the loss of her chance of ever tasting a steak or pumpkin pie again, and you get the idea.

resolves the key legal issues in their case. In some instances she will give them a written opinion explaining her legal choices, and some of these find their way into the reported opinions. But since at trial the judge pays most attention to the historical part of the case, deciding what happened, she usually keeps her explanations at the relatively informal oral level. As a result other judges will not find these opinions reported anywhere; they cannot discover them even if they try. Hence few trial judges create precedents even though they resolve legal issues.

Thus the masses of legal precedents that fill the shelves of law libraries mostly emerge from the appellate process. You should not, however, lose sight of the fact that lawyers use many of the same legal reasoning techniques when they base their recommendations to their clients on appellate precedents to avoid trials as well as when they manipulate precedents to their advantage in litigation.

Stage Three: The Three-Step Process of Reasoning by Example   Legal reasoning often involves reasoning from the examples of precedents. Powerful legal traditions impel judges to solve problems by using solutions to similar problems reached by judges in the past. Thus a judge seeks to resolve conflicts by discovering a statement about the law in a prior case—the example—and then applying this statement or conclusion to the current case. Lawyers who seek to anticipate problems and prevent conflicts follow much the same procedure. Professor Levi calls this a three-step process in which the judge sees a factual similarity between the current case and one or more prior cases, announces the rule of law on which the earlier case or cases rested, and applies the rule to the current case.[8]

Stage Four: How Reasoning by Example Perpetuates Unpredictability in Law
To understand this stage we must return to the first step in the three-step description of reasoning by example, the step in which the judge decides which precedent governs. The judge must *choose* the facts in the current case that resemble or differ from the facts in the case, or line of cases, in which prior judicial decisions first announced the rule. The judge no doubt accepts the obligation, made powerful by legal tradition, to "follow precedent," but the judge is under no obligation to follow any particular precedent. He completes step one *by deciding for himself* which of the many precedents are similar to the facts of the case before him and *by deciding for himself* what they mean.

No judicial opinion in a prior case can require that a judge sift the facts of the present case one way or another. She is always free to do this herself. A judge writing an opinion can influence a future user of the precedent she creates by refusing to report or consider some potentially important facts revealed in the trial transcript. But once she reports them, judges in later similar cases can use the facts in their own way. They can call a fact critical that a prior judge reported but deemed irrelevant; they can make a legal molehill out of what a prior judge called a mountain. Thus the present judge, the precedent user, retains the freedom to choose the example from which the legal conclusion follows.

I call this judicial freedom to choose the governing precedent by selectively sifting the facts *fact freedom.* Our inability to predict with total accuracy how a judge will use

---

[8]Edward Levi, *An Introduction to Legal Reasoning* (Chicago: University of Chicago Press, 1949), p. 2. Please do not confuse the six analytical stages I use in this chapter with the three-step reasoning process inherent in our legal system itself.

fact freedom is the major source of uncertainty in law. Thus we cannot say that "the law" applies known or given rules to diverse factual situations because we don't know the applicable rules until after the judge uses fact freedom to choose the precedent.

Stage Five: An Illustration of Unpredictability in Law   Consider the following example from the rather notorious history of enforcing the Mann Act. The Mann Act, passed by Congress in 1910, provides in part that "Any person who shall knowingly transport or cause to be transported . . . in interstate or foreign commerce . . . any woman or girl for the purpose of prostitution or debauchery, or for any other immoral purpose . . . shall be deemed guilty of a felony." Think about these words for a minute. Do they say that if I take my wife to Tennessee for the purpose of drinking illegal moonshine whiskey with her I have violated the Mann Act? What if I take her to Tennessee to rob a bank? Certainly robbing a bank is an "immoral purpose." Is it "interstate commerce"? But we are jumping prematurely to Chapter 3. For the moment, you should see only that the Congress has chosen some rather ambiguous words and then move to the main problem: choosing the "right" example to decide the following case.

Mr. and Mrs. Mortensen, owners and operators of a house of prostitution in Grand Island, Nebraska, went with two employees on a well-earned vacation to Yellowstone and Salt Lake City. The girls did lay off their occupation completely during the entire duration of the trip, and they paid for many of the trip expenses themselves. Upon their return they resumed their calling. Over a year later federal agents arrested the Mortensens and, on the basis of the vacation trip, charged them with violation of the Mann Act. The jury convicted the Mortensens. Their lawyer appealed to an appellate court judge.

Unpredictability in law arises when the judge cannot automatically say that a given precedent is or isn't factually similar. To simplify matters here, let us now assume that only one precedent exists, the decision of the U.S. Supreme Court in *Caminetti v. United States*, announced in 1917.[9] How does this example determine the result in *Mortensen?* Assume that in *Caminetti* two married men took two young women (ages 19 and 20), who were not their wives, from Sacramento, California, to a cabin near Reno, Nevada, where they had sexual relations. The girls went voluntarily; they were neither prostitutes nor known to be "fast." By traveling to Reno, the men may have hoped to avoid prosecution by California state officials. On these facts the Supreme Court in *Caminetti* upheld the conviction under the Mann Act. Does this case seal the Mortensens' fate? Does this precedent require the courts to find Mr. and Mrs. Mortensen guilty under the Mann Act? To answer these questions the judge must decide whether this case is factually similar to *Mortensen.* Is it?

In one sense, of course it is. In each case the defendants transported women across state lines, after which sex out of wedlock occurred. In another sense, it isn't. Without going to Reno the girlfriends might not have slept with the defendants. But if the Mortensens had not sponsored the vacation, the women would have continued their work. The Mortensens's transportation *reduced* the frequency of prostitution. The two

---

[9]*Caminetti v. United States*, 242 U. S. 470 (1917). *Caminetti's* facts and holding cover noncommercial as well as commercial sexual immorality. For a much fuller discussion of *Caminetti*, which in fact was a head-line-making national scandal involving, among many players, a U.S. attorney general who went on to sit on the U.S. Supreme Court, see this book's final chapter, pp. 158–161.

boyfriends maintained or increased "illicit sex." Should this difference matter? The judge is free to select one interpretation of the facts or the other in order to answer this question. Either decision will create a new legal precedent. It is precisely this freedom to decide either way that increases unpredictability in law.

Stage Six: *Reasoning by Example Facilitates Legal Change* Why does judicial fact freedom make law change constantly? Legal rules change every time they are applied because no two cases ever have exactly the same facts. Although judges treat cases as if they were legally the same whenever they apply the rule of one case to another, deciding the new case in terms of the rule adds to the list of cases a new and unique factual situation. To rule in the Mortensens' favor, as the Supreme Court did in 1944, gave judges new ways of looking at the Mann Act.[10] With those facts, judges after 1944 could, if they wished, read the Mann Act more narrowly than they did in *Caminetti*. *Mortensen* thus potentially changed the meaning of the Mann Act, thereby changing the law.

But as the situation turned out, the change did not endure. In 1946 the Court upheld the conviction, under the Mann Act, of certain Mormons, members of a branch known as Fundamentalists, who took "secondary" wives across state lines. No prostitution at all was involved here, but the evidence did suggest that some of the women did not travel voluntarily. Fact freedom worked its way again.[11] The Court extended *Caminetti* and by implication isolated *Mortensen*. The content of the Mann Act, then, has changed with each new decision and each new set of facts.

Is law always as confusing and unclear as these examples make it seem? In one sense certainly not. To the practicing lawyer, most legal questions the client asks possess clear and predictable answers. But in such cases—and here we return to the definition of legal conflicts in Chapter 1—the problems probably do not get to court at all. Uncertainty helps convert a human problem into a legal conflict. We focus on uncertainty in law because that is where reason in law takes over.

In another sense, however, law never entirely frees itself from uncertainty. Lawyers always cope with uncertainties about what happened, uncertainties that arise in the historical part of law. If they go to trial on the facts, even if they think the law is clear, the introduction of new evidence or the unexpected testimony of a witness may raise new and uncertain legal issues the lawyers didn't consider before the trial. Lawyers know they can never fully predict the outcome of a client's case, even though much of the law is clear to them most of the time.

IS UNPREDICTABILITY IN LAW DESIRABLE?

Is it desirable that legal rules do not always produce clear and unambiguous answers to legal conflicts? Should the legal system strive to reach the point where legal rules solve problems in the way, for example, that the formula for finding square roots of numbers provides automatic answers to all square root problems?

[10]*Mortensen v. United States*, 322 U.S. 369 (1944).
[11]*Cleveland v. United States*, 329 U.S. 14 (1946).

Despite the human animal's natural discomfort in the presence of uncertainty, some unpredictability in law is desirable. Indeed, if a rule had to provide an automatic and completely predictable outcome before courts could resolve conflicts, society would become intolerably repressive, if not altogether impossible. There are two reasons why.[12]

First, since no two cases ever raise entirely identical facts, society must have some way of treating different cases *as if they were the same* in a way litigants accept as fair. But if the legal system resolved all conflicts automatically, people would have little incentive to *participate* in the process that resolves their disputes. If the loser knew in advance he would surely lose, he would not waste time and money on litigation. He would not have the opportunity to try to persuade the judge that his case, always factually unique, *ought* to be treated by a different rule. Citizens who lose will perceive a system that allows them to "make their best case" as fairer than a system that tells them they lose while they sit helplessly.

Only in unpredictable circumstances will each side have an incentive to present its best case. Because the law is ambiguous, each side thinks it might win.[13] This produces an even more important consequence for society as a whole, not just for the losers. The needs of society change over time. The words of common law, statutes, and constitutions must take on new meanings. The participation that ambiguity encourages constantly bombards judges with new ideas. The ambiguity inherent in reasoning by example gives the attorney the opportunity to persuade the judge that the law *ought* to say one thing rather than another. Lawyers thus keep pushing judges to make their interpretation of "the law" fit newer shared beliefs about right and wrong.

I am not encouraging legislators and judges to create or applaud legal uncertainty. Rather, I am arguing that uncertainty in law is unavoidable. This uncertainty is, however, more a blessing than a curse. The participation that uncertainty in law encourages gives the legal process and society itself a vital capacity to change its formal rules as less formal and official human needs and values change.

THE OTHER SIDE OF THE COIN: STARE DECISIS AS A STABILIZING AND CLARIFYING ELEMENT IN LAW

I hope that this discussion of unpredictability in law has not left the impression that law is never clear at all. If rules of law amounted to nonsense—lacked any meaning—government by law could not function. If society is to work, most law must be clear much of the time. We must be able to make wills and contracts, to insure ourselves against disasters, and to plan hundreds of other decisions with the confidence that courts will back our decisions if the people we trust with our freedom and our property fail us.

There is indeed a force pushing toward stability within reasoning by example itself: Once judges determine that a given precedent is factually similar enough to determine the outcome in the case before them, then in normal circumstances they follow the precedent. We call this the doctrine of *stare decisis,* "we let the prior decision stand."

---

[12]Levi, *An Introduction to Legal Reasoning,* pp. 1–6.
[13]The process also has the desirable effect of encouraging negotiation and compromise. Each side has an incentive to settle because each side knows it could lose.

Stare decisis operates in two dimensions. Stare decisis in the first, or *vertical*, dimension acts as a marching order in the chain of judicial command. Courts in both the state and federal systems are organized in a hierarchy within their jurisdictions. Thus the supreme courts of Georgia and of the United States each sit at the top of an "organization chart" of courts. The rulings of the highest court in any jurisdiction legally control all the courts beneath it. Stare decisis stabilizes law vertically because no court should ignore a higher authoritative decision on a legal point. As long as the U.S. Supreme Court holds that airplanes are not "vehicles" within the NMVTA, all courts beneath it must legally honor that ruling in any future airplane theft case that may arise under the act.

There is, however, a more interesting *horizontal* dimension to stare decisis. What if a supreme court makes a decision but then, either a few years or many decades later, decides that its own precedent now states "bad" law and policy? When should a court follow its own "bad" precedent? The U.S. Supreme Court's decision in June of 1992 to continue to follow *Roe v. Wade*—and to reaffirm that the Constitution implicitly grants a female a right to choose whether to continue a pregnancy prior to viability—amounted to a debate on this very question. The *New York Times* quoted on its front page the essence of the Court's stare decisis reasoning. Justice O'Connor extolled the importance of keeping law clear and stable. "Liberty finds no refuge in a jurisprudence of doubt . . . ," her opinion began. Justice Kennedy wrote of the importance of respecting the interest in relying on the law: "An entire generation has come of age free to assume Roe's concept of liberty in defining the capacity of women to act in society, and to make reproductive decisions." And Justice Souter spoke eloquently of preserving the Court's image: "A decision to overturn . . . would address error, if error there was, at the cost of both profound and unnecessary damage to the Court's legitimacy, and to the Nation's commitment to the rule of law."[14]

As you begin to wrestle with the intricacies of horizontal stare decisis, please note that the concept applies only after a judge has reason to doubt the policy or wisdom of the precedent. Judges do not need to resort to the doctrine to justify following the example of a case whose analysis and outcome are as convincing as the alternatives. Note also that stare decisis does not substitute for reasoning by example. Judges can seek guidance from the doctrine only after they have used their fact freedom to conclude that a questionable or outright "bad" case from the past legally governs or controls the case at bar. Professor Thomas S. Currier has stated well the values that justify the principle of horizontal stare decisis. He suggests five values that should lead judges toward continuing to follow otherwise "bad" precedents:

> 1. *Stability.* It is clearly socially desirable that social relations should have a reasonable degree of continuity and cohesion, held together by a framework of reasonably stable institutional arrangements. Continuity and cohesion in the judicial application of rules [are] important to the stability of these institutional arrangements, and society places great value on the stability of some of them. Social institutions in which stability is recognized as particularly important include the operation of government, the family, ownership of land, commercial arrangements, and judicially created relations. . . .

---

[14]*New York Times,* June 30, 1992, p. A1, and *Planned Parenthood v. Casey,* 112 S.Ct. 2791 (1992).

2. *Protection of Reliance.* [T]he value here is the protection of persons who have ordered their affairs in reliance upon contemporaneously announced law. It is obviously desirable that official declarations of the principles and attitudes upon which official administration of the law will be based should be capable of being taken as determinate and reliable indications of the course that such administration will in fact take in the future. . . . This value might be regarded as a personalized variation on the value of stability; but it is broader in that it is recognized even where no social institution is involved, and stability as such is unimportant.

3. *Efficiency in the Administration of Justice.* If every case coming before the courts had to be decided as an original proposition, without reference to precedent, the judicial workload would obviously be intolerable. Judges must be able to ease this burden by seeking guidance from what other judges have done in similar cases.

4. *Equality.* By this is meant the equal treatment of persons similarly situated. It is a fundamental ethical requirement that like cases should receive like treatment, that there should be no discrimination between one litigant and another except by reference to some relevant differentiating factor. This appears to be the same value that requires rationality in judicial decision making, which in turn necessitates that the law applied by a court be consistently stated from case to case. The same value is recognized in the idea that what should govern judicial decisions are rules, or at least standards. The value of equality, in any event, appears to be at the heart of our received notions of justice.

5. *The Image of Justice.* By this phrase I do not mean that any judicial decision ought to be made on the basis of its likely impact upon the court's public relations, in the Madison Avenue sense, but merely that it is important not only that the court provide equal treatment to persons similarly situated, but that, insofar as possible, the court should appear to do so. Adherence to precedent generally tends not only to assure equality in the administration of justice, but also to project to the public the impression that courts do administer justice equally.[15]

The next chapters will describe more precisely the circumstances in which Currier's reasons for horizontal stare decisis do and do not compel a judge to follow rather than depart from a precedent. Here you should simply note that, in fact, most law is clear enough to prevent litigation most of the time. Lawyers can advise us on how to make valid wills and binding contracts. We do know that if someone steals our car and takes it to another state, federal officials, under the authority of the National Motor Vehicle Theft Act, can try to track down the car and the criminal. Without a system of precedents it would be harder for us to predict judicial decisions and therefore more difficult for us to plan to avoid legal conflicts.

These forces in law pushing toward predictability and stability should not, however, obscure this chapter's main conclusion. Cases routinely arise where the best possible legal reasoning *cannot* provide a "right answer." New mixes of facts and legal rules pop up literally every day. This book discusses many socially important legal issues, but let me make the point here with a deliberately minor example: Some years

[15]Thomas S. Currier, "Time and Change in Judge-Made Law: Prospective Overruling," 51 *Virginia Law Review* 201 (1965), pp. 235–238. See also James Hardisty, "Reflections on Stare Decisis," 55 *Indiana Law Journal* 41 (1979).

ago a federal appellate court had to wrestle with the legal definition of "doll" because the new tariff laws imposed a 12 percent import tariff on "dolls" but allowed importing "toy soldiers" duty free. Question: Is the item, made in Hong Kong, known as "G.I. Joe" a doll, like Barbie, or a toy soldier? The lawyers for Joe's seller, Hasbro, pointed out that, like older metal toy soldiers', but unlike most dolls', Joe's clothes were painted on. Hasbro lost. Just as in politically heated areas like abortion, so in little cases like this one, we and the parties want to know *why*. Only through legal reasoning can judges justify their answers.

ILLUSTRATIVE CASES

In the federal judicial system it is common for the intermediate appellate courts to hear cases in panels of three judges, with the outcome determined by majority vote. Here are two opinions written by Learned Hand sitting on two separate panels. The first is a precedent for the second. Notice that they were decided just a month apart. You should read the second case initially to see how Judge Hand uses his fact freedom to distinguish *Repouille* from *Francioso,* then to see how Judge Frank uses fact freedom a different way, and finally to explore the possibility that both judges in *Repouille* have used their fact freedom foolishly.

United States v. Francioso
164 F.2d 163 (Nov. 5, 1947)

L. HAND, Circuit Judge.

This is an appeal from an order admitting the appellee, Francioso, to citizenship. At the hearing the "naturalization examiner" objected to his admission upon the ground that he had married his niece and had been living incestuously with her during the five years before he filed his petition. Upon the following facts the judge held that Francioso had been "a person of good moral character" and naturalized him. Francioso was born in Italy in 1905, immigrated into the United States in 1923, and declared his intention of becoming a citizen in 1924. His wife was born in Italy in 1906, immigrated in 1911, and has remained here since then. They were married in Connecticut on February 13, 1925, and have four children, born in 1926, 1927, 1930, and 1933. Francioso was the uncle of his wife, and knew when he married her that the marriage was unlawful in Connecticut and that the magistrate would have not married them, had they not suppressed their relationship. They have always lived together in apparent concord, and at some time which the record leaves indefinite, a priest of the Catholic Church—of which both spouses are communicants—"solemnized" the marriage with the consent of his bishop.

In United States ex rel. *Iorio v. Day,* in speaking of crimes involving "moral turpitude" we held that the standard was, not what we personally might set, but "the commonly accepted mores": i.e., the generally accepted moral conventions current at the time, so far as we could ascertain them. The majority opinion in the United States ex rel. Berlandi v. Reimer perhaps looked a little askance at that decision; but it did not overrule it, and we think that the same test applies to the statutory standard of "good moral character" in the naturalization statute. Would the moral feelings, now prevalent generally in this country, be outraged because Francioso continued to live with his wife and four children between 1938 and 1943? Anything he had done before that time does not count; for the statute does not search further back into the past.

In 1938 Francioso's children were five, eight, eleven and twelve years old, and his wife was 31; he was morally and legally responsible for their nurture and at least morally responsible for hers. Cato himself would not have demanded that he should turn all five adrift. True, he might have left the home and supported them out of his earnings; but to do so would deprive his children of the protection, guidance and solace of a father. We can think of no course open to him which would not have been regarded as more immoral than that which he followed, unless it be that he should live at home, but as a celibate. There may be purists who would insist that this alone was consistent with "good moral conduct"; but we do not believe that the conscience of the ordinary man demands that degree of ascesis; and we have for warrant the fact that the Church— least of all complaisant with sexual lapses—saw fit to sanction the continuance of this union. Indeed, such a marriage would have been lawful in New York until 1893, as it was at common law. To be sure its legality does not determine its morality; but it helps to do so, for the fact that disapproval of such marriages was so long in taking the form of law, shows that it is condemned in no such sense as marriages forbidden by "God's law." It stands between those and the marriage of first cousins which is ordinarily, though not universally, regarded as permissible.

It is especially relevant, we think, that the relationship of these spouses did not involve those factors which particularly make such marriages abhorrent. It was not as though they had earlier had those close and continuous family contacts which are usual between uncle and niece. Francioso had lived in Italy until he was eighteen years of age; his wife immigrated when she was a child of four; they could have had no acquaintance until he came here in August, 1923, only eighteen months before they married. It is to the highest degree improbable that in that short time there should have arisen between them the familial intimacy common between uncle and niece, which is properly thought to be inimical to marriage. . . .

Order affirmed.

Repouille v. United States
165 F.2d 152 (Dec. 5, 1947)

L. HAND, Circuit Judge.

The District Attorney, on behalf of the Immigration and Naturalization Service, has appealed from an order, naturalizing the appellee, Repouille. The ground of the objection in the district court and here is that he did not show himself to have been a person of "good moral character" for the five years which preceded the filing of his petition. The facts are as follows. The petition was filed on September 22, 1944, and on October 12, 1939, he had deliberately put to death his son, a boy of thirteen, by means of chloroform. His reason for this tragic deed was that the child had "suffered from birth from a brain injury which destined him to be an idiot and a physical monstrosity malformed in all four limbs. The child was blind, mute, and deformed. He had to be fed; the movements of his bladder and bowels were involuntary, and his entire life was spent in a small crib." Repouille had four other children at the time towards whom he has always been a dutiful and responsible parent; it may be assumed that his act was to help him in their nurture, which was being compromised by the burden imposed upon him in the care of the fifth. The family was altogether dependent upon his industry for its support. He was indicted for manslaughter in the first degree; but the jury brought in a verdict of manslaughter in the second degree with a recommendation of the "utmost clemency"; and the judge sentenced him to not less than five years nor more than ten, execution to be stayed, and the defendant to be placed on probation, from which he was discharged in December 1945. Concededly, except for this act he conducted himself as a person of "good moral character" during the five years before he filed his petition. Indeed, if he had waited before filing his petition from September 22, to October 14, 1944, he would have had a clear record for the necessary period, and would have been admitted without question.

Very recently we had to pass upon the phrase "good moral character" in the Nationality Act; and we said that it set as a test, not those standards which we might ourselves approve, but whether "the moral feelings, now prevalent generally in this country" would "be outraged" by the conduct in question: that is, whether it conformed to "the generally accepted moral conventions current at the time."[a] In the absence of some national inquisition, like a Gallup poll, that is indeed a difficult test to apply; often questions will arise to which the answer is not ascertainable, and where the petitioner must fail only because he has the affirmative. Indeed, in the case at bar itself the answer is not wholly certain; for we all know that there are great numbers of people of the most unimpeachable virtue, who think it morally justifiable to put an end to a life so inexorably destined to be a burden on others, and—so far as any possible interest of its own is concerned—condemned to a brutish existence, lower indeed than all but the lowest forms of sentient life. Nor is it inevitably an answer to say that it must be immoral to do this, until the law provides security against the abuses which would inevitably follow, unless the practice were regulated. Many people—probably most people—do not make it a final ethical test of conduct that it shall not violate law; few of us exact of ourselves or of others the unflinching obedience of a Socrates. There being no lawful means of accomplishing an end, which they believe to be righteous in itself, there have always been conscientious persons who feel no scruple in acting in defiance of a law which is repugnant to their personal convictions, and who even regard as martyrs those who suffer by doing so. In our own history it is only necessary to recall the Abolitionists. It is reasonably clear that the jury which tried Repouille did not feel any moral repulsion at his crime. Although it was inescapably murder in the first degree, not only did they bring in a verdict that was flatly in the face of the facts and utterly absurd—for manslaughter in the second degree presupposes that the killing has not been deliberate—but they coupled even that with a recommendation which showed that in the substance they wished to exculpate the offender. Moreover, it is also plain, from the sentence which he imposed, that the judge could not have seriously disagreed with their recommendation.

One might be tempted to seize upon all this as a reliable measure of current morals; and no doubt it should have its place in the scale; but we should hesitate to accept it as decisive, when, for example, we compare it with the fate of a similar offender in Massachusetts, who, although he was not executed, was imprisoned for life. Left at large as we are, without means of verifying our conclusion, and without authority to substitute our individual beliefs, the outcome must needs be tentative; and not much is gained by discussion. We can say no more than that, quite independently of what may be the current moral feeling as to legally administered euthanasia, we feel reasonably secure in holding that only a minority of virtuous persons would deem the practise morally justifiable, while it remains in private hands, even when the provocation is as overwhelming as it was in this instance.

However, we wish to make it plain that a new petition would not be open to this objection; and that the pitiable event, now long passed, will not prevent Repouille from taking his place among us as a citizen. The assertion in his brief that he did not "intend" the petition to be filed until 1945, unhappily is irrelevant; the statute makes crucial the actual date of filing.

Order reversed; petition dismissed without prejudice to the filing of a second petition.

FRANK, Circuit Judge (dissenting).

This decision may be of small practical import to this petitioner for citizenship, since perhaps, on filing a new petition, he will promptly become a citizen. But the method used by my colleagues in disposing of this case may, as a precedent, have a very serious significance for many another future petitioner whose "good moral character" may be questioned (for any one of a variety of reasons which may be unrelated to a "mercy killing") in circumstances where the necessity of filing a new petition may cause a long and injurious delay. Accordingly, I think it desirable to dissent.

---

[a]United States v. Francioso, 164 F.2d 163, (2d Cir., 1947). [Footnote in original.]

The district judge found that Repouille was a person of "good moral character." Presumably, in so finding, the judge attempted to employ that statutory standard in accordance with our decisions, i.e., as measured by conduct in conformity with "the generally accepted moral conventions at the time." My colleagues, although their sources of information concerning the pertinent mores are not shown to be superior to those of the district judge, reject his finding. And they do so, too, while conceding that their own conclusion is uncertain, and (as they put it) "tentative." I incline to think that the correct statutory test (the test Congress intended) is the attitude of our ethical leaders. That attitude would not be too difficult to learn; indeed, my colleagues indicate that they think such leaders would agree with the district judge. But the precedents in this circuit constrain us to be guided by contemporary public opinion about which, cloistered as judges are, we have but vague notions. (One recalls Gibbon's remark that usually a person who talks of "the opinion of the world at large" is really referring to "the few people with whom I happened to converse.")

Seeking to apply a standard of this type, courts usually do not rely on evidence but utilize what is often called the doctrine of "judicial notice," which, in matters of this sort, properly permits informal inquiries by the judges. However, for such a purpose (as in the discharge of many other judicial duties), the courts are inadequately staffed, so that sometimes "judicial notice" actually means judicial ignorance.

But the courts are not helpless; such judicial impotence has its limits. Especially when an issue importantly affecting a man's life is involved, it seems to me that we need not, and ought not, resort to our mere unchecked surmises, remaining wholly (to quote my colleagues' words) "without means of verifying our conclusions." Because court judgments are the most solemn kind of governmental acts—backed up as they are, if necessary, by the armed force of the government— they should, I think, have a more solid foundation. I see no good reason why a man's rights should be jeopardized by judges' needless lack of knowledge.

I think, therefore, that, in any case such as this, where we lack the means of determining present-day public reactions, we should remand to the district judge with these directions: The judge should give the petitioner and the government the opportunity to bring to the judge's attention reliable information on the subject, which he may supplement in any appropriate way. All the data so obtained should be put of record. On the basis thereof, the judge should reconsider his decision and arrive at a conclusion. Then, if there is another appeal, we can avoid sheer guessing, which alone is now available to us, and can reach something like an informed judgment.[b]

QUESTIONS ABOUT THE CASES

1. What legal questions does Judge Hand ask about Mr. Francioso's behavior? How does he answer them?
2. What facts about the *Repouille* case make *Francioso* factually similar enough to serve as a precedent?
3. The problem in both cases is how a court should determine whether an applicant for naturalization has the required good moral character. In *Francioso* Judge Hand uses a method that permits him to conclude that Francioso should become a citizen. How does he do so?
4. Does Judge Hand use the same method in *Repouille?* If so, what facts distinguish the two cases so that, even though Francioso won, Mr. Repouille lost?
5. What method would Judge Frank use? How, if at all, does it differ from Hand's method? Which of these two do you prefer? Why?

[b]Of course, we cannot thus expect to attain certainty, for certainty on such a subject as public opinion is unattainable. [Footnote in original.]

For Further Thought

1. Stanley Fish, the literary theorist, has strongly criticized the belief that rules of law dictate "correct" answers to legal conflicts. Which points made in the first two chapters does Fish's analogy to basketball illustrate?

> Suppose you were a basketball coach and taught someone how to shoot baskets and how to dribble the ball, but had imparted these skills without reference to the playing of an actual basketball game. Now you decide to insert your student into a game, and you equip him with some rules. You say to him, for instance, "Take only good shots." "What," he asks reasonably enough, "is a good shot?" "Well," you reply, "a good shot is an 'open shot,' a shot taken when you are close to the basket (so that the chances of success are good) and when your view is not obstructed by the harassing efforts of opposing players." Everything goes well until the last few seconds of the game; your team is behind by a single point; the novice player gets the ball in heavy traffic and holds it as the final buzzer rings. You run up to him and say, "Why didn't you shoot?" and he answers, "It wasn't a good shot." Clearly, the rule must be amended, and accordingly you tell him that if time is running out, and your team is behind, and you have the ball, you should take the shot even if it isn't a good one, because it will then *be* a good one in the sense of being the best shot in the circumstances. (Notice how both the meaning of the rule and the entities it covers are changing shape as this "education" proceeds.) Now suppose there is another game, and the same situation develops. This time the player takes the shot, which under the circumstances is a very difficult one; he misses, and once again the final buzzer rings. You run up to him and say "Didn't you see that John (a teammate) had gone 'back door' and was perfectly positioned under the basket for an easy shot?" and he answers "But you said . . . ." Now obviously it would be possible once again to amend the rule, and just as obviously there would be no real end to the sequence and number of emendations that would be necessary. Of course, there will eventually come a time when the novice player (like the novice judge) will no longer have to ask questions; but it will not be because the rules have finally been made sufficiently explicit to cover all cases, but because explicitness will have been rendered unnecessary by a kind of knowledge that informs rules rather than follows from them.[16]

2. In February of 1996, I took my students to attend a sitting of the Colorado Supreme Court. During the morning's oral arguments the court wrestled with an insurance claim. The plaintiff, while riding in a car, had been hurt in a random drive-by shooting. Her auto policy covered losses suffered from injuries suffered in an autombile accident. The insurance company refused to pay, insisting that the shooting was deliberate, not accidental. It turned out that Colorado law had never defined the word "accident." How would you decide? If you had been injured in the 1995 Oklahoma City bombing, would you have felt injured by an "accident?" What if you had, just before the bomb went off, gone into the federal office building by mistake, perhaps because you were new in town and thought it was the post office? Should this distinction determine who recovers on their insurance and who doesn't? Is it not *inevitable* that judges will have to choose among different possible meanings of the word "accident," and does it not make more sense to choose a definition, in the

---

[16]Stanley Fish, *"Fish v. Fiss,"* 36 *Stanford Law Review* 1325 (1984), pp. 1329–1330.

context of insurance policies, that will achieve the goals of insurance coverage, rather than to decide in the abstract the "true" meaning of the word "accident"?

3. Professor Cass Sunstein has noted recently that analogical reasoning—what I have called "reasoning by example," is not the only form of reasoning that judges may, in theory, use to reach decisions. Other reasoning tools could include:

   a. Deductive reasoning from general theories. For example, general theories of economics claim to determine the most efficient result in certain types of situations.

   b. Compromise (sometimes called "reflective equilibrium"). Here judges might "work from the outside in" toward the best balance between inevitably competing interests. Recent affirmative action rulings fall somewhere between the position that "the Constitution is colorblind" and the position that past discrimination grants racial minorities automatic preferences.

   c. Reasoning from practical experience, not precedents.

   d. Means-ends rationality.

   The traditions of judicial justification do not condone judges who overtly reason in only these ways. You will, however, discover in the rest of this book examples of judges who manage to integrate these techniques into their justifications, usually slipping them in via the social background facts and/or the values doors.[17]

---

[17]Cass Sunstein, "On Analogical Reasoning," 106 *Harvard Law Review* 741. And see Cass Sunstein, *Legal Reasoning and Political Conflict* (New York: Oxford University Press, 1996).

CHAPTER 3

Statutory Interpretation

Whoever hath an absolute authority to interpret any written or spoken laws, it is he who is truly the lawgiver, to all intents and purposes, and not the person who first spoke or wrote them.

—Benjamin Hoadly

It is of course dangerous that judges be philosophers—almost as dangerous as if they were not.

—Paul Freund

WHAT ARE STATUTES?

"Statutes"—a dusty and unromantic word. One thinks of endless rows of thick books in inadequately illuminated library stacks. The librarians have the mildew under control, but its odor remains faintly on the air.

To understand better the significance of statutory law, we must abandon our reaction to statutes as dull and musty words; we must see them as vital forces in society. Statutes are the skeleton of the body politic. Our elected representatives officially speak to us through the statutes they enact. They form the framework that gives political power its leverage. People in government, when fortified by statutory authority, can take our property, our freedom, and our lives. Political campaigns and elections, indeed much in public life that does excite us, matter because they directly influence the making of statutory policies that can dramatically affect the quality of our lives.

In the United States, the special legal meaning of statutes rests on two fundamental principles of government. First, although all officials, including judges, can and do make law, legislatures possess primary authority for doing so.[1] When legislatures

---

[1]This familiar principle of legislative supremacy has one important exception: Courts in the United States possess the authority to reject statutory supremacy when they conclude that the enforcement of a statute would violate a legal norm expressed in or implied by the constitutions of the states or the nation. Where

make policy to address a public problem, in theory that policy controls or supersedes the policies of presidents, administrators, or judges. Second, legislatures can communicate their chosen policies in a legally binding way only by voting favorably on a written proposal. Without the vote by the legislature, no matter how forcefully individual legislators or political parties advocate a policy decision, they create no law. Committee reports, floor speeches, and so forth, may help us make sense of the law, but only the duly enacted statute has the force of law.

Statutes say, in effect: "Society has a problem. This is how society shall cope with it." Some statutory policies are incredibly general. Early antitrust statutes said that society has a problem preserving effective business competition, and it shall hereafter be illegal to restrain competition. In 1890 a nearly unanimous Congress passed with very little debate the Sherman Antitrust Act. Its first two sections state: (1) "Every contract, combination in the form of a trust or otherwise, or conspiracy, in restraint of trade or commerce among the several States, or with foreign nations, is hereby declared to be illegal"; and (2) "Every person who shall monopolize, or attempt to monopolize . . . any part of the trade or commerce among the several States, or with foreign nations, shall be deemed guilty of a misdemeanor. . . ." Such general language leaves to judges much freedom to shape and refine law. Other statutes create extremely detailed rules. Current tax laws say that government shall raise revenues, but it takes literally thousands of pages of rules and regulations to specify how government shall do it.

The first two chapters (and the appendix) introduce a number of statutes. At the national level we have already studied the Mann Act, the National Motor Vehicle Theft Act, and the Nationality Act, and at the state level the blood test and burden of proof statutes in the Wisconsin's paternity cases. In each of the cases covered, the statute did *not* automatically resolve the conflict. Chapter 2 suggested reasons why this legal ambiguity has positive as well as negative consequences. In statutory law, there is an additional benefit. Legislatures, as we shall see, cannot think of every specific case that might come up in a problem area. Statute writers must write policy in general language, which means questions and ambiguities, like whether an airplane is a vehicle under the NMVTA, inevitably pop up. How realistic is it that the drafters of Michigan's first degree murder statute would anticipate and cover precisely the circumstance of doctor-assisted suicide? In July of 1992 a Michigan trial judge threw out charges against Dr. Jack Kevorkian, who prepared methods of suicide by lethal injection and carbon monoxide which his patients voluntarily triggered.[2]

A statute that states how society shall cope with business monopoly or stolen vehicles or any of thousands of other problems does instruct judges to settle legal conflicts in

judges find a violation, their expression of constitutional values becomes supreme, and this political dynamic is part of the familiar set of checks and balances that American government contains.

[2]See "Murder Charges Against Kevorkian Are Dismissed," *New York Times,* July 22, 1992, p. A6. In April of 1996, frustrated Michigan authorities tried prosecuting Kevorkian again. This time the prosecution admitted that no Michigan statute declared assisted suicide as wrong, but the prosecution instead followed an unusual Michigan precedent that seemed to permit prosecution for common law crimes. Legal scholars said the move was "highly unusual," and made "no legal sense, except as a way to give the state a tool to go after Kevorkian." See "Kevorkian Is Facing Prosecution Without a Statute's Being Cited," *New York Times,* April 17, 1996, p. A8. For a comprehensive review of all the political and interpretive issues involved in statute making and implementation, see William D. Popkin's *Materials on Legislation: Political Language and the Political Process* (Westbury, N.Y.: The Foundation Press, 1993).

one way rather than another. How should judges decide in concrete cases what statutes mean? When judges resolve specific cases in terms of statutes, they should seek first the guidance of earlier case precedents dealing with the same interpretive problem. But what if the problem has never arisen before? We call this *statutory interpretation in the first instance.* When judges decide what uncertain statutes "really" mean the first time, without any help from precedents, they must try to decipher what policy the statute adopts, not what they think good policy ideally ought to be. *McBoyle* and *Caminetti* each had to decide, in the first instance, how to unravel statutory uncertainties. Judge Richard Posner likens the problem to a field commander in combat who radios his superiors for instructions. He hears the instruction "Go . . ." but immediately loses contact with headquarters. The field commander must decide to go forward or back, but he knows he cannot stay where he is, even if that seems the wisest course to him.[3]

A judge must address directly such questions as these: What problem does this statute try to solve? Is the case before me an example of such a problem? If so, how does this statute tell me to solve it? The judge who approaches statutory interpretation in the first instance this way acknowledges legislative supremacy. It is not the judge's idea of the problem that resolves the case. Rather, the judge must identify the problem and decide the case in the way the statute communicates that problem and its solutions.

Judges who approach statutes wisely also know that they cannot treat the words as a series of Webster's definitions strung together. Wise judges intuitively appreciate the saying, "The greatest difficulty with communication is the illusion that it has been achieved." They know that words gain meaning not from dictionaries, but from their context. They know that a sign on an outdoor escalator reading "Dogs Must Be Carried" does not mean that everyone riding the escalator must carry a dog.[4] They know that the words of statutes become meaningful only when they are applied sensibly to the solution of public problems.

THREE WAYS JUDGES MISTAKENLY INTERPRET STATUTES

We have just outlined how judges should interpret statutes in the first instance. The rest of the chapter fills in the details. We must begin, however, by seeing that judges actually interpret statutes in ways that violate the principles of democracy and of common sense that we've just described.[5]

First Mistake: Sticking to the Literal Meaning of Words

Perhaps the most celebrated problem of statutory interpretation in American jurisprudence involves the seemingly straightforward and rather boring statutes governing

---

[3]See Posner's "Legal Formalism, Legal Realism, and the Interpretation of Statutes and the Constitution," 37 *Case Western Reserve Law Review* 179 (1986–1987), p. 189.

[4]My thanks to Professor Allan Hutchinson for this illustration.

[5]The persistence of what sometimes verges on downright silliness in statutory interpretation thus illustrates a critical point made near the beginning of Chapter 2: The law's language, practices, and traditions, like those in any field of organized human action, tend to perpetuate themselves even when they no longer square well with contemporary social background facts and values, i.e., they perpetuate bad legal reasoning.

inheritances. When someone with property dies with a valid will, statutes direct that the property go to the named heirs. When a person dies without a will, statutes designate which relatives—spouses, children, parents, siblings, and so on—take priority, and in what order. Until specific cases arose, these statutes said nothing to prevent people who committed murder in order to get an inheritance, either under a valid will or by statute, from getting the money. In an Ohio case, where the statute said the children would inherit from a parent who died without a spouse and without a will, one Elmer Sharkey took out mortgages on his mother's real estate and then murdered her. The court held that the law entitled him—or rather his debtors, since Elmer had since been hanged—to the money because the statute did not, by its literal words, forbid murderers from inheriting from their victims. The Ohio court reviewed a New York case holding that a grandson named to inherit in his grandfather's will should, despite the law, *not* inherit after he poisoned his grandfather. The Ohio court nevertheless reasoned: "[W]hen the legislature, not transcending the limits of its power, speaks in clear language upon a question of policy, it becomes the judicial tribunals to remain silent." Is this good legal reasoning? The New York court had reasoned that it would not serve any valid statutory purpose to let someone inherit who had murdered to do so.[6]

In 1912 Lord Atkinson, speaking for the British House of Lords in its appellate judicial role, said:

> If the language of a statute be plain, admitting of only one meaning, the Legislature must be taken to have meant and intended what it has plainly expressed, and whatever it has in clear terms enacted must be enforced though it should lead to absurd or mischievous results.[7]

Lord Atkinson, no doubt, respected legislative powers and responsibilities—in this case, those of the House of Commons. The problem he perceived, we can safely guess, is this: If courts can go beyond the words at all, they can go anywhere they want, setting their own limits and destroying legislative supremacy in the process.

Legislative supremacy is important, but how would the good Lord react to this hypothetical statute: "A uniformed police officer may require any person driving a motor vehicle in a public place to provide a specimen of breath for a breath test if the officer has reasonable cause to suspect him of having alcohol in his body." Presumably Lord Atkinson would not exempt women from this law just because the last sentence reads "him" rather than "him or her." The earlier use of the word "person," even to a literalist, can cover both sexes. But how would he handle the following argument by an equally literalistic defendant? "The statute plainly says the officer may require the specimen from a person driving. I may have been slightly inebriated when the officer pulled me over, but when the officer required the specimen I was *not* 'driving a motor vehicle.' I wasn't even in my car. I was doing my imitation of a pig in the middle of the pavement

---

[6]*Deem v. Millikin*, 6 O.C.C. Rep 357 (1892), 360, and 53 Ohio St. 668 (1895); *Riggs v. Palmer*, 115 N.Y. 506 (1889). See the discussion in Hart and Sacks, above (fn 7, p. 4), beginning at page 75. See also Richard Posner, *The Problems of Jurisprudence* (Cambridge: Harvard University Press, 1990), pp. 105–107. For Ronald Dworkin's famous discussion of this classic problem, see his *Taking Rights Seriously* (Cambridge: Harvard University Press, 1977), pp. 23–31. And see Joel Levin's discussion of the same problem in his *How Judges Reason* (New York: Peter Lang, 1992), Chapter 6.

[7]*Vacher and Sons, Ltd., v. London Society of Compositors*, A.C. 107 (1912), 121.

when the officer requested the specimen."[8] This result is absurd, but Lord Atkinson seems willing to accept absurd results. Should he be?

American judges have also been seduced by the appeal of adhering to the words. A Virginia statute stated: "No cemetery shall be hereafter established within the corporate limits of any city or town; nor shall any cemetery be established within two hundred and fifty yards of any residence without the consent of the owner. . . ." In 1942, after the legislature passed this statute, the town of Petersburg, Virginia, bought an acre of land within its corporate limits on which to relocate bodies exhumed during a road-widening project. The acre adjoined and would be incorporated into a long-established cemetery. A city resident well within the proscribed distance of the added acre brought suit to prevent the expansion and cited the statute. He lost. Justice Gregory wrote for the appellate court:

> If the language of a statute is plain and unambiguous, and its meaning perfectly clear and definite, effect must be given to it regardless of what courts think of its wisdom or policy. . . .
>
> The word, "established," is defined in *Webster's New International Dictionary,* second edition, 1936, thus: "To originate and secure the permanent existence of; to found; to institute; to create and regulate. . . ."
>
> Just why the Legislature, in its wisdom, saw fit to prohibit the establishment of cemeteries in cities and towns, and did not see fit to prohibit enlargements or additions, is no concern of ours. Certain it is that language could not be plainer than that employed to express the legislative will. From it we can see with certainty that . . . a cemetery . . . may be added to or enlarged without running counter to the inhibition found in [the statute]. . . . Our duty is to construe the statute as written.[9]

Judges, like Justice Gregory, who cling to the literal meaning of words fail to appreciate that the dictionary staff did not sit in Virginia's legislature. By sticking to the words, the judges prevent themselves from asking what problem the legislature sought to address. Just why the legislature might purposely allow enlargement but not establishment of cemeteries in cities and towns *is* Justice Gregory's concern. Unless he tries to solve that puzzle, we can have no confidence that he has applied the statute to achieve its purpose.

Second Mistake: The Golden Rule

Of course, Lord Atkinson could have solved his problem another way, by sticking to the words except when they produce absurd results. The Golden Rule of statutory interpretation holds that judges should follow

> the grammatical and ordinary sense of the words . . . unless that would lead to some absurdity, or some repugnance or inconsistency with the rest of the instrument,

[8]See Sir Rupert Cross, *Statutory Interpretation* (London: Butterworths, 1976), p. 59. Or imagine a city ordinance requiring all liquor stores "to cease doing business at 10:00 P.M." Does the ordinance permit them to reopen at 10:01 P.M.?

[9]*Temple v. City of Petersburg,* 182 Va. 418 (1994), pp. 423–424. Responding to the vague words of the Mann Act (quoted in Chapter 2), Justice Day wrote in his majority opinion in *Caminetti,* "Where the language is plain and admits of no more than one meaning the duty of interpretation does not arise. . . ." Was the language of the the Mann Act plain?

in which case the grammatical and ordinary sense of the words may be modified, so as to avoid the absurdity and inconsistency, but no farther.[10]

The Golden Rule solves the problem of the clever intoxicated driver. It would be absurd and possibly dangerous to require that the officer ride with him and collect the specimen while weaving down the road.

But the Golden Rule, unfortunately, does not solve much more because it does not tell us how to separate the absurd from the merely questionable. To test this weakness in the rule, ask yourself two questions: (1) Is it absurd to allow expansion of existing graveyards while prohibiting the creation of new ones, or only questionable? (2) Is it absurd to use the Mann Act to prevent the transportation of willing girlfriends and mistresses across state lines along with unwilling "white slaves" and prostitutes, or merely questionable? The Golden Rule provides no answer.

Both the literal approach and the superficially more sensible Golden Rule fail. They deceive judges into believing that words in isolation can be and usually are clear and that the words communicate by themselves. But they don't. The word "establish" in *Temple* (the graveyard case), the phrase "immoral purpose" in *Caminetti* (our first Mann Act case), and the word "vehicle" in *McBoyle* (the airplane theft case) simply are not clear, and no blunt assertion to the contrary will make them so. Even when words in isolation do seem unambiguous, the process of coordinating them with the facts of a particular case may make them unclear. The judge who simply examines the words by themselves and asserts that they are clear seeks only an easy exit. Taking Webster's definition of "establish" as an example, the responsible judge would at least have to explain why the city of Petersburg was not originating and securing "the permanent existence of" the new acre for a cemetery. Justice Gregory did not explain this. Interpreting words in isolation rather than in context, then, is a danger because it leads judges to believe that they have thought a problem through to its end when they have only thought it through to its beginning.

To summarize, words become meaningful only in context. In statutory interpretation, judges must analyze two contexts, the legislative context—what general problem exists and what kind of policy response to it the legislature has created; and the case context—what the litigants are disputing and whether their dispute involves the problem the statute addresses. To say that words are clear or unclear depending on the context really means that the words would become clear if we could imagine a different case or context arising under each of the same statutes this book has mentioned so far. If Mr. McBoyle had stolen a car, or if Mr. Caminetti had abducted a Mexican-American immigrant girl, judges would have had no difficulty concluding that the statutory words clearly and unambiguously determine the case. Judges would similarly not have hesitated to prohibit Petersburg from opening a brand new cemetery within the city limits.

The idea that words read literally will mislead has been around a very long time. In 1615, Galileo explained in a letter to the Grand Duchess of Tuscany the same idea. After strongly affirming that "the Bible can never speak untruth," Galileo went on to write that the Bible

is often very abstruse, and may say things which are quite different from what its bare words signify. Hence in expounding the Bible if one were always to

---

[10]*Grey v. Pearson*, 6 H.L. Cas. 61 (1857), 106, quoted in Cross, p. 15.

confine oneself to the unadorned grammatical meaning, one might fall into error. Not only contradictions and propositions far from true might thus be made to appear in the Bible, but even grave heresies and follies.

Literally read, the Bible would have God forgetting the past and clueless about the future, clearly contradictory to church teachings about the omnipotence of God. It is not too much to expect that judges learn what Galileo taught the Grand Duchess.

Third Mistake: Legislative Intent and Legislative History

Idle Armchair Speculation   One common way in which judges try to justify their interpretations of statutes is to try to discover what the legislature "intended" its statutory words to mean. I shall try in a moment to persuade you that "legislative intent" is a most slippery and misleading concept. For now, think carefully about the following use of legislative intent. How much more comfortable are you with Chief Justice Rugg's reasoning in the next case than you were with Lord Atkinson's literal approach or Justice Gregory's reasoning in the cemetery case or Justice Day's argument in *Caminetti?*

Shortly after it became a state, and long before the Nineteenth Amendment to the United States Constitution enfranchised women, Massachusetts passed a statute providing that "a person qualified to vote for representative to the General Court [the official name of the Massachusetts legislature] shall be liable to serve as a juror." Ten years after the passage of the Nineteenth Amendment, one Genevieve Welosky, a criminal defendant, found herself facing a Massachusetts jury that excluded all women. Welosky protested the exclusion, appealed, and lost. Under the literal or Golden Rule approaches she would surely have won, for "person" includes women, and women were "qualified to vote." Even before the days of women's liberation, we would hardly label it absurd to allow female jurors.

But Massachusetts Chief Justice Rugg invoked the intent of the legislature:

> It is clear beyond peradventure that the words of [the statute] when originally enacted could not by any possibility have included or been intended by the General Court to include women among those liable to jury duty.... Manifestly, therefore, the intent of the Legislature must have been, in using the word "person" in statutes concerning jurors and jury lists, to confine its meaning to men.[11]

The legislature didn't intend women to become jurors when they passed the statute because at that time women could not vote. Despite the literal meaning of the words, women cannot therefore sit on juries.

---

[11]*Commonwealth v. Welosky,* 276 Mass. 398 (1931), pp. 402–406. A similar issue arose in a 1985 U.S. Supreme Court case where plaintiffs challenged, on right to counsel grounds, a statute that allowed a maximum fee of ten dollars to be paid an attorney who represents veterans seeking benefits before the Veterans Administration. The statutory maximum was passed at the close of the Civil War in 1864! Does it not make more sense to assume that inflation has defeated the purpose of the original maximum? Plaintiffs lost. In an angry dissent, Justice Stevens, joined by Justices Brennan and Marshall, wrote, "The fact that the $10-fee limitation has been on the books since 1864 does not, in my opinion, add any force at all to the presumption of validity." *Walters v. National Association of Radiation Survivors,* 105 S.Ct. 3180, at 3213.

The title of this section offered the hope that judges can find statutory truth by discovering legislative intent. The Massachusetts court has identified an uncontested social background fact—that women could not vote when the statute was passed—and concluded logically that the legislature did not intend women to sit on juries. This logic is straightforward enough, but the *Welosky* opinion is a virtual fraud. Rugg says the simple sequence of historical events reveals the legislature's intent; because the statute came before the amendment, the legislature did not intend to include women. But Rugg's first quoted sentence sends us on a wild goose chase. It is plausible that the legislature did not consider the possibility of women—or for that matter immigrant Martians—becoming jurors. But it is simultaneously plausible that the Massachusetts legislature "intended" to settle the problem of who may sit as a juror once and for all by simply gearing jury liability automatically to all future changes in the voting laws. A legislature that did so would hardly act absurdly. Rugg completely fails to show that it did not so act.

Does the hope that legislative intent will reveal the meaning of statutory language hence fail? Ultimately it does fail, but not because of poorly reasoned cases like *Welosky*. The quest for legislative intent is a search for hard evidence. It is detective work in the legal field, not Rugg's idle armchair speculations, so we should not abandon the field of legislative intent so quickly.

Judges have many sleuthing techniques for discovering "hard evidence" of intent, of which we now review three of the most prominent. What do you think of them?

Other Words in the Statute   The brief excerpt from the cemetery case may have treated Justice Gregory unfairly, for he did not simply rest his opinion on Webster's dictionary. He continued by pointing out that another section of the cemetery statute of Virginia

> affords a complete answer to the question of legislative intent in the use of the word "established" in Section 56, for the former section [Section 53] makes a distinction between "establish" and "enlarge" in these words: "If it be desired at any time to establish a cemetery, for the use of a city, town, county, or magisterial district, or to enlarge any such already established, and the title to land needed cannot be otherwise acquired, land sufficient for the purpose may be condemned. . . ."
>
>   The foregoing language, taken from Section 53, completely demonstrates that the legislature did not intend the words "establish" and "enlarge" to be used interchangeably, but that the use of one excluded any idea that it embraced or meant the other.[12]

Similarly, Justice McKenna, dissenting in *Caminetti,* found support in the official title of the Mann Act:

> For the context I must refer to the statute; of the purpose of the statute Congress itself has given us illumination. It devotes a section to the declaration that the "Act shall be known and referred to as the 'White Slave Traffic Act.'" And its prominence gives it prevalence in the construction of the statute. It

---

[12]*Temple v. City of Petersburg*, p. 424.

cannot be pushed aside or subordinated by indefinite words in other sentences, limited even there by the context.[13]

The title of the statute tells Justice McKenna that Congress did not intend to police the activities of willing girlfriends. Willing girlfriends are not white slaves; the conclusion sounds sensible.

The Expressed Intent of Individual Legislators and Committee Reports   Like Justice Gregory, Justice McKenna, in his *Cominetti* dissent, made more than one argument to support his conclusion.[14] In fact, he went directly to the words of the bill's author and quoted extensively from Representative Mann:

> The author of the bill was Mr. Mann, and in reporting it from the House committee on interstate and foreign commerce he declared for the committee that it was not the purpose of the bill to interfere with or usurp in any way the police power of the states, and further, that it was not the intention of the bill to regulate prostitution or the places where prostitution or immorality was practiced, which was said to be matters wholly within the power of the states, and over which the Federal government had no jurisdiction. . . . [Mann stated]:
>
> "The White Slave Trade—A material portion of the legislation suggested and proposed is necessary to meet conditions which have arisen within the past few years. The legislation is needed to put a stop to the villainous interstate and international traffic in women and girls. The legislation is not needed or intended as an aid to the states in the exercise of their police powers in the suppression or regulation of immorality in general. It does not attempt to regulate the practice of voluntary prostitution, but aims solely to prevent panderers and procurers from compelling thousands of women and girls against their will and desire to enter and continue in a life of prostitution." *Congressional Record,* vol. 50, pp. 3368, 3370.
>
> In other words, it is vice as a business at which the law is directed, using interstate commerce as a facility to procure or distribute its victims.

Judges rarely argue that the expressed views of any one legislator necessarily convey legislative intent, but they frequently cite committee reports and statements of authors as proof of intent. This is a curious practice, for it seems to allow a minority of legislators to determine what the law holds in spite of the fact that in a legislature the majority rules.

Other Actions, Events, and Decisions in the Legislature   To establish legislative intent, judges may also look at how the legislature handled related legislation. In *Welosky,* Chief Justice Rugg noted that the Massachusetts legislature had in 1920 changed several laws relating to women in order to make them conform to the

---

[13]*Caminetti v. United States,* p. 497.

[14]Appellate judges often give multiple arguments for the conclusions in their opinions, but they rarely articulate whether one argument, by itself, would justify the same result. They don't, in other words, spell out the relative importance of the arguments they use.

Eighteenth and Nineteenth Amendments, but said nothing about the problem of female jurors. He argued regarding the 1920 legislation:

> It is most unlikely that the Legislature should, for the first time require women to serve as jurors without making provision respecting the exemption of the considerable numbers of women who ought not to be required to serve as jurors, and without directing that changes for the convenience of women be made in court houses, some of which are notoriously over-crowded and unfit for their accommodation as jurors.

Judges may even find in the physical evidence presented to committees the key to intent. In the 1940s the postmaster general refused to grant the preferential lower postage rate to books, like workbooks and notebooks, that contained many blank pages. Congress then amended the relevant statute to grant the preferential postal rates to books with space for notes. However, the postmaster general continued to refuse the rate to so-called looseleaf notebooks with blank pages on the basis that they were not permanently bound. A shipper of such notebooks eager for the cheaper postage rate sued for an order granting the preferential rate.

The opinion of Judge Groner concluded that Congress did intend to give the preferential rate to looseleaf notebooks because the many physical exhibits placed before the committee that handled the bill included some such notebooks. Groner wrote, "[I]t follows logically that textbooks of the make and quality of those of appellant were considered and purposely included by Congress in the list of publications entitled to the book rate."[15]

The list of possibilities in this category could continue for pages. For example, judges are fond of finding legislative intent by discovering that one house's version of a bill contained a clause that does not appear in the final law, approved by both houses. They conclude from this discovery that the legislature intended that the remaining words *not* mean what the dropped clause meant. Superficially, these discoveries of "hard evidence" of legislative intent appeal to us because they seem to reveal the purpose of the statute. But comparing the examples of sleuthing with our "first principles" of statutory interpretation reveals that legislative intent fails as badly as our other two approaches. Only the statute, the words for which the majority of both houses of the legislature voted, has the force of law.

When Judge Groner concludes "logically" that the legislature intended to include looseleaf notebooks for the preferential rate, he is logically completely incorrect. He does not give one shred of evidence that any legislator, much less the majority, actually thought about the physical exhibits when they voted. Of course, Representative Mann's thoughts give us some clue to his intent, but we do not know that a majority heard or read his thoughts. Even if a majority in the House and Senate did know what Mann intended, we don't know that they agreed with him. After all, the statute uses the word *prostitution* without Mann's qualifications. Maybe the majority voted for the act because they wanted a tougher response than did Mann.

---

[15]*McCormick-Mathers Publishing Co. v. Hannegan,* 161 F.2d 873 (D.C. Cir. 1947), p. 875. See Arthur Phelps, "Factors Influencing Judges in Interpreting Statutes," 3 *Vanderbilt Law Review* 456 (1950).

Why then, precisely, does legislative intent fail as a tool of statutory interpretation? A legislature is an organizational unit of government. By itself a legislature can no more intend something than can a government car or an office building. *People* intend things, and, because the elected representatives in a legislature are people, they may intend something when they vote. If all members of the voting majority intended the same thing, then that might well state the purpose of the statute. Here three difficulties fatal to the cause of legislative intent arise.

First, intent is subjective. It is usually impossible to tell with 100 percent certainty what anyone, ourselves included, intends. Thus, if a majority of legislators were fortunate enough to intend the same thing, it is highly unlikely that judges could actually discover what that thing was. For centuries, the difficulties of knowing a person's actual intentions have led common law principles of contract and tort to reject the relevance of evidence about the actual intentions of the parties. Instead the law asks what a reasonable and prudent person would think or do in such a situation.

Second, we know enough about politics to know that in all likelihood the individuals making up the voting majority do not intend the same thing. Most will not have read the statute they vote on. By casting their vote some will intend to repay a debt, or to be a loyal follower of their party leaders, or to encourage a campaign contribution from a private source in the future. If we want to deduce collective intent on anything, we must take a poll, and the only poll we ever take of legislators is when the presiding officer of the house calls for the vote to enact or defeat a bill. "Yes" voters intend to vote "yes," and "No" voters intend to vote "no," but that's about all we can accurately say about their intentions.

The third and most serious difficulty is that if by a miracle we overcome the first two difficulties, so that we actually know that the majority intended the same thing about a statute, it is highly unlikely, if not absolutely impossible, that they intended anything about the unique facts of the case before the court. In all probability the facts of cases such as *Mortensen* or *Cleveland* arose long after the lawmaking legislature disbanded. Just as in the *Repouille* case, a general feeling about an issue in the abstract does not necessarily resolve concrete cases, yet legislators at best intend only such general directions. Pose the Mann Act Congress problems of migrating Mormons or vacationing prostitutes and you would probably get a gruff instruction to "ask a judge about the details." And of course by the time those cases actually arose, the majority of the makers of the Mann Act were, if not in their graves, surely no longer in Congress.

We shall see later that the evidence we falsely ascribe to legislative intent can sometimes help define the purpose of the statute, the problems the statute tries to solve. But this evidence is rarely decisive alone.

WORDS, INTENT, AND HISTORY DO NOT REACH "CORRECT" INTERPRETATIONS

This chapter provides as powerful a group of illustrations of judicial confusion as any to be found in this book. Hart and Sacks have written, "The hard truth of the matter is that American courts have no intelligible, generally accepted, and consistently applied theory of statutory interpretation."[16] Three characteristics of the reasoning process help explain the frequency of unpersuasive statutory interpretations.

The Disorderly Conduct of Words

Linguistics and the philosophy of language are abstruse and difficult subjects. Much of our knowledge of the complexity of language is quite recent. Few lawyers—hence few judges—study the disorderly conduct of words, and this is the first characteristic that helps to explain interpretive confusion. To understand this we must master generality, vagueness, and ambiguity in language.

First, words are often necessarily *general.* General language allows us to think of many specific possibilities simultaneously. Advertisers often use generalities to good advantage. An advertisement that says "Dynamic Motors cars over the last five years have needed fewer and less costly repairs than Universal Motors cars" wants us to believe that all Dynamic Motors (DM) cars perform more reliably than all Universal Motors (UM) cars. Of course, even if the ad is completely true, it does not mean that. It certainly does not mean that DM's bottom line models perform more reliably than UM's top line models. But this is a helpful generalization, especially if you are debating whether to invest in DM or UM stock. Statutes necessarily speak in general language in order to control the wide variety of specific cases that are part of the social problem with which the statute copes, but judges must take care to discover what the generalization does *not* mean.

Second, language can be *vague.* The Dynamic Motors ad may be general (it may also be factually wrong!), but it is not vague because we can easily tell DM-built cars from UM-built cars. But consider this statement: "Bigger cars are safer than little cars." Vagueness in language refers to uncertainty about how much or of what degree of something a statement encompasses. We do not know how much car is enough to make it big, and we don't know whether bigness is size, weight, or both.

Third, and most important, words turn out to communicate *ambiguous* ideas; that is, words allow us to think of two simultaneously inconsistent concepts. Sometimes ambiguity in language arises when one or just a few words have mutually inconsistent meanings, because the dictionary itself permits such a clash of meanings. What does this statute mean? "It shall be a misdemeanor to sleep at a railway station." Does the word "at" include those comfortably asleep in their upper berths while their train rests at the station? Sleep can mean (1) being in a state of unconscious repose or (2) deliberately bedding down and spending the night. The first definition would cover both the hobo

---

[16]Henry M. Hart, Jr., and Albert M. Sacks, *The Legal Process* (Cambridge: Harvard Law School, 1958), p. 1201. And see Arthur Murphy, "Old Maxims Never Die: The 'Plain Meaning Rule' and Statutory Interpretation in the 'Modern' Federal Courts," 75 *Columbia Law Review* 1299 (1975), p. 1308. Murphy asserts, "[T]he courts have no clear idea about what the plain meaning rule is and, what is more, . . . they really do not care." The leading proponent of the plain meaning approach today is Supreme Court Justice Antonin Scalia. His jurisprudence has been strongly criticized from many quarters. For criticism from a highly respected judge, see Particia Wald, "The Sizzling Sleeper," 39 *American University Law Review* 277 (1990). See also Richard Brisbin, *Justice Antonin Scalia and the Conservative Revival* (Baltimore: The Johns Hopkins University Press, 1997), and David Schultz and Christopher Smith, *The Jurisprudential Vision of Justice Antonin Scalia* (Lanham, Md: Rowman & Littlefield, 1996). Scalia himself refers to those who disagree with him as "vigilantes." See his "Vigilante Justices" in *The National Review,* February 10, 1997, p. 32.

sprawled on a bench and the tired commuter dozing upright while waiting for the delayed train. The second meaning would spare the commuter but not the hobo.[17]

Language may also possess syntactic ambiguity. In this case, it is the ordering of the words, not varying dictionary definitions, that causes a problem. A statute regulating bank loans might say, "The banker shall require the borrower promptly to repay the loan." Does this mean the banker shall require the borrower to repay as soon as the law permits the banker to do so, or does this mean that the borrower must repay quickly once the banker begins requiring repayment, whenever that might be? Relocating the position of the word "promptly" in the sentence would have avoided the ambiguity.[18]

This chapter has emphasized the importance of interpreting the meaning of words by examining their context.[19] If the sentence proscribing sleeping in train stations augments a statute controlling vagrancy, the context of vagrancy solves the problem. If the neighboring language in the bank statute governs bankers on one hand or borrowers on the other, that ambiguity would disappear. But despite this chapter's lecture about the importance of context, context can create as well as eliminate ambiguity. This was one of the problems created by the wording of the Mann Act. While "prostitution" normally carries a fairly clear meaning, placing it in the context of the "White Slave" act potentially changes the word's interpretation. While prostitutes as a rule need not be unwilling, maybe *these* prostitutes must be unwilling before the statute applies.

Once we realize that the context of statutes can sometimes render them ambiguous rather than clear, we must face this reality: The linguistically honest judge will, from time to time, have to admit that the statute does not, through its words, communicate any clear-cut solution to the case and context before her. We'll see later what this judge must then do.

The Booming Canons of Statutory Construction

In the past, judges have defended themselves against the imprecision of words by arming themselves with interpretive weapons called "canons of construction." Judges have often used these weapons unwisely, and this unwise use of the canons is another source of confusion in statutory interpretation.

A canon of construction or interpretation (they are, for our purposes, the same), is really a rule for interpreting rules, a device designed to make vague or ambiguous words appear precise. Here is an example:

---

[17]Linguists call this semantic ambiguity. See Reed Dickerson, *The Interpretation and Application of Statutes* (Boston: Little, Brown, 1975) pp. 45–46. It may help you to understand these distinctions if you figure out why the general and vague statements about cars are not semantically ambiguous, or syntactically or contextually ambiguous either, as the next few paragraphs define these concepts.

[18]Dickerson, pp. 46–47. The meaning of "ambiguity" here is much narrower than in Chapter 2, where it encompassed all sources of imprecision in law.

[19]The classical illustration in the literature is from Wittgenstein, one I have modernized here. Suppose a father takes his child to Las Vegas, hires a croupier, and says, "Teach the kid some games." Would the father be disappointed to find the croupier taught the boy the fine points of Monopoly? If the father had uttered the same sentence to a baby-sitter at home, he could be equally disappointed to discover the child gambling his college savings on the chance of drawing to an inside straight in seven-card stud. The context—Las Vegas versus living room—makes all the difference.

Where general words follow a statutory specification, they are to be held as applying only to persons and things of the same general kind or class of thing to which the specified things belong.

This canon, called *ejusdem generis,* may not mean much to you until you apply it in the context of a specific case. Fortunately, we have already covered two legal problems to which this canon could apply.

In the first, *McBoyle,* which involved the theft of an airplane, the relevant statute forbade transportation across state lines of a stolen "automobile, automobile truck, automobile wagon, motorcycle or any other self-propelled vehicle not designed for running on rails." Is an airplane such a vehicle? By invoking the ejusdem generis canon ("of the same kind"), a judge could conclude that the general words "or any other self-propelled vehicle" refer only to items *like* (in the same genus as) the objects the statute specifically mentions (the species). In this case, all the specific items run on land. Therefore, an airplane is not a vehicle.

Similarly, Justice Day invoked the ejusdem generis canon in reaching the conclusion that the Mann Act did cover concubines. He said that the general words "other immoral purposes" refer only to sexual immorality because all the specific examples fit that genus. If you take your mother or a female friend across a state line to rob a bank, you will not violate the Mann Act even though "immoral," by its plain meaning, clearly includes robbery.

Before we consider why the canons represent a vice rather than a virtue in statutory interpretation, it will help to review a few more examples from among dozens of canons that judges utilize. One frequently cited canon instructs judges to interpret criminal statutes narrowly. This means that when a judge finds that the statute does not clearly resolve his case, he should resolve it in favor of the defendant. Again *McBoyle* can illustrate. Justice Holmes wrote for the Supreme Court in that case:

> [I]t is reasonable that a fair warning should be given to the world in language that the common world will understand of what the law intends to do if a certain line is passed. To make the warning fair, so far as possible the line should be clear.

Holmes argues, in other words, that unless judges interpret criminal statutes narrowly, judges will send to jail people who had no clear notice that they had committed a crime.[20]

Holmes's concern for fairness in *McBoyle* reminds us that the canons are not totally ineffective or undesirable weapons. Felix Frankfurter said that "even generalized restatements from time to time may not be wholly wasteful. Out of them may come a sharper rephrasing of the conscious factors of interpretation; new instances may make them more vivid but also disclose more clearly their limitations."[21] Nearly every canon that judges have created contains at least a small charge of sensibility. Canons exist to support each of the principles of proper interpretation that this chapter covers. For

---

[20]*McBoyle v. United States,* p. 27. A narrow interpretation may produce a very different decision from that of a literal interpretation. A literal interpretation of the words "other immoral purposes" in the Mann Act *would* make the act cover my taking my wife to another state to rob a bank. A narrow interpretation would not.

[21]Felix Frankfurter, "Some Reflections on the Reading of Statutes," 2 *Record of the Association of the Bar of the City of New York* 213 (1947), p. 236.

example, the canon *noscitur a sociis* ("it is known by its associates") states that words are affected by their context. One British court used this canon to confine a statute regulating houses "for public refreshment, resort and entertainment" only to places where people received food and drink and excluded musical and other theatrical places, refreshing though their shows might be. The statute bore the title Refreshment House Act.[22] Again we must ask why the canons are part of the problem rather than part of the solution.

By making disorderly words appear orderly, canons deceive judges into thinking they have found a sensible and purposeful application of the statute to the case. In fact, the canons often allow judges to evade the difficult task of untangling statutory purpose and of weighing all four elements of legal reasoning. One example of this judicial evasion of purpose occurred after Congress passed a statute in 1893 designed to promote railway safety.[23] In part, Section 2 of the statute reads:

> [I]t shall be unlawful for any . . . common carrier [engaged in interstate commerce] to haul or permit to be hauled or used on its line any car . . . not equipped with couplers coupling automatically by impact, and which can be uncoupled without the necessity of men going between the ends of the cars.

Section 8 of the Act placed the right to sue for damages in the hands of "any employee of any such common carrier who may be injured by any locomotive, car or train in use contrary to the provisions of this act. . . ." At common law, the injured employee often had no right of action against his employer; Section 8 created that right. Additionally, the act imposed criminal penalties on railroads that failed to comply.

A workman was injured while positioned between a locomotive and a car. He had tried to couple them by hand because the locomotive did not possess a coupler that coupled automatically with the car. He sued for damages and lost both in the trial court and in the U.S. Court of Appeals, the latter holding that the statute did not require locomotives to possess the same automatic couplers. Judge Sanborn fired canon after canon in defense of his conclusion that the statutory word "cars" did not include locomotives:

- "The familiar rule that the expression of one thing is the exclusion of the others leads to [this] conclusion."
- "A statute which thus changes the common law must be strictly construed."
- "This is a penal statute, and it may not be so broadened by judicial construction as to make it cover and permit the punishment of an act which is not denounced by the fair import of its terms."
- "The intention of the legislature and the meaning of a penal statute must be found in the language actually used."[24]

Do any of these canons convince you that this statute does not require locomotives to have automatic couplers? Again, the canons are not themselves absurd; the damage occurs when they seduce judges into applying them simplistically and into thinking the

---

[22]Cross, p. 118. The list of canons is lengthy. Karl Llewellyn cites and provides judicial citations for 56 canons in "Remarks on the Theory of Appellate Decision and the Rules or Canons about How Statutes Are to Be Construed," 3 *Vanderbilt Law Review* 395 (1950), pp. 401–406.

[23]27 Stat. c. 196, p. 531.

[24]*Johnson v. Southern Pacific Co.*, 117 Fed. 462 (C.C.A. 8th 1902). Fortunately the United States Supreme Court reversed, 196 U.S. 1 (1904).

canon gives *the* answer when the canon only justifies *an* answer. Does not Judge Sanborn's reasoning at least create the suspicion in your mind that he wanted, for whatever reasons, to rule for the railroads, and that the easy availability of canons only provided convenient camouflage for his personal preferences?

The vice of the canons resembles the familiar law of mechanics. For each and every canon there is an equal and opposite canon. Llewellyn organizes his 56 canons noted in footnote 22 into 28 sets of opposing canons: "THRUST BUT PARRY," he calls them. The judge who, for whatever reason, reaches any conclusion can find a canon to defend it.

Consider this example of Llewellyn's point: A federal statute prohibits the interstate shipment of any "obscene . . . book, pamphlet, picture, motion-picture film, paper, letter, writing, print or other matter of indecent character." One Mr. Alpers shipped interstate some phonograph records that, admitted for the sake of argument, were obscene. On the basis of ejusdem generis and "strict construction of criminal statutes," two canons, we might expect Mr. Alpers to win his case. After all, the genus to which all the species belong is "things comprehended through sight." Instead, Justice Minton, for the Supreme Court, alluded to noscitur a sociis, another canon, and upheld the conviction.[25]

In short, the canons themselves are at war. In *Caminetti,* ejusdem generis pushes toward conviction, but "narrow construction" pushes toward acquittal. Shall judges flip coins?

Judicial Naiveté about the Legislative Process

The last and most serious source of judicial confusion in statutory interpretation involves the naive assumptions judges often make about how legislatures make laws. An old political aphorism holds: "There are two things that the public should never see being made: sausages and laws." Judges often ignore the mundane realities of legislative life. The frequent judicial discoveries of the intent of the legislature, when in all probability the legislature intended nothing with respect to the unique factual situation before the court, best illustrate the problem.

Much can be (and has been) said for abandoning the concept of legislative intent permanently. The ever-skeptical Holmes wrote, "I don't care what their intention was, I only want to know what the words mean." And Frankfurter added, "You may have observed that I have not yet used the word 'intention.' All these years I have avoided speaking of the 'legislative intent' and I shall continue to be on my guard against using it."[26] A few pages back I introduced the reasons why the concept of intent fails. Let me expand those observations in three directions here.

First, legislatures respond to public problems by creating general public policies. The problem is nearly always an accumulation of many different specific instances, like vehicle thefts, white slavery, juror selection, or controlling of the location of cemeteries. Legislatures simply do not confront the concrete and always unique factual case. In this sense, as former Attorney General Levi once said, "Despite much gospel to the contrary, a legislature is not a fact-finding body. There is no mechanism, as there is with a court, to require the legislature to sift facts and to make a decision about specific

---

[25]*United States v. Alpers,* 338 U.S. 680 (1950).
[26]Frankfurter, pp. 227–228.

situations."[27] In all probability no one in the legislature foresaw the precise problem facing the judge, and it is even less likely that the legislature consciously intended to resolve the case one way or another.

The candid judge looking for firm evidence of intent often won't find it. A candid Rugg would, for example, have concluded, "I simply can't say whether the Massachusetts legislature thought about women becoming jurors or not." The names Holmes and Frankfurter endure more prominently than Rugg because they were especially able to make such candid judgments.[28]

For further illustration of this point, consider one final problem. A federal immigration statute requires that immigrants receive an immigration permit prior to leaving their home country and that they present the permit on arrival before being allowed to enter and move about the United States. Imagine that on a voyage of immigration from China a woman with a permit gives birth to a child. While the mother can present her permit and enter, her new infant cannot. There is no shred of evidence in the legislative history of the immigration law that Congress ever once thought about this problem. Must the infant (and presumably its mother) return to China?[29]

Second, although the United States government prints reams of information about legislation in Congress—committee hearings, committee reports, speeches, and so forth—judges often have no access to this kind of information about how state legislatures operate. Even if we could count on this information to reveal the true intent of legislators (which we can't), much of the time judges won't get the information in the first place.

The *third* and most important set of reasons that judges misunderstand the legislative process is that they hide from the mundane facts of political life. Consider:

- The institutional dynamics of contemporary policy making are so complex and the political cross-pressures so intense that Congress often makes garbled policy and sends conflicting messages. Reviewing Martha Derthick's disturbing study, *Agency Under Stress: The Social Security Administration in American Government,* Martin Shapiro summarized the condition succinctly:

  Presidents, energized by their electoral mandates, seek to institute transformations in policy and do so with a rationalizing bias and a remoteness from the practicalities of field implementation. Conflicts between president and Congress lead to unclear and inconsistent statutory direction to administrators. Congress itself—responding to its multiple constituency, electoral connection—keeps changing its signals. And although it fails to care enough about administration to do a good job, it often resorts to detailed commands to administrators for policy or political reasons while simultaneously seeking to minimize the costs of administration.[30]

---

[27]Edward H. Levi, *An Introduction to Legal Reasoning* (Chicago: University of Chicago Press, 1949), p. 31.

[28]The eminent jurisprudent John Gray wrote, "The fact is that the difficulties of so-called interpretation arise when the Legislature has had no meaning at all; when the question which is raised on the statute never occurred to it. . . ." *The Nature and Sources of the Law* (New York: Macmillan, 1927), p. 173.

[29]Charles Curtis, "A Better Theory of Legal Interpretation," 3 *Vanderbilt Law Review* 407 (1950), p. 413.

[30]Book review, 85 *American Political Science Review* 1020 (1991), p. 1021. Cf. W. Lance Bennett, *The Governing Crisis* (New York: St. Martin's Press, 1992).

• We saw earlier (on pg. 46) that Judge Groner could not logically conclude that the Congress intended to include looseleaf notebooks in the preferential rate just because one committee's exhibits contained samples of them. The conclusion appears even shakier once we acknowledge that a lobbyist, with or without conscious help from a busy committee chairman, might have deliberately planted that evidence before the committee. The lobbyist may not aggressively try to influence the committee, but he would hope to persuade the judge later in litigation that the planted evidence proves legislative intent and thereby win a favorable judicial ruling for the lobbyist's client. As long ago as 1947, Archibald Cox wrote that "it is becoming increasingly common to manufacture 'legislative history' during the course of legislation."[31]

• Both houses of a bicameral legislature must approve the identically worded bill before it becomes law. Often when the two houses disagree, special joint committees form to negotiate the compromise. Whatever force committee reports and speeches might have had on the passage of the original bill in each house, it is difficult, if not impossible, to discern the grounds on which the two houses compromise. Often the compromise package includes a decision to leave a question deliberately unanswered simply to avoid stalemate. The process of deciding on a compromise also often means, in practice, that one house may ratify without debate a bill containing provisions it never considered one way or another when it debated and passed its own bill.

• Judges often claim to distill congressional intent from the formal speeches and remarks of legislators printed in the *Congressional Record,* as if the entire body of legislators sat in rapt attention, devouring and ultimately approving the tenor of the remarks. But the bulk of the *Record*'s comments simply appear there at the request of the legislator. Even when debate precedes the vote, the floor usually contains virtually no one but debaters and a very few listeners. The *Record* tells nothing about how many rushed in to record their votes without hearing the floor debate.

• Often there is no real legislative history at all. Most state legislatures still do not produce complete documentation of proceedings that most lawyers can access. Even Congress sometimes acts without hearings or meaningful debate. In practice, a legislative aide often drafts the legislation after getting advice from a variety of members of Congress and its committees. The drafter will construct, as best he or she sees it, the language that accommodates the competing interests within Congress. Thus, practically, this drafter will be the only person who thinks fully about where the purposes of a particular piece of legislation stop. If that person is an attorney (and this is usually the case), the attorney-client privilege actually forbids communication with the courts about the actual intentions of the people whom he or she represented in the drafting process!

• Most voting legislators never read the bill on which they vote at all; more likely, they hurriedly glance at the committee report. Most often, the voting legislator relies on party leadership, or on the advice of an aide who has reviewed the

[31]Archibald Cox, "Some Aspects of the Labor Management Relations Act, 1947," 61 *Harvard Law Review* 1 (1947), p. 44. Justice Antonin Scalia has recently reemphasized this same argument. See "With Rights Act Comes Fight to Clarify Congress's Intent," *New York Times,* November 18, 1991, p. A1.

problem, or on the record of public opinion, or on the private urging of a lobbyist. They may do any or all of these without giving any detailed thought to the bulk of the words and sentences in the act (drafted most likely by administrators, aides, and lobbyists in combination—not by legislators) that lawyers piously debate later in court.[32]

• Finally, judges often ignore the possibility that the lawmaking process might purposely create unclear law because legislatures *want* the courts to fill in the details. This may amount to buck-passing in the hope that the courts will take the pressure for an unpopular result. But legislators may also believe that case-by-case judicial action is the best way to decide precisely what the statute should include and exclude. The judge who fails to look for that purpose evades his own judicial responsibilities.

These examples of legislative realities should make judges wary of concluding that the legislature ever intended anything. "Legislative intention," Professor Horack wrote,

> is useful as a symbol to express the gloss which surrounds the enacting process—the pre-legislative history, the circumstances and motivations which induced enactment. . . . Society cannot act effectively on subjectivity of intent; and, therefore, legislative intention becomes not what the legislature in fact intended but rather what reliable evidences there are to satisfy the [judicial] need for further understanding of the legislative action.[33]

The ultimate danger in all of these methods of statutory interpretation—the literal and Golden Rule approaches, the use of canons, and the search for legislative intent in legislative history—is that each allows the judge to reach a conclusion without ever struggling with the fundamental question of whether one interpretation or another actually copes with social problems effectively. These methods, in other words, perpetuate decisions that may not promote law's basic goal—social cooperation. The next section describes a better way for judges to interpret statutes.

HOW JUDGES SHOULD INTERPRET STATUTES IN THE FIRST INSTANCE

Statutory interpretation so frequently seems inadequate because judges face an unavoidable necessity. Judges must say what the law "is" in order to resolve the case before them. I call this a necessity for judges because our society, our culture, believes that judges act unfairly when they do not decide on the basis of what the law says and is.

---

[32]On his retirement late in 1986, long-time senator (and 1964 presidential candidate) Barry Goldwater told an interviewer, "We don't work . . . Monday. We don't work Friday or Saturday. So we work a three-day week. . . . People don't get here for 9 o'clock meetings until 9:15 A.M., and 9:30 A.M. . . . We were elected to serve our country and yet we don't do it very well." "Retiring Goldwater fires parting shots, says Congress doesn't serve nation well," *Atlanta Journal and Constitution*, November 27, 1986, p. 2N. See also the comments of a former congressman, Judge Abner Mikva, "How Well Does Congress Support and Defend the Constitution," 61 *North Carolina Law Review* 587 (1983).

[33]Frank E. Horack, Jr., "The Disintegration of Statutory Construction," 24 *Indiana Law Journal* 335 (1949), pp. 340–341.

Judges cannot hear a case and then refuse to render a decision because they cannot determine the legal answer.[34] We do not pay judges to say, "Maybe the law is X. Maybe the law is Y. I'll guess Y. You lose!" (Or worse, "I don't care if it's X or Y. You still lose!") In order to render justice in our culture, judges must persuade us to believe with certainty that which is inherently uncertain.

Making the murky and muddled appear clear and composed (the *art* in judging and in everything else) is particularly difficult in statutory interpretation. In common law and in constitutional law, the courts know that they have authority to make law. In these realms judges can say, "The law ought to be X, not Y. Therefore the law is X." But legislative supremacy bars judges from interpreting statutes so boldly. They must try to find the "oughts" somewhere in the legislative process, an uncertain and distant process in which judges themselves play little part. It is like sending forth a knight with orders to find the Holy Grail, requiring him to return in a week with anything he finds as long as he can persuade us that what he found is the Grail, and repeating this order week after week.

Judges will continue to make uncertain statutes certain in their application by creating and asserting that certainty can and does emerge from the generality, the vagueness, and the ambiguity in words, and from the disorderly world of politics. They can do so persuasively by identifying the *purpose* of the statute, i.e., the problem statutory language tries to solve.

The Centrality of Statutory Purpose

Judges should believe, almost as an article of faith, that words by themselves never possess a plain or clear or literal meaning. Statutes become meaningful only to the extent that their words fit some intelligible purpose. The problem the statute addresses always gives direction to the search for purpose. A dictionary never does.

Judges must satisfy themselves that their application of a statute to the case before them serves the statute's purpose. Sometimes a statute seems automatically to determine a case. We saw that this would occur if McBoyle had transported a stolen automobile instead of an airplane. But judges must understand that no conclusion is totally automatic. We can imagine that an individual could transport an automobile across state lines, knowing the car to be stolen, and yet not violate the act: an FBI agent driving the car back to its owner. The agent does not violate the act because he is not part of the problem the act tries to solve—he is part of the solution.

Let me explain this a slightly different way. The questions people ask determine the answers they receive. The right answer to the wrong question should never satisfy a judge. In statutory interpretation, the right questions always begin with questions about statutory purpose: What social problems does this statute try to correct? Does the case before us in court now represent the problem the statute addresses? Think of the difference it can make in *Johnson* (the locomotive coupling case) to ask (1) "Is a locomotive a railroad car?" versus (2) "Is protecting the safety of workers coupling locomotives to cars as well as cars to cars a sensible part of the problem this law tries to cope with?"

---

[34]This is true of most formal legal systems. For example, the French Civil Code dating from 1804 states, "A judge who refuses to enter judgment on the pretext of silence, obscurity, or inadequacy of the statute is subject to prosecution for the denial of justice."

Notice that whenever a judge inquires into the purpose of the legislation he must inevitably inquire into the social background facts that reveal the nature of the social problems involved in the case and how the statute tries to cope with them.

To illustrate, consider a contemporary variation on the Mann Act. Suppose some imaginary international legislature passed a law making it a crime "to transport women or girls from one nation to another for purposes of prostitution, debauchery, or any other immoral purpose." In interpreting the purpose of such a statute, it would be entirely appropriate for courts to consider evidence that the monstrous trading in unwilling women, Representative Mann's original concern, persists to this day. In late 1995, the *New York Times* headlined a story, "From a Bangkok Grocery to a Brothel in New York." The story told of a Thai woman who, promised a free airline ticket and a job in New York, left home, only to find herself kept behind barred doors and windows until she had slept with enough customers to pay off her plane ticket. And in late 1996, the *Bangkok Post* headlined "Asia's Trafficking Shame." The story, which reported on the recent World Congress Against Exploitation of Children held in Sweden, noted that approximately one million females worldwide are sold into forced prostitution each year and that approximately 35 percent of these are under age 18. The story noted how the ease of traveling between Thailand, Burma, Laos, Cambodia, Vietnam, and the Yunan province of China helped traffickers evade prosecution.[35]

Determining Purpose: Words Can Help

It is the language of a statute that alone has the force of law. Nothing else that individual legislators or legislative bodies say or do legally binds a judge. Some legislation includes specific definitions of key words. These definitions in statutes may or may not agree with a dictionary definition, but they are law and they bind the judge. Legislation, though lacking an internal dictionary, always contains words whose ordinary definitions unambiguously shape its purpose. By including the word *prostitution,* the Mann Act unambiguously covers more than white slavery because by no ordinary definition are prostitutes necessarily enslaved in that occupation. Judges must never give words a meaning that the words, in their context, cannot bear. Except for its euphemistic title, the "White Slave Act" contains not one word to indicate that the women whose transportation it forbids must be unwilling. It is in this context that the word *prostitution* unambiguously shapes the Mann Act's meaning.

Context is always crucial. Some contexts require courts to decide precisely the opposite of the literal command of words. If, through some printing error, the officially published version of a statute omits a key word, judges properly include the word if the context makes such a purpose clear. Suppose that a statute prohibiting some very undesirable behavior omits in its official version the key prohibitory word "not." Although the statute would then literally permit or even require the unwarranted behavior, judges may apply the statute as if it contained the missing and critical "not."

Canons of interpretation may help reassure judges that a given word, phrase, or sentence has a certain meaning in a specific context. They may serve as shorthand

[35]*New York Times*, September 12, 1995, p. A12; *Bangkok Post*, September 18, 1996, p. C3.

reminders of ways of thinking about purpose. But a canon should never dictate to a judge that words must have one meaning regardless of context. The canons of ejusdem generis and of narrow construction of criminal statutes may help a judge exclude airplanes and obscene records from the reach of those two statutes, but they do not compel that conclusion, as the next section illustrates.

Noscitur a sociis can also be a helpful reminder for a way of thinking about purpose. The context of neighboring words may crystallize the meaning of an ambiguous phrase. What, for example, is "indecent conduct"? In the abstract, we might agree that it depends on individual perceptions and moralities and that we can't really tell what it is. But consider two statutes, one that prohibits "indecent conduct at a divine service of worship" and another that prohibits "indecent conduct at a public beach or bathing place." The contexts of worship and beach could both classify total nudity as indecent conduct, but only one context would classify playing a game of volleyball in string bikini bathing suits as indecent.

Let me put this even more strongly. In life, not just in law, things don't exist "in the abstract." In the abstract, there is no such thing as, say, "indecent conduct." We might, trying to pick an extreme and hence conclusive example, say that cannibalism is automatically "indecent conduct." Jeffrey Dahmer's crimes certainly were, but when the survivors of a plane crash high in the Andes consume the flesh of the dead in the hope of staying alive, does not the specific context change our feelings drastically about the moral meaning of cannibalism?

Determining Purpose: The Audience

Legislatures direct different statutes to different kinds of audiences. Some statutes, especially criminal statutes, communicate to the community at large. Criminal statutes thus have the purpose of communicating general standards of conduct to large populations containing people of widely varying degrees of literacy and local customs and habits. Judges properly interpret such words according to the common meanings they may expect these words to convey to this diverse population. Other perhaps highly technical laws may communicate only to special classes of people, such as commercial television broadcasters or insurance underwriters. Here the words may assume technical meanings that only the special audience understands. Similarly, judges should hold that a statute purposely changes a long-held principle of common law or the legality of a behavior widely believed proper in the past only when they think a statute makes that purpose unambiguously clear.

Determining Purpose: The Assumption of Legislative Rationality and the Uses of Legislative History

In determining whether an issue in a lawsuit is part of the problem that a statute purposely tries to address, judges should treat the people who make laws and the process of lawmaking as rational and sensible, "reasonable persons pursuing reasonable purposes reasonably," as Hart and Sacks put it.[36] This assumption helps judges determine

---

[36]Hart and Sacks, p. 1415.

purpose because it forces them to determine what portion of the law, prior to the enactment of the statute, worked so poorly that a rational legislature wanted to change it.[37]
Again, think about how the result in the locomotive coupling case would differ if the
court had approached the problem this way. Finally, what purposes would a rational
legislator have for inserting the "good moral character" test in our nationalization laws?
Is such a purpose well served by making moral judgments about incest or mercy-killing
in the abstract?

The judge who thinks about lawmaking as a logical process also recognizes that no
statute exists in isolation, for rational lawmakers understand that no one act can completely define where its policy stops and another competing policy ought, instead, to
govern. Members of Congress realize (and the courts grasp that they know) that state
law, not federal law, assumes the major responsibility for defining and policing criminal
behavior. Knowing that state laws purposely define and prohibit sexual immorality limited the purpose the Court attributed to the Mann Act in *Mortensen*.

Sometimes, as we have seen, no helpful legislative history exists at all. But at other
times courts can generate sensible conclusions about the purpose of statutes from the
statements of legislative committees, sponsors of the bill, and so forth. This history
may allow a judge to understand what aspects or consequences of prior law failed to
cope with a social problem so that the legislature needed to create a new law.
Legislative history may also clarify where one policy should give way to another.
Legislative history relating to specific applications of the statute, as in the looseleaf
notebook case, only helps the judge to the extent that it provides good evidence of the
legislation's general purpose.

Illustrations of Statutory Purpose

Three Easy Cases   You should now have little difficulty resolving comfortably some
of this chapter's cases. Despite the ambiguities in the statutory language, you should
not hesitate (1) to allow the officer to collect the breath specimen from a driver standing on the shoulder of the road, not while the driver weaves down the highway; (2) to
prohibit the liquor store from reopening at 10:01 (see footnote 8); and (3) to allow the
sleepy commuter to doze upright on the bench while prohibiting the hobo from
encamping in a corner. The words don't require these conclusions and judges probably
lack any legislative history for these state and local laws, but judges can still reach sensible results. The words can bear these interpretations, and our knowledge of social
problems and purposes compels these conclusions. Notice, by the way, how the solution
to each of these three cases hinges on the judge's realistic assessment of the social background facts and widespread public values that bear on these cases, not merely on the
rules and case facts alone.

Of course, other cases could arise under these same statutes in which the words themselves would not bear the interpretation claimed for them. Our officer cannot collect
breath specimens in parking lots and driveways outside cocktail parties at midnight, even
if he safely assumes that many will soon drive home and even if we believe it a highly wise
social policy to prevent intoxicated drivers from driving in the first place. This action might

---

[37]Lord Coke originated this helpful approach, sometimes labeled the *mischief rule*, in 1584.

be an effective preventive, but it is not found in the meaning and purpose of this law because the words make "driving" a prerequisite for demanding the specimen.

The Case of the Lady Jurors, or Why Legislative Intent Does Not Necessarily Determine Statutory Purpose   Recall briefly Chief Justice Rugg's justification for excluding women from jury liability despite the fact that they could vote and despite the fact that the statute required jury duty of "persons" (not "men") qualified to vote. The legislature did not intend "person" to include females because females could not then vote, he said.

Like the case of the automatic couplers, *Welosky* offers a classic example of a judge reaching the right answer to the wrong question. Of course the legislature did not intend to include women, but that doesn't answer the right question. The proper question is, "What purpose does legislation serve that gears jury liability to voter eligibility?"

Efficiency is one possible answer because this policy spares the legislature from repeatedly rehashing the question of who should sit on juries. Quality is another, for this policy provides a test of qualifications that will insure at least the same minimum degree of responsibility, competence, education, and permanence of residence for both jurors and voters. Both voting and jury duty are general civic functions of citizens. Gearing the right to practice medicine, for instance, to voting eligibility would not make much sense, but gearing these two similar civic functions sounds reasonable. But where does turning the problem around leave us? Does it serve a purpose to pass a statute saying, in effect, "If you are qualified to vote, you are qualified to serve as a juror; however, any changes in voter eligibility hereafter enacted won't count because we haven't thought of them yet."? If the legislation had this purpose, why didn't it simply list the desirable qualifications for jurors? Read the statute as Rugg did and the gearing loses purpose. Rugg did not treat the policy process as rational and sensible. He did not admit that juror qualifications could have been purposely designed to change with the times.

The difference between a search for legislative intent and a search for purpose, then, is the difference in the evidence judges seek. Judges who believes they must show intent will examine reports, speeches, and prior drafts of bills. This evidence probably won't give clear meaning to the statute because it will contain internal inconsistencies or raise issues only in general terms. Moreover, judges who thinks they must find intent can fool themselves into believing that they have found it in the evidence. On the other hand, judges who feels they must articulate a sensible statement of purpose will necessarily search much further, into dictionaries, canons, verbal contexts, and competing social policies as well as history itself. They will coordinate the materials in order to reach a confident articulation of purpose. They will perform the judicial function as Benjamin Cardozo described it. (See the epigraph that opens this book.) They will work harder than will judges who stop when they have found a nugget of legislative history, which is why so many judges, possessing the all-too-human tendency to laziness, are satisfied with the nugget.

Statutory Purpose in the Cases of Criminal Commerce: Caminetti, McBoyle, and Alpers   In each of these three cases, Congress, under the authority of the commerce clause of the U.S. Constitution, forbade citizens from moving what Congress

deemed evil from one state to another. Let us assume that every state had laws to deal with each of the evil things—statutes punishing theft, prostitution, and pornography. What purpose, then, does additional *federal* legislation on these matters serve? For each of the federal statutes we possess records of committee reports, floor speeches, and other legislative history. In no case, however, does the solid data of legislative history reveal whether the purpose of the statute does or does not include the cases of our defendants. After a delightfully detailed review of the House and Senate reports on the Mann Act and of the discussions reported in the *Congressional Record* showing, if not total confusion about the act, at least much disagreement about its specific meaning, Levi concludes, "The Mann Act was passed after there had been many extensive governmental investigations. Yet there was no common understanding of the facts, and whatever understanding seems to have been achieved concerning the white-slave trade seems incorrectly based. The words used were broad and ambiguous."[38]

These cases resemble each other not only in their constitutional origins but also because the canons of construction could resolve each of them. The canon dictating narrow construction of criminal statutes could allow a judge to reverse the three convictions, since the law does not unambiguously apply to any of these special factual situations. A judge who adopted Holmes's belief that criminal laws must communicate to a general lay audience with a clarity the average man can understand would reach the same result. Following ejusdem generis, however, Mr. Caminetti might go to jail, but McBoyle, the airplane thief, and Alpers, the seller of obscene records, would still go free.

Despite these similarities, these cases do not come out this way. The smut peddler and the boyfriend went to jail. McBoyle went free. The three judicial opinions together articulate no coherent linkages between purposes and outcomes. To link purposes and outcomes, we must begin with the right question: Why would Congress, "reasonable persons pursuing reasonable purposes reasonably," pass laws making actions crimes when all the states already have, through their criminal laws, expressed a policy? Does not the purpose lie in the fact that movement from state to state makes it difficult for the states to detect or enforce the violation? A car owner who has his car stolen may have trouble tracking it in another state. The prosecutor in the state where citizens receive wanted or unwanted pornography cannot reach the man who peddles by mail from another state. Men who hustle girls far from home may make both detection and social pressure to resist prostitution impossible. Movement has consequences. It makes objects and behaviors physically harder to locate. It makes apprehension and prosecution more difficult because police and prosecutors in one jurisdiction don't have authority in another. The presence of physical movement thus helps to reveal purpose.

In *McBoyle,* then, the proper questions ought to look something like this: (1) Do airplanes, because they are movable, complicate the task of catching people who steal them? (2) Does it, secondarily, serve any purpose to assume that McBoyle thought flying a stolen airplane to another state was legal because of the ambiguities in the word *vehicle?* Is it, in other words, unfair to McBoyle to convict him under this act because

---

[38]Levi, p. 40, and see pp. 33–40. Virtual enslavement of girls for "sale" as prostitutes is, in many parts of the world, a major moral and public health problem. Murray Kempton reports an estimate of 200,000 child prostitutes in Thailand in 1992. See Kempton's "A New Colonialism," *The New York Review of Books,* November 19, 1992, p. 39.

the act does not unambiguously include airplanes? You should reach your own conclusion, but I would answer the first question with a yes, the second with a no, and respectfully dissent from Justice Holmes.

You should ask one other question about *McBoyle*. Suppose McBoyle's lawyer had argued that when the Motor Vehicle Theft Act was passed, air travel was in such infancy that Congress probably did not intend to include airplanes. Notice that this argument should matter to you only if you think it important to ask what Congress intended. If you instead consider legislation as policy designed to adjust to future technological and other changes that lawmakers cannot in the present foresee, and if you ask instead what kind of crimes call for the kind of law enforcement help that this act provides, you would find McBoyle's lawyer's argument trivial.

Is *Alpers* any different? It might be, particularly if you see the case as presenting a constitutional problem of free expression. The purpose of this statute might be said to be to prevent exposing children or unwilling people, people who open mail or see magazines left around, to visual pornography. Is this purpose served by prohibiting the shipment of obscene records?

I find *Alpers* an especially difficult case. Unlike Mr. McBoyle, Mr. Alpers could reasonably have interpreted the act as not banning records for two reasons. First, the competing principle of free expression does set limits on government interference with the communication of ideas. No such principle limits governmental interference with the movement of property known to be stolen. Second, the purpose of the Motor Vehicle Theft Act specifically seems to apply to airplanes. They are very transportable. The act's purpose may therefore especially apply to airplanes. However, one reading of the purpose of the statute in *Alpers*—visual pornography left around may offend but a phonograph record lying around does not—reduces its applicability to *Alpers*. But, although it reduces it, it doesn't eliminate it. The recipient might play the dirty record for an unwilling person and cause that person great offense. However, does not the *McBoyle* example provide a strong argument for excusing Alpers? Isn't transporting stolen property at least as morally ambiguous as pornography?

Finally, consider the man who brings in a willing girlfriend from out of state for a night or for the big-game weekend. Conceivably, the Mann Act could purposely try to police all forms of sexual immorality involving, somehow, interstate transportation. But what are the probabilities that this legislation has such purpose in light of (1) the title of the act; (2) the canons of narrow construction of and clear communication in criminal statutes; (3) the problem arousing public concern at the time; (4) the fact that states are just as able, if they so choose, to discover and crack down on noncommercial illegal sex as the FBI; (5) Representative Mann's report and the widespread belief that the general police powers reside in state and not federal hands?

Notice how only by using many different techniques of interpretation together do we begin to develop confidence about the purpose of the Mann Act.

A Final Complication

This summary of sensible judicial approaches to statutes may, I fear, have misled you in one critical respect. You may now feel that in every case the "right-thinking" judge will find the one "right" solution simply by uncovering a single purpose of the statute. This chapter's illustrations all make sense when we analyze them in terms of purpose. *We may, however, still honestly disagree about purpose.* Justice does not reside in judges who find the one right solution as much as it resides in judges who decide cases of first instance in terms of purpose. The task of judging is choosing among plausible alternative possibilities, not solving an algebra problem. Even judges who work to discover purpose may disagree about the resolution of a specific case.

To illustrate, suppose Holmes had said in *McBoyle,*

> The purpose of this act is to permit federal assistance to states in finding easily moved and hidden vehicles. But airplanes, while easily moved, are really like trains, which the act expressly excludes, because, like trains, they are tied to places where they cannot be hidden—airports. What goes up must come down, and only in certain places. One black Ford may look like a thousand other black Fords almost anywhere, but an airplane is much more like a train in this respect. Therefore, since we believe states, not the federal government, possess primary police powers, this act does not cover airplanes.

Finally, suppose in the cemetery case Justice Gregory argued,

> Establishment and expansion of cemeteries differ because the people near an expanded cemetery are already used to its presence, but to create a new cemetery in a place where residents had not planned on seeing funeral processions and graves and other unwanted reminders of life's transience is another matter.

Whether we agree or disagree with these analyses, at least these analyses rest on purpose. We should prefer them to the automatic citation of a canon, a quotation from a dictionary, or to any technique of interpretation that allows judges to evade the difficult task of determining statutory purpose.

STARE DECISIS IN STATUTORY INTERPRETATION

This chapter has reviewed some of the most enticing problems in legal reasoning. These problems and their solutions appeal to our instinctive quest for sensibility, not just in law but in all our affairs. They show us that reason, our reason, can give us the confidence to assert that some judicial choices are wiser than others. The discovery that we can make sense of important and apparently complex legal issues can give us, more generally, a feeling of independence and competence in an increasingly complex society. Democracy will not survive in conditions of high complexity if most citizens conclude that government and politics have become too complicated for them to understand and influence.

In nearly all of this chapter, we have thus far studied an atypical occurrence in statutory interpretation, interpretation *in the first instance.* This may already have puzzled you, for Chapter 2 stated that reasoning by example—using precedents as guides for resolving legal conflicts—is central to legal reasoning. So far, however, this chapter has not mentioned reasoning by example at all. In the interpretation of statutes in the first instance, courts by definition have no precedents with which to work. In this chapter, we have examined some methods for interpreting statutes in the first instance, but these methods do not resolve the more typical problem: Once a court has given direction and meaning to a statute by interpreting it in the first instance, when should courts in the future follow that interpretation? When, conversely, should courts prefer a different interpretation and ignore or overrule an earlier court's first effort to make sense of the statute's meaning?

Let me make this point more sharply. Assume that the *McBoyle* decision wrongly interpreted the National Motor Vehicle Theft Act because its purpose does cover the theft of airplanes. Or assume that *Caminetti* wrongly applied the Mann Act to include the transportation of girlfriends. Should a court facing a new airplane or girlfriend case feel bound to accept that interpretation? Once a precedent or series of precedents gives a clear answer on a point of law, should courts leave it to legislatures to change that questionable interpretation by statutory amendment? In what circumstances should judges adhere to stare decisis in statutory interpretation?

It might seem sensible to you to answer these questions by referring to the justifications for stare decisis that appeared near the end of Chapter 2. When adherence to a prior interpretation or series of cases interpreting a statute promotes stability in law and this stability in turn allows citizens to plan their affairs by relying on specific legal rules— in short, when stability promotes the paramount social goal of cooperation—courts should not abandon stare decisis. Similarly, if a citizen now deserves to receive the same treatment a citizen in a precedent did, or if we feel stare decisis would preserve efficient judicial administration or a positive public image of justice, then courts should honor it. When stare decisis does not promote these goals, courts should freely ignore it. Thus, assuming a court felt that both *McBoyle* and *Caminetti* were wrongly decided, normal stare decisis theory would permit overruling *Caminetti* but not *McBoyle*. It injures no citizen to declare that something once held criminal is no longer so, but it does seem unfair to convict someone after declaring that his actions were not crimes.

Unfortunately, some judges and legal scholars believe that judges should invariably follow the first judicial attempt to find statutory meaning even when they have doubts about the wisdom of the first attempt and, worse, when the characteristics of the problem do not call for stare decisis. We shall first review an example of this "one-shot theory" of statutory interpretation in action.[39] Then we shall evaluate its shortcomings. We shall see that, in part, it fails because it depicts judges once again misunderstanding how legislatures operate and how courts should reason from legislative action and inaction. We shall also see in this example considerable judicial ignorance about stare decisis itself.

MAJOR LEAGUE BASEBALL, HAVILAND'S DOG AND PONY SHOW, AND GOVERNMENT REGULATION OF BUSINESS

The power of the federal government to regulate business derives from the constitutional clause empowering Congress to make laws that regulate commerce "among the several states." Armed with this authority Congress has passed many statutes regulating

---

[39]William Eskridge calls the theory "the super-strong presumption against overruling statutory precedents." "Overruling Statutory Precedents," 76 *Georgetown Law Journal* 1361 (1988) at 1363. Eskridge's very thorough analysis agrees in nearly all respects with the position I take in this chapter. Calling the notion "a very odd doctrine," he analyzes cases from 1961–1987 and finds that "in only twenty-six instances (or one per term) has the Court explicitly repudiated both the reasoning and the result of a statutory precedent." p. 1368. He concurs with Justice Scalia's statement that "vindication by Congressional inaction is a canard." p. 1405n.

wages, hours of work, safety and health standards, and so forth in businesses. Such laws apply not only to businesses and businesspersons that physically cross state lines or transact business among states. They also apply to businesses operating within one state entirely, on the theory that these businesses nevertheless may compete with and affect businesses operating from other states.[40] Modern economic and political theory also suggest that the collective health of small businesses and of labor can and does affect the national welfare.

Among the many such statutes regulating business, we shall consider only two. The more substantial of the two, the federal antitrust laws, responded to the huge cartels and monopolies that emerged in the nineteenth century by prohibiting certain activities that restrain competition in business. (See p. 38.) They authorize criminal and civil proceedings by government and by citizens privately when they feel they are damaged by anticompetitive business practices. The antitrust laws were in the news in the 1990s after the Justice Department filed suit against MIT and the eight elite Ivy League universities because the admissions officials had met annually to decide how much financial aid to offer individual students with applications at more than one of these elite schools. The Justice Department argued that the schools were conspiring to fix the "price" of top-quality students. The same kind of collusion in business to avoid costly price competition presumptively would violate the antitrust prohibitions. MIT alone defended the lawsuit, insisting the law did not apply to that situation.[41] This story confirms the basic assumption on which antitrust law rests: Despite popular rhetoric, economic competition is *not* the "natural" state of affairs; cooperation is. Cooperation reduces risks and uncertainties to parties but imposes external costs on those excluded, here the students and other less elite universities.

The Animal Welfare Act of 1970, our second statutory example, specifies a variety of requirements for handling animals in a humane manner.[42] The statute requires "exhibitors" of animals "purchased in commerce or the intended distribution of which affects commerce or will affect commerce" to obtain an exhibitor's license. The statute explicitly includes carnivals, circuses, and zoos. It empowers the Agriculture Department to administer its regulatory provisions.

Within the context of these two statutes, we shall now observe a truly wondrous phenomenon in contemporary law. Within the past twenty years courts have held: (1) that the multimillion-dollar industry of professional baseball, with all its national commercial television coverage and travel from state to state and to foreign countries, *is not* a business in interstate commerce such that the antitrust laws govern the owners of baseball clubs; and (2) that "Haviland's Dog and Pony Show," consisting of a maximum of two ponies and five dogs traveling the rural byways of the American Midwest and earning a handful of dollars weekly, *is* a business in interstate commerce that must therefore meet the requirements of the Animal Welfare Act.[43]

We need say little more about the *Haviland* case. Haviland refused to obtain an exhibitor's license. The court held that he was wrong to refuse. Given the current legal definition of commerce, the interpretation is entirely defensible constitutionally. This

[40]*United States v. Darby*, 312 U.S. 100 (1941), and *Wickard v. Filburn*, 317 U.S. 111 (1942).
[41]See "What's An A Student Worth?", *Newsweek*, July 6, 1992, p. 52.
[42]15 U.S.C. 1 et seq. and 7 U.S.C. 2131 et seq.
[43]*Flood v. Kuhn*, 407 U.S. 258 (1972); *Haviland v. Butz*, 543 F.2d 169 (D.C. Circuit 1976).

interpretation and result also make sense in terms of the presumed purpose of the statute. Owners of dog-and-pony shows, we can assume, are no less likely to abuse their animals than is the staff of the San Diego Zoo; rather more likely, I should think.

But why don't antitrust statutes regulate major league baseball? Rigid adherence to stare decisis in statutory interpretation provides the answer, as the following chronology of decisions illustrates.

1922   The "Federal Baseball Club of Baltimore," a member of a short-lived third major league, sued the National and American Leagues claiming that the two leagues had, in violation of the antitrust laws, bought out some Federal League clubs and induced other owners not to join the league at all. The Baltimore franchise found itself frozen out and sued to recover the financial losses caused by the anticompetitive practices of the other leagues. The case reached the United States Supreme Court, where Justice Holmes's opinion held that the essence of baseball, playing games, did not involve interstate commerce. The travel from city to city by the teams, Holmes thought, was so incidental that it did not bring baseball within the scope of the act. Thus, without reaching the question whether the defendants did behave anti-competitively within the meaning of the statute, Holmes ruled that the act did not apply to professional baseball any more than it would apply to a Chautauqua lecturer traveling the circuit.[44]

      Comment: We should not hastily condemn Holmes's reasoning. His opinion predated by 20 years the final shift in the legal meaning of commerce that solidified in the holding of *Wickard v. Filburn,* so we cannot blame him for an antiquated definition. Also, to his credit, Holmes did not try to discover whether Congress intended to include baseball within the scope of the antitrust laws. There is nothing in the opinion that stamps its results with indelibility, nothing that says if the commercial character of baseball changes, baseball club owners would nevertheless remain free to behave monopolistically. For its time, *Federal Baseball* rested on defensible if not indisputable reasoning.

1923   A year later Justice Holmes addressed the applicability of the antitrust laws in the field of public entertainment. In this case, the plaintiff, a Mr. Hart, acted as a booking agent and manager for a variety of actors. He specialized in negotiating contracts between vaudeville performers, on one hand, and large theater chains sponsoring vaudeville shows on the other. Hart sued the Keith Circuit, the Orpheum Circuit, and other theatrical chains, claiming that, in violation of the antitrust laws, they colluded to prevent any of his actors from obtaining contracts in their theaters unless Hart granted them what we would today call kickbacks. Holmes noted that some of these contracts called for the transportation of performers, scenery, music, and costumes. Distinguishing *Federal Baseball,* he held that "in the transportation of vaudeville acts the apparatus sometimes is more important than the performers and . . . the defendant's conduct is within the [antitrust] statute to that extent at least."[45]

[44]*Federal Baseball Club of Baltimore v. National League of Professional Baseball Clubs,* 259 U.S. 200 (1922).

    [45]*Hart v. B. F. Keith Vaudeville Exchange,* 262 U.S. 271 (1923), p. 273.

Comment: Note fact freedom at work here. Holmes does not, despite vaudeville's obvious resemblance to baseball, find that the two are factually similar enough to govern vaudeville by baseball's precedent. There was, he said, a difference. Some of the disputed contracts did involve transportation itself. Holmes could have chosen to follow the previous year's precedent. The travel is still incidental to local performance of either baseball or vaudeville. Compare this with what happened in 1953.

1948   Blacklisted by the major league owners because he had once chosen to play in Mexico rather than for the major leagues, an outfielder named Danny Gardella sued. The Second Circuit Court of Appeals ruled that, in part due to increased radio and television revenues, baseball was interstate commerce and subject to the Sherman Act. The court also called the major league's treatment of the players a "shockingly repugnant" form of slavery, outlawed by the Thirteenth Amendment after the Civil War.[46]

Question: Do you believe by now, since the business aspects of baseball had changed, since the constitutional basis for *Federal Baseball* had evaporated, and since an appellate court had ruled that baseball was now covered by the antitrust laws, that the baseball owners had *any* reason to rely on the *Federal Baseball* precedent?

1953   Baseball again, but not an alleged attempt to prevent the formation of a third league. Now it was the players' turn to allege violation of the antitrust laws. The violation took the form of the well-publicized reserve clause,[47] or so players claimed. The players contended that the clause prevented open competition for better salaries. In *Toolson v. New York Yankees* the Supreme Court ruled in an unsigned (*per curiam*) opinion that baseball still did not fall under the coverage of the antitrust laws. It so held despite the efforts of Justices Burton and Reed, who dissented, to marshall extensive evidence of baseball's dramatic growth since 1922. The majority opinion stated:

> Congress has had the [*Federal Baseball*] ruling under consideration but has not seen fit to bring such business under these laws by legislation having prospective effect. The business has thus been left for thirty years to develop, on the understanding that it was not subject to existing antitrust legislation. The present cases ask us to overrule the prior decision and, with retrospective effect, hold the legislation applicable. . . . Without reexamination of the underlying issues, the judgments below are affirmed on the authority of *Federal Baseball* . . . so far as that decision determines that Congress had no intention of including the business of baseball within the scope of the federal antitrust laws.

Questions: Did Justice Holmes conclude in 1922 that "Congress had no intention of including the business of baseball within the scope of the federal antitrust laws?" Do you believe that because Congress has not legislated

---

[46]See Andrew Zimbalist, *Baseball and Billions* (New York: Basic Books, 1992), p. 13. See also Stephen Jay Gould's "Dreams That Money Can Buy," *The New York Review of Books,* November 5, 1992, pp. 41–45.
[47]*Toolson v. New York Yankees,* 346 U.S. 356 (1953), pp. 362–363.

on the subject of baseball and the antitrust laws, therefore professional baseball does not fall within the act? Remember that not only had baseball
become more businesslike since 1922, but the definition of commerce had
also changed so that travel or movement from state to state did not have to
be an essential part of a business's activities in order to put it under the act.
Why is it necessary to follow the 1922 precedent? Why could not the *Toolson*
opinion simply say that both the law and the sport have changed and the
owners have no justified expectation to rely on an outdated judicial ruling?
Do you think, in other words, that because in 1922 the Court told the established leagues they could try to prevent the formation of a third league, they
therefore rightly planned in 1946 to deal with their players by contracts that
prevented free competition in that business?

1955   In *United States v. Shubert*, Chief Justice Warren, speaking for the Supreme
Court, upheld the government's claim that theater owners who monopo-
lized the booking of theater attractions violated the antitrust laws.[48] The
Court acknowledged *Hart*, though only in passing. It refused to follow
Toolson, calling it "a narrow application of the rule of *stare decisis.*"

Question: One purpose of stare decisis is to promote equality. On what
basis should the law treat actors and baseball players unequally, as this case
concludes the law must?

Chief Justice Warren, in a companion case to *Shubert*, held that professional boxing did fall within the scope of antitrust laws.[49] He distinguished
Toolson for the same reasons he gave in Shubert.

Questions: How equally do you think baseball players felt the courts
applied the law in 1955? If you had managed the Boxing Club, would you
have relied on the *Toolson* decision? Would you think of boxing as any
more a business than baseball? Would the new boxing decision possibly
surprise you?

1957   In *Radovich v. National Football League*, the lower appellate court, mysti-
fied by the distinction between baseball and boxing that the Supreme Court
had created, decided that football did not fall under the antitrust laws
because football, like baseball but unlike boxing, was a team sport. The
Supreme Court reversed.[50]

Comment: "Foolish consistency is the hobgoblin of little minds."

1971   The Supreme Court held that the antitrust laws did govern professional
basketball.[51]

Question: By now do you think the Court could safely overrule *Federal
Baseball?*

1972   Fifty years after *Federal Baseball*, Curt Flood's challenge to the reserve
clause reached the Supreme Court. After a panegyrical review of baseball's
history, replete with references to Thayer's "Casey at the Bat" and a long

---

[48]*United States v. Shubert*, 348 U.S. 222 (1955).
[49]*United States v. International Boxing Club of New York, Inc.*, 348 U.S. 236 (1955).
[50]*Radovich v. National Football League*, 352 U.S. 445 (1957).
[51]*Heywood v. National Basketball Association*, 401 U.S. 1204 (1971).

and curious list of baseball's greats (the list includes such immortals as Three-Finger Brown and Hans Lobert but omits Stan Musial, Joe DiMaggio, Ted Williams, and Hank Aaron), Justice Blackmun refused to abandon *Toolson* or stare decisis. Flood lost. Blackmun wrote:

> [W]e adhere once again to *Federal Baseball* and *Toolson* and to their application to professional baseball. We adhere also to *International Boxing* and *Radovich* and to their respective applications to professional boxing and professional football. If there is any inconsistency or illogic in all this, it is an inconsistency and illogic of long-standing that is to be remedied by the Congress and not by this Court. If we were to act otherwise, we would be withdrawing from the conclusion as to congressional intent made in *Toolson* and from the concerns as to retrospectivity therein expressed. Under these circumstances, there is merit in consistency even though some might claim that beneath that consistency is a layer of inconsistency.[52]

Justice Douglas dissented. He wrote, "The unbroken silence of Congress should not prevent us from correcting our own mistakes."[53]

That's enough of the chronology of judicial decisions. In the wake of judicial and congressional failure to deal with the reserve clause, the baseball players struck in the early 1970s. The strike successfully freed the players from the clause, and recent increases in players' salaries can be credited to this change.

What went wrong here? In the immediate case of sports and the antitrust laws, *Toolson*'s utterly inaccurate insistence that *Federal Baseball* means that Congress did not intend to include baseball wreaked the most havoc. *Toolson,* to paraphrase, says, "The highest lawmaking body in the country, Congress, has determined that the antitrust laws should not apply to professional baseball. Therefore the owners of baseball teams have made many business arrangements in reliance on this state of the law. It would be wrong to upset these expectations legitimized by the intent of Congress." This position is pure nonsense. Congress did not intend to exclude baseball. Holmes in *Federal Baseball* never said Congress so intended. As my questions at the end of the *Toolson* excerpt imply, the baseball owners had no reason to rely on *Federal Baseball,* at least not in 1953, given intervening precedents. Stability and reliance do not in this instance require the Court to invoke stare decisis and follow *Federal Baseball. Toolson* reached that different result by merely saying, without supporting evidence, that Congress so commanded.

Unfortunately, the Supreme Court's reasoning in these cases is worse than that. At least, you might say, baseball owners probably did honestly believe that they had a good chance of escaping the antitrust laws and acted on that basis. There is some

---

[52]*Flood v. Kuhn,* p. 284.

[53]The mess created by these decisions will not go away. In 1996 the Court returned to them in *Brown v. Pro Football, Inc., dba Washington Redskins,* 116 S.Ct. 2116 (1996). See particularly Justice Stevens's dissent, where he cites *Federal Baseball, Toolson, Radovich,* and *Flood.* The lawsuit alleged that the National Football League's unilateral arrangement to pay "taxi squad" members a flat rate of $1000 per week violated the Sherman Antitrust Act.

merit in the reliance argument. But if stare decisis seeks to assist people to make plans in reliance on stable law, then surely owners of football, basketball, and boxing franchises and athletes had every bit as much reason for relying on *Federal Baseball* or *Toolson* as did the baseball owners. After all, in terms of the antitrust law, there is no difference among these sports that ought to induce baseball owners to rely on the original precedent while preventing those in the other sports from doing so.

In the name of stare decisis, then, we have a series of decisions that hardly seems stable, that violates reliance expectations to the extent that there are any, and that does not treat equals equally. To complete the list of justifications for adhering to precedent, do these decisions strike you as efficient judicial administration? What image of justice do these cases flash in your mind? Crazy, perhaps?

Fortunately, I have deliberately chosen an extreme example. Faced with statutory precedents, courts do not invariably invoke stare decisis in order to wreak havoc on the very justifications for stare decisis. Nevertheless, this critical question remains: *If* a judge feels that an existing judicial interpretation of a statute is erroneous and *if* the judge also feels that he may overrule it without doing violence to the five justifications of stare decisis, do *any* aspects of the court's relationship to the legislature nevertheless compel adherence to the questionable interpretation? I believe the proper answer to this question is no. However, on two analytical levels, judges and legal scholars have at times reached a different conclusion. Let us review their reasons for the "one-shot theory" on both levels.

The Case Against Increased Adherence to Precedent in Statutory Interpretation

The first, and more superficial, analytical level holds that the legislature may take certain actions that compel the courts to adhere to precedent. In *Toolson,* for example, the Supreme Court seemed to say that since Congress had not passed a statute to cover baseball by the antitrust laws, Congress had somehow converted *Federal Baseball* into statutory law. Would any of the following events in Congress, or in any legislature, strengthen such a conclusion?

- Many bills were introduced to cover baseball, but none of them passed.
- Many bills were introduced to exempt baseball, but none of them passed.
- Congress reenacted the relevant antitrust provisions, with some modifications, none of which attempted to cover or exempt baseball specifically.
- Congress passed a statute explicitly placing, say, professional boxing prior to 1955, under the antitrust laws but makes no mention of baseball's status.
- Congress passed a joint resolution that officially states that baseball is hereinafter to be considered "The National Pastime of the United States."

Judges often buttress their adherence to precedents on such grounds, but these grounds are insufficient. Congress possesses no power to make law other than by passing statutes. Statutes are, among other items, subject to presidential veto power. Not even joint resolutions, which escape presidential veto, therefore create law. To say that any of the legislative acts I just listed create law is to give Congress a lawmaking power not found in the Constitution.

Furthermore, consider these reasons that a legislature might not, in fact, directly respond to a judicial interpretation by law.[54]

- Legislators never learn of the judicial interpretation in the first place.
- Legislators don't care about the issue the interpretation raises.
- Legislators care but feel they must spend their limited time and political resources on the other more important matters.
- Legislators like the proposed new statute or amendment but feel it politically unwise to vote for it.
- Legislators decide to vote against the bill because they do not like another unrelated provision of the bill.
- Legislators feel the bill does not go far enough and vote against it in hopes of promulgating more comprehensive law later.
- Legislators don't like the bill's sponsor personally and therefore vote negatively.
- Legislators believe, in the words of Hart and Sacks, "that the matter should be left to be handled by the normal process of judicial development of decisional law, including the overruling of outstanding decisions to the extent that the sound growth of the law requires. . . ."[55]

Do not all these possibilities, especially the last, convince you that courts should not speculate about the meaning of a statutory interpretation by guessing at why the legislature didn't pass a law affecting the interpretation?

Professor Beth Henschen writes:

> Congress rarely responds to the statutory decisions of the Court in at least . . . labor and antitrust policy. . . . Over a 28-year period, Congress considered legislation constituting reactions to only 27 of 222 cases in which the Court interpreted labor and antitrust statutes. . . . Moreover, only 9 of those decisions . . . were modified by the enactment of a bill that was signed into law.[56]

In a more recent and more comprehensive survey, William Eskridge calculates that from 1967 to 1990, the Supreme Court issued approximately 1900 opinions interpreting statutes. In the same period, the Congress overrode or substantially modified 121 decisions, some of which (including *Caminetti*) predated the period. Eskridge does find that the contemporary Congress considers bills to revise court interpretations much more frequently than in the past. He estimates that half of the Supreme Court's decisions get some kind of review. The majority of these efforts die in committee. Eskridge's data reveal some important political observations. Thirty-eight percent of the overrides overrode distinctly conservative Court decisions while 20 percent overrode liberal decisions. More interesting for our purposes, Eskridge coded the reasons Congress gave for overriding into such categories as bad interpretation, confusion in law, bad or outdated policy, and need to clarify law. If the courts were doing a consistently bad job of interpretation, we would expect "bad interpretation" to crop up frequently. If, on the other hand, the Congress was doing a consistently bad job of writing statutes, we would

---

[54]Hart and Sacks, pp. 1395–1396.
[55] Ibid, p. 1396.
[56]Beth Henschen, "Statutory Interpretations of the Supreme Court: Congressional Response," 11 *American Politics Quarterly,* 441 (1983).

expect other reasons, like "bad policy" or "confusion," to crop up more frequently. Of the total of 311 congressional actions so coded (including overrides of lower court decisions and of multiple aspects of the same statute), only 40 actions (13 percent) cited bad or unfair interpretation as the reason. On the other hand, Eskridge lists bad or unfair policy as the reason for overriding in 240 of the 311 cases (77 percent). From this we might conclude that the courts faithfully implement a foolish policy six times more often than they interpret a statute poorly.[57]

The second analytical level is more complex. Sophisticated proponents of the "one-shot" theory of statutory interpretation admit that legislative silence is meaningless.[58] They worry instead about the proper apportionment of legislative and judicial responsibilities. Their argument goes this way: Legislatures deliberately use ambiguous language in statutes, not simply to bring many somewhat different specific events under one policy roof but also to allow room for the compromises necessary to generate a majority vote. Once written, the words of a statute will not change, but because they are general, vague, and ambiguous, courts will certainly have the opportunity to interpret those same words in many different ways.

If, the argument continues, words have different meanings at different times and places, the legislature's power to make law becomes pointless, or at least quite subordinated to judicial power of interpretation. Courts must find one meaning. They do so by determining legislative intent. The judiciary insults the legislature if it says that at one time the legislature intended the words to carry one meaning and at another time another meaning. To say this is to say of the legislature that it had no intent and that it did not understand its actions. That assertion would embarrass the legislature, to say the least.

The argument thus holds that part of the judicial responsibility to the legislature is to reinforce the concept that the legislature did in fact have a specific intention because that is what the public expects of legislatures. The first half of this chapter has, I trust, revealed why this argument fails.

Fortunately, the argument does not stop there. Levi asserts:

> Legislatures and courts are cooperative law-making bodies. It is important to know where the responsibility lies. If legislation which is disfavored can be interpreted away from time to time, then it is not to be expected, particularly if controversy is high, that the legislature will ever act. It will always be possible to say that new legislation is not needed because the court in the future will make a more appropriate interpretation. If the court is to have freedom to reinterpret legislation, the result will be to relieve the legislature from pressure. The legislation needs judicial consistency. Moreover, the court's own behavior in the face of pressure is likely to be indecisive. In all likelihood it will do enough to prevent legislative revision and not much more. Therefore it seems better to say that once a decisive interpretation of legislative intent has been made, and in that sense a direction has been fixed within the gap of

---

[57]William Eskridge, Jr., "Overriding Supreme Court Statutory Interpretation Decisions," 101 *Yale Law Journal* 331 (1991). See more generally Eskridge's *Dynamic Statutory Interpretation* (Cambridge: Harvard University Press, 1994).

[58]See especially Levi, pp. 31–33.

ambiguity, the court should take that direction as given. In this sense a court's interpretation of legislation is not dictum. The words it uses do more than decide the case. They give broad direction to the statute.[59]

Levi's argument cuts too deeply. Indeed, there are instances in which legislators breathe sighs of relief that courts have taken delicate political problems from them. (Curiously enough, courts most often do so by applying constitutional standards to legislation, and in this area Levi does not demand similarly strict stare decisis.) But Levi's position is simply inaccurate in its assumption that most questions of interpretation raise highly charged public issues that legislatures ought to deal with but won't if the Court does it for them. For the most part, judicial errors in statutory interpretation involve borderline application of statutes. The interpretations may do considerable injustice to the parties who find themselves in borderline situations without, in any significant way, damaging the central purposes of the statutory policy as a whole. In the large majority of cases, then, it is wholly unrealistic to assume that either overruling or adherence will affect how legislators perform. Try to imagine, for example, how Congress would have reacted had the Supreme Court held in 1946 that the traveling bigamous Mormons did not violate the Mann Act. I suspect with a yawn.[60]

To conclude, notice how many of the problems that courts have created for themselves regarding the place of stare decisis in statutory interpretations would evaporate if only judges convinced themselves to seek the purpose of a statute and not to speculate about legislative intent from inconclusive legislative evidence. The inadequate conclusions that judges reach when they reason on the first and more superficial analytical level would disappear altogether. At the more sophisticated level, the concept that the courts embarrass legislatures by implying the rather obvious truth that the legislators probably had no intent with respect to the precise issue before the court would also disappear. Is this truth so awful? Of course not. That statutes speak in general terms is a simple necessity in political life. Such generality explains and justifies the existence of courts.

A SUMMARY STATEMENT OF THE APPROPRIATE JUDICIAL APPROACH TO STATUTORY INTERPRETATION

Judges should follow precedents when the justifications of stare decisis so dictate. Their primary obligation to the legislature is to apply the statutes it creates so as to achieve,

---

[59]Ibid., p. 32.

[60]However, nearly three-quarters of a century after the *Caminetti* decision, Congress quietly rewrote the Mann Act in the Child Sexual Abuse and Pornography Act of 1986. The amendments eliminated the reference to "white slavery," substituted "individual" for "female" and "woman or girl," and instead of debauchery or immoral purpose wrote "any sexual activity for which any person can be charged with a criminal offense. . . ." This presumptive tightening of the law still leaves some hypothetically questionable applications. Consensual oral sex between married people remains a criminal offense in the state of Georgia. If a spouse flies a spouse who is temporarily working out of state home to Georgia for a romantic visit, would this violate the purpose of the Mann Act? What if this separated couple periodically reunites to reduce the temptations to have adulterous liaisons while lonely and apart?

as best judges can determine it, the intelligible solution of problems the statute exists to solve. Judges should try to determine purpose accurately, but they will err from time to time. It is no embarrassment to the legislature for judges to admit that they erred in determining statutory purpose and applying it to cases properly before them. They should therefore give stare decisis no special weight in statutory interpretation. They should do so with the confidence that to the extent that they can predict legislative behavior at all, they can predict that the legislature is no less likely to correct them if they err today than if they erred yesterday. Of course, legislation needs judicial consistency. Affixing proper legislative responsibility will occur only when courts consistently discern sensible statutory purposes.[61]

ILLUSTRATIVE CASE

The next opinion's format will seem unfamiliar to you because the case comes from England over a century ago. Note that this report summarizes the positions of the attorneys as well as the opinions of each of the judges. The reference at the very beginning is the citation to the statute that the court must interpret. Also, the word "personate" is the same as our modern "impersonate." Hart and Sacks used this case to good advantage in their materials, cited frequently in this book.

Whiteley v. Chappell
L.R. 4 Queen's Bench 147 (1868)

The following is the substance of the case:—

By 14 & 15 Vict. c. 105, s. 3, if any person, pending or after the election of any guardian [of the poor], shall wilfully, fraudulently, and with intent to affect the result of such election . . . "personate any person entitled to vote at such election," he is made liable on conviction to imprisonment for not exceeding three months.

The appellant was charged with having personated one J. Marston, a person entitled to vote at an election of guardians for the township of Bradford; and it was proved that Marston was duly qualified as a ratepayer on the rate book to have voted at the election, but that he had died before the election. The appellant delivered to the person appointed to collect the voting papers a voting paper apparently duly signed by Marston.

The magistrate convicted the appellant.

The question for the Court was, whether the appellant was rightly convicted.

Mellish, Q.C. (with him *McIntyre*), for the appellant. A dead person cannot be said to be "a person entitled to vote;" and the appellant therefore could not be guilty of personation under 14 & 15 Vict. c. 105, s. 3. Very possibly he was within the spirit, but he was not within the letter, of

---

[61]The "one-shot theory" is, sadly, alive and well. In *Neal v. United States,* 116 S.Ct. 763 (1996), the Court in 1996 insisted on following its own interpretation of a 1986 drug law. The Court had concluded in 1991 that LSD dealers should be sentenced based on the weight of the LSD they sold *plus* the weight of the blotter paper that contained it. The United States Sentencing Commission subsequently concluded that the blotter paper weight should *not* count toward the amount of LSD sold. Justice Kennedy's opinion for the Court made the standard "one-shot" argument for following precedent blindly and ignoring the Sentencing Commission rules. The Court also ignored the fact that the Court, not Congress, created the "blotter paper rule" in the first place.

the enactment, and in order to bring a person within a penal enactment, both must concur. In Russell on Crimes . . . under a former statute, in which the words were similar to those of 2 Wm. 4, c. 53, s. 49, which makes it a misdemeanor to personate "a person entitled or supposed to be entitled to any prize money," &c., *Brown's Case* (1) is cited, in which it was held that the personation must be of some person prima facie entitled to prize money. In the Parliamentary Registration Act . . . the words are "any person who shall knowingly personate . . . any person whose name appears on the register of voters, whether such person be alive or dead;" but under the present enactment the person must be entitled, that is, could have voted himself.

Crompton, for the respondent. *Brown's Case* is, in effect, overruled by the later cases of *Rex v. Martin,* and *Rex v. Cramp,* in which the judges decided that the offence of personating a person "supposed to be entitled" could be committed, although the person, to the knowledge or belief of the authorities, was dead. Those cases are directly in point. The gist of the offence is the fraudulently voting under another's name; the mischief is the same, whether the supposed voter be alive or dead; and the Court will put a liberal construction on such an enactment; *Reg. v. Hague.*

Mellish, Q.C., in reply. "Supposed to be entitled" must have been held by the judges in the cases cited to mean supposed by the person personating.

LUSH, J. I do not think we can, without straining them, bring the case within the words of the enactment. The legislature has not used words wide enough to make the personation of a dead person an offence. The words "a person entitled to vote" can only mean, without a forced construction, a person who is entitled to vote at the time at which the personation takes place; in the present case, therefore, I feel bound to say the offence has not been committed. In the case of *Rex v. Martin,* and *Rex. v. Cramp,* the judges gave no reason for their decision; they probably held that "supposed to be entitled" meant supposed by the person personating.

HANNEN, J. I regret that we are obliged to come to the conclusion that the offence charged was not proved; but it would be wrong to strain words to meet the justice of the present case, because it might make a precedent, and lead to dangerous consequences in other cases.

HAYES, J., concurred.

Judgment for the appellant.

QUESTIONS ABOUT THE CASE

1. If a student attends class one day dressed in a 10-gallon hat, Western boots, and chaps, is it linguistically possible to say that he is "impersonating" a cowboy? Is it linguistically possible to define *impersonation* as any act in which someone pretends to be someone other than his or her real self?
2. If it is possible to impersonate a general type of character, or a fictitious character, is it not linguistically possible to violate the statute simply by pretending to be a voter entitled to vote?
3. Does not the question in *Whiteley* inescapably boil down to what purpose it would serve, if any, for the legislature to make it a crime to impersonate a live person but not a dead person at an election?
4. What important background facts does your determination of the purpose of this statute depend on? Is it not true that impersonating a live registered voter might deprive such a person of his right to vote, whereas this plaintiff did not so deprive anyone? But the statute does not distinguish between an attempt to vote in the name of a living person before, rather than after, that person successfully votes. Or does

it? Do we not suspect that the main purpose is to protect the integrity of the voting system, rather than an individual right to vote? If so, what conclusion should the court have reached in this case?

FOR FURTHER THOUGHT

1. For a fascinating review of the political lobbying in Congress that preceded the *Toolson* case, see Zimbalists' *Baseball and Billions,* cited in footnote 46. In 1951 the Subcommittee on the Study of Monopoly Power of the U.S. House of Representatives, chaired by Emmanuel Celler, held extensive hearings but sent no bill to the floor. Most observers concluded that the committee agreed that the *Gardella* precedent in 1948 had ended the matter. But, as Zimbalist writes,

> It appears that the Congress and the Supreme Court were playing a game of cat and mouse. Congress did not enact legislation because it believed the 1948 Court of Appeals decision removing baseball's exemption was good law, not the Holmes decision. The Supreme Court putatively did not reverse the . . . Holmes decision because it interpreted congressional inaction in 1951 as an endorsement of baseball's exemption. (Zimbalist, p. 15)

   Serious baseball fans will find fascinating information and insights on every page of Zimbalist's book. Nonfans should at least note Zimbalist's conclusion, that the *Toolson* decision had vast and unpredictable consequences on the entire sport of professional baseball. Condensed into one sentence, Zimbalist agrees with former player and manager Whitey Herzog: "It's hard to imagine any group of people less sensible and less practical than the people who run baseball."[62] Is it not true that, at the time of *Toolson,* the Supreme Court had immense amounts of social background facts about the nature of monopoly versus competitive business and could have made at least some crude predictions about the consequences of allowing baseball, or any business, to continue operating like a nineteenth-century corporate fiefdom? When courts have such overwhelming information, are they not obligated to pay attention to it in order to avoid making palpably bad law?
2. Recall the federal statute at issue in the obscene phonograph record case (*Alpers,* p. 52, above). Suppose the same language governed communications on the Internet. How would you rule regarding the prosecution of someone who maintained a Web site that, for purposes of argument, was concededly obscene? If you followed the "idle armchair speculation" of the lady juror case (*Welosky*), how would you rule? How would you rule if you followed the reasoning of the *McBoyle* case? More generally, try to imagine that you are a legislative aide responsible for drafting a statute that would punish obscene uses of the Internet but would permit exchange of medical information about the human body. Would you not inevitably find yourself drawing some lines and making some compromises in order to achieve not the "right" solution but a workable solution?
3. In December 1995, the Supreme Court unanimously resolved the following case: Title 18, Section 924(c) (1) of the United States Code (the official codification of federal statutory law) creates a separate crime for anyone who, "during and in relation to any . . . drug trafficking crime . . . uses or carries a firearm." One petitioner was

---

[62]Zimbalist, *Baseball and Billions,* p. 29.

convicted when, upon being stopped for a traffic violation and found to possess in his car a saleable quantity of cocaine, police also found a loaded gun in his car's trunk. In another case, whose appeal was consolidated with the first, the police had found an unloaded gun in a drug dealer's home. Both were charged under Section 924(c) (1). Did they "use" a gun? A recent precedent interpreting the same language held that a person who bartered a gun in exchange for illegal drugs did "use" a gun within the meaning of the statute. If you speculated about the purpose of this statute, would you not start from the premise that "use" is different from "possession"? Why is this distinction important? The Court unanimously reversed the two convictions, but the majority opinion by Justice O'Connor is actually quite tortured. It makes no reference to statutory purpose, but instead tries to construct a dictionary definition of the word *use* that includes bartering but does not include carrying a loaded weapon in one's trunk for protection.[63]

[63]*Bailey v. United States*, 133 L. Ed 2d 472 (1995).

CHAPTER 4

Common Law

The life of the law has not been logic; it has been experience. The felt necessities of the time, the prevalent moral and political theories, intuitions of public policy, avowed or unconscious, even the prejudices which judges share with their fellow-men, have had a good deal more to do than the syllogism in determining the rules by which men should be governed.

—OLIVER WENDELL HOLMES, JR.

We begin this chapter with a puzzle: Common law is judge-made law, a process distinct from statutory interpretation and constitutional law. However, the examination of reason in statutory interpretation reveals that judges inevitably make law when they interpret statutes. Chapter 5 will explain how courts inevitably exercise even broader lawmaking power when they interpret the Constitution. How then is common law any more judge-made than any other kind of law?

The short, and therefore inadequate, answer lies in our legal tradition, which empowers judges to resolve conflicts when no statute or constitutional provision addresses the problem. When a statute speaks to the issue, the judge must look to the statute for his solution. But when no statute speaks, the judge resolves the conflict by reasoning from common law cases that judges have decided in the past and from the doctrines that emerge from them.

The origins of a better answer come from the complex history of English law.[1] To make sense of this history, let me ask you to start by joining in role-playing.

ORIGINS OF COMMON LAW

Put yourself in the position of William the Conqueror. You are, like many of your Norman kin, a shrewd politician. You have just managed the remarkable political feat,

---

[1]Plucknett's "concise" history of the subject is over 700 pages long. Theodore F. T. Plucknett, *A Concise History of the Common Law*, 5th ed. (Boston: Little, Brown, 1956). For real conciseness try Frederick G. Kempin, *Historical Introduction to Anglo-American Law in a Nutshell*, 2nd ed. (St. Paul:

at least for the eleventh century, of assembling thousands of men and the necessary supporting equipment to cross the English Channel and to win title to England in battle. In these feudal days, title means ownership, and in a real sense you own England as a result of the Battle of Hastings.

However, your administrative headaches have just begun. On the one hand you must reward your supporters—and your supporters must reward their supporters—with grants of your land. On the other hand, you don't want to give up any of the land completely. You deserve to and shall collect rents—taxes are the modern equivalent—from the landholders beneath you. You must give away with one hand but keep a legal hold with the other.

Furthermore, you must keep the peace, not only among the naturally restless and resentful natives but also among your supporters. As time goes on and their personal loyalty to you dwindles, they will no doubt fight more readily over exactly who owns which lands. And, of course, you have a notion that you and your successors will clash with that other group claiming a sort of sovereignty, the Church.

You must, in short, develop machinery for collecting rents, tracking ownership, and settling disputes.

Fortunately, you have conquered a relatively civilized land. At the local level some degree of government already exists on which you can build. In what we would call counties, but which the natives call shires, a hereditary *shire reeve* (our sheriff) cooperates with a bishop representing the Church to handle many of the problems of daily governance. These shires have courts, as do the smaller villages within them. You hope that, in the next century at least, your successors will be able to take control of them.

Meanwhile you take the action of any good politician. You undertake a survey, a sort of census, of who owns what lands—the *Domesday Book*. You organize all the lords (to whom you granted large amounts of land), church leaders, and many of the major native landlords who swear allegiance to you, into a Great Council. They advise you (and you thus co-opt their support) on the important policy questions before you. You start appointing the local sheriffs yourself. You also create a permanent staff of bureaucrats—personal advisors who handle and resolve smaller problems as they arise.

You succeed in creating a new political reality, one in which it soon becomes somehow right to govern in the name of the ultimate landlord, the king.

So much for the role-playing.

William in no sense developed the contemporary common law system, but he did create the political reality in which that development had to happen: governing in the king's name—settling land disputes, collecting rents, and keeping the peace—meant rendering justice in the king's name. William's personal advisors (his staff) often traveled about the country administering *ad hoc* justice in the king's name. Additionally, many of the more serious offenses, what we would today call *crimes,* came directly to the Great Council for decision because they were offenses against the king's peace.

One hundred years later, Henry II began the actual takeover of the lower local courts. Initially, the king insisted on giving permission to the local courts before they

West, 1973). To contrast common law systems with the deductive or "code-based" systems of law on the European continent I recommend John Henry Merryman, *The Civil Law Tradition* (Stanford: Stanford University Press, 1969).

could hear any case involving title to his land. A litigant would have to obtain from London a *writ of right* and then produce it in court before the court could hear the case. Shortly thereafter the king's council began to bypass the local courts altogether on matters of land title. Certain council members heard these cases at first, but, as they became more and more specialized and experienced, they split off from the council to form the king's Court of Common Pleas.

Similarly, the council members assigned to criminal matters developed into the Court of the King's Bench. The Court of the Exchequer, which handled rent and tax collections, evolved in similar fashion.

Only three problems remained. The first concerned the rules of law these judges should use. One solution, ultimately adopted in many continental jurisdictions, was simply to use the old Roman codes. In England, however—partly because it was easy and partly because it possessed considerable local political appeal—the king's judges adopted the practice of the pre-Conquest local courts. This practice of the lower courts consisted of adopting the local customs of the place and time and applying to daily events what people felt was fair. We might call this the custom of following custom.

The custom of following custom, however, produced the second problem. In a sparsely populated area—a primitive area by today's standards of commerce and transportation—customs about crimes, land use, debts, and so forth varied considerably from shire to shire, village to village, and manor to manor. But the king's judges could hardly decide each case on the basis of whatever local custom or belief happened to capture the fancy of those living where the dispute arose. To judge that way would amount to judging on shifting and inconsistent grounds. Judging would not occur in the name of the king but in the name of the location where the dispute arose. Following local custom would undercut William's long-range political objectives.

Hence the royal courts slowly adopted some customs and rejected others in an attempt to rule consistently in the king's name. Because justice in England rested on the custom of customs, the customs that the royal courts adopted and attempted to apply uniformly became the customs *common* to all the King's land. Thus the royal courts did not just follow custom; they created new common customs by following some, rejecting others, and combining yet others into new customs.

Of course, by doing this the courts no longer ruled by custom, strictly speaking. Because they sought to rule in the king's name, they sought to rule consistently. In doing so, the courts rejected some customs. Although judges no doubt felt that what they decided was right because it had its roots in some customs, it would be wiser to say they created not common custom but common law—law common throughout England.

With the solution of the third problem as follows, the story of the origins of common law ends. If judges adopt today a custom by which to govern other similar cases before the royal courts tomorrow, then tomorrow the judges must have some way of remembering what they said today. By the year 1250, the problem of faulty judicial memory so bothered one judge, Henri de Bracton, that he wrote a huge treatise attempting to solve it. Plucknett describes the work this way:

> [Bracton] procured, for his own private use, complete transcripts of the pleadings in selected cases, and even referred to the cases in the course of his treatise. This great innovation gives to his work in several places a curiously modern

air, for like modern law writers he sometimes praises and sometimes criticises his cases. At the beginning of his book he explains, however, that the contemporary bench is not distinguished by ability or learning, and that his treatise is, to some extent, a protest against modern tendencies. He endeavours to set forth the sound principles laid down by those whom he calls "his masters" who were on the bench nearly a generation ago; hence it is that his cases are on the average about twenty years older than his book. Of really recent cases he used very few. It must not, therefore, be assumed that we have in Bracton the modern conception of case law. He never gives us any discussion of the authority of cases and clearly would not understand the modern implications of *stare decisis*. Indeed, his cases are carefully selected because they illustrate what he believes the law ought to be, and not because they have any binding authority; he freely admits that at the present moment decisions are apt to be on different lines. Bracton's use of cases, therefore, is not based upon their authority as sources of law, but upon his personal respect for the judges who decided them, and his belief that they raise and discuss questions upon lines which he considers sound. Although it is true that the use of cases as a source of law in the modern sense was still far in the future, nevertheless Bracton's use of cases is very significant. He accustomed lawyers of the thirteenth and early fourteenth centuries to read and to discuss the cases which he put in his book, and this was a great step towards the modern point of view.[2]

Bracton's great work, together with smaller pamphlets of other judges and lawyers, were followed within half a century by "year-books," annual reports of court proceedings and decisions that heavily emphasized procedure. Procedure in England, the correct way and the incorrect way to proceed in court, had rapidly become rigid, and lawyers who could not master it and who could not remember all the strict technicalities lost their cases. They needed to write the technicalities down to remember them. Out of necessity, Bracton and his successors began the tradition—very much expanded today—of writing down the essential conclusions of the courts and using these writings as guides for future judicial choices.

As Plucknett reminds us, however, Bracton and his followers did not create the practices of reasoning by example and stare decisis as we know them. Indeed, until the American Revolution, men actively rejected the notion that judges actually made law as they decided cases. Men believed rather in natural law, if not God's law at least nature's own. To them the proper judicial decision rested on true law. The decision that rested elsewhere was in a sense unlawful. This was, after all, the problem facing Bracton. Prior to and throughout most of the eighteenth century, lawyers and judges thought of common law as a collected body of correct legal doctrine, not the process of growth and change that reasoning by example, to say nothing of the changes and compromises in political life, makes inevitable.

Additional reasons explain why common law only rather recently began to emphasize reasoning from precedents. Bracton's treatise and the many that followed it did not

---

[2]Plucknett, pp. 259–260. For a recent and particularly concise review of how slowly and fitfully common law judges came to appreciate that they inevitably make law as they decide each case, see Roger Cotterrell, *The Politics of Jurisprudence* (London: Butterworth and Co., 1989) Chapter 2.

reliably report the factual details of each and every case. These were unofficial, incomplete, and often critical commentaries. Not even a judge who wanted to follow the examples of precedents could use them with confidence. Only the radical and recent change in viewpoint and the recognition that law comes from politicians and not from God or nature, coupled with accurate court reporting, permitted reasoning by example and stare decisis to flourish.[3]

It is time to close this historical circle. In calling common law judge-made law we mean that, for a variety of historical reasons, a large body of legal rules and principles exist because judges without legislative help have created them. As long as judges continue to apply them, they continue to re-create them with each application. The fact that judges for most of this history thought they simply restated divine or natural law matters relatively little to us today. What matters is that the twentieth-century United States has inherited a political system in which, despite legislative supremacy, judges constantly and inevitably make law. How they do so—how they reason, in other words—thus becomes an important question in the study of politics and government themselves; one of the central questions in this book is not *whether* courts should make law but *what* law to make, and *how*.

REASONING BY EXAMPLE IN COMMON LAW

Much of the everyday law around us falls into the category of common law. Although modern statutes have supplanted some of it, particularly in the important area of commercial transactions, even these statutes for the most part preserve basic definitions, principles, and values articulated first in common law. One of the most important common law categories, also probably the one least touched by statute today, concerns the law of tort. Tort law wrestles with these problems: What defines and limits a person's liability to compensate those he hurts? What counts as a hurt serious enough to merit compensation? Breaking someone's leg? Embarrassing someone? When does law impose liability on me if I threaten someone with a blow (assault)? If I strike the blow (battery)? If I publicly insult another (libel and slander)? If I do careless things that injure other people (negligence)? These questions may sound like questions of criminal law to you, but they are not, for the law of torts does not expose the lawbreaker to punishment by the state. The law of torts—while much of it overlaps criminal law—defines at what times people who hurt other people's bodies, their property, their reputations, or their freedom must compensate them for their hurt.

In this section, indeed for the bulk of the chapter, we illustrate common law in action with problems of tort law, mostly of negligence. But we do not discuss tort law in its entirety, of course, for it would take books triple the size of this one to review all the subtleties and uncertainties in the law of tort. We shall instead focus in some detail

---

[3]Kempin, p. 85, suggests that as late as 1825 in the United States and 1865 in England stare decisis rested on very shaky ground. Anthropologists are quite comfortable with the conclusion that rules of law in contrast to imperfectly articulated customs and interpersonal understandings play a relatively insignificant role in many if not most of the world's justice systems. See Stanley Diamond, "The Rule of Law vs. the Order of Custom," 51 *Social Research* 387 (1984).

on an important and perennial question in the law of tort: At what point do the rights and privileges of owning property stop and at what point does our legal obligation not to hurt others begin? Because the common law of tort has continuously evolved for more than a century, we begin with some old cases that may seem fairly irrelevant today. In the nineteenth and early twentieth centuries the legal question often took the following form: To what extent may we hurt other people without incurring a legal liability to compensate those we hurt *because we hurt them on our own land?*

By the end of this chapter, you will see that the common law process has transformed essentially the same question into this one: Where do the rights and privileges of being private and free stop and our legal obligation to step in to help a stranger in need begin? For example, does a bar (barroom) have an obligation to let a good samaritan use the bar's private phone to call the police 911 number for assistance in an emergency across the street from the bar? No doubt, fifty years from now the question will have modulated yet again. Common law is a process of continual incremental adjustment, a story always with more chapters to write.

Let us begin with a review of the basic rules of common law that seemed to govern in the middle of the last century. First, the common law of negligence required one to act in a way a reasonable and prudent person would act and to refrain from acting in a way a reasonable and prudent person would refrain from acting. Lawyers would say that a "standard of care" existed. Second, the law defined the classes of persons to whom a "duty" to act carefully was and was not owed. Third, law imposed liability upon those who in fact carelessly violated the "reasonable man" standard. Whether a person in fact acted negligently in a specific case is one of those legal history questions juries often decide. Fourth, someone to whom a duty is owed must actually suffer an injury as a result of the hurt. Juries often make this factual decision also. Thus the critical legal questions in negligence cases involve the definition of the standard and the duty.

Similarly, the law of battery commands us not to strike another deliberately unless a reasonable person would do so, as in self-defense. If we strike another unreasonably, then we become liable as long as we owe a duty to the injured person not to strike.

As you may already suspect, the requirement of a duty before liability attaches can make a great difference. One of the common law principles of the last century quite plainly said that people do not owe a duty to avoid injuring, carelessly or deliberately, people who *trespass* (encroach without express or implied permission) on their property.

We shall examine three common law cases to illustrate some of the main features of reasoning in common law. These cases provide evidence, or clues, that support some basic truths about the common law process:

- General principles, including the rules of negligence and battery just described, do not neatly resolve legal problems.
- Precedents do not neatly resolve legal problems, either.
- In reasoning from precedents, judges do make choices and do exercise fact freedom; it is this exercise that best describes how and why they decide as they do.
- Social background facts often influence case outcomes more powerfully than the facts in the litigation itself.
- The beliefs and values of individual judges do influence law.

- The precise meaning of common law rules—here of trespass and of duty—changes as judges decide each new case.
- Over time, as fundamental social values change, common law also changes in a fundamental way to reflect these changes in social values.
- Judges have shifted their conception of their role—from a belief that their role requires them to apply divine or natural law toward a recognition of the inevitability of judicial lawmaking and its consequences.

Here are the three cases.

The Cherry Tree

It is summer in rural New York. The year is 1865. The heat of midday has passed. Sarah Hoffman, a spinster living with her brother, a country doctor, sets out at her brother's request to pick ripe cherries for dinner.

A cherry tree stands on her brother's land about two feet from the fence separating his land from that of his neighbor, Abner Armstrong. Sarah's previous cullings have left few cherries on Hoffman's side of the fence. Hence, nimbly enough for her age, Sarah climbs the fence and from her perch upon it begins to take cherries from the untouched branches overhanging Abner's yard.

Angered by this intrusion, Abner runs from his house and orders her to stop picking his cherries. She persists. Enraged, he grabs her wrist and strongarms her down from the fence. Ligaments in the wrist tear. She cries from the pain and humiliation. She sues at common law for battery. The trial jury awards her $1000 damages.

Abner appealed. He claimed that *he,* not Sarah nor her brother, owned the cherries overhanging his land. Because he owned the cherries, he had every right to protect them, just as he could prevent Sarah from pulling onions in his garden with a long-handled picker from her perch. In other words, Sarah was not a person to whom Abner owed a duty. By her trespassing and her interference with Abner's property, Sarah exposed herself to Abner's legal battery committed in defense of his property.

Abner's lawyer cited many legal sources in support of his argument. He began with the maxim, *cujus est solum, ejus est usque ad coelum et ad inferos,* sometimes translated as "he who has the soil, has it even to the sky and the lowest depths." He then referred the appellate judge to the great English commentator, Blackstone, quoting: "Upwards, therefore, no man may erect any building, or the like to overhang another's land." He also cited *Kent's Commentaries,* the Bouvier *Institutes, Crabbe's Text on Real Property,* and seven cases in support of his position. One of these, an English case titled *Waterman v. Soper,* held "that if A plants a tree upon the extremest limits of his land and the tree growing extends its roots into the land of B next adjoining," then A and B jointly own the tree.[4]

Sarah's lawyer responded that, in law, title to the tree depends on who owns title to the land from which the tree grows. Sarah did not trespass; therefore, Abner owed her the duty not to batter her. In support he cited several commentaries, Hilliard's treatise on real property, and four cases. Sarah's lawyer relied especially on a case, *Lyman v. Hale,* decided in Connecticut in 1836.[5] In *Lyman* the defendant picked and refused

---

[4]*Waterman v. Soper,* 1 Ld Raymond 737 (opinion undated).
[5]*Lyman v. Hale,* 11 *Conn. Rep.* 177 (1836).

to return pears from branches overhanging his yard from a tree the plaintiff had planted four feet from the line. The *Lyman* opinion explicitly rejected the reasoning of the English precedent, *Waterman*. Despite the antiquated language, *Lyman* is a remarkably sensible, unlegalistic opinion. The court held that *Waterman*'s "roots" principle is unsound because of the practical difficulties in applying it:

> How, it may be asked, is the principle to be reduced to practice? And here, it should be remembered, that nothing depends on the question whether the branches do or do not overhang the lands of the adjoining proprietor. All is made to depend solely on the enquiry, whether any portion of the roots extend into his land. It is this fact alone, which creates the [joint ownership]. And how is the fact to be ascertained?
>
> Again; if such [joint ownership] exist, it is diffused over the whole tree. Each owns a certain proportion of the whole. In what proportion do the respective parties hold? And how are these proportions to be determined? How is it to be ascertained what part of its nourishment the tree derives from the soil of the adjoining proprietor? If one joint owner appropriates . . . all the products, on what principle is the account to be settled between the parties?
>
> Again; suppose the line between adjoining proprietors to run through a forest or grove. Is a new rule of property to be introduced, in regard to those trees growing so near the line as to extend some portions of their roots across it? How is a man to know whether he is the exclusive owner of trees, growing, indeed, on his own land, but near the line; and whether he can safely cut them, without subjecting himself to an action?
>
> And again; on the principle claimed, a man may be the exclusive owner of a tree, one year, and the next, a [joint owner] with another; and the proportion in which he owns may be varying from year to year, as the tree progresses in its growth.
>
> It is not seen how these consequences are to be obviated, if the principle contended for be once admitted. We think they are such as to furnish the most conclusive objections against the adoption of the principle. We are not prepared to adopt it, unless compelled to do so, by the controuling force of authority. The cases relied upon for its support, have been examined. We do not think them decisive.[6]

In effect the *Lyman* opinion says property titles must be clear to help us plan our affairs, to help us know whether we can or can't cut down a tree for winter firewood, for example. Given the inescapable background facts about trees, the roots rule introduces inevitable uncertainty. We must therefore reject it.

The appellate court in New York found *Lyman* most persuasive and followed it. Sarah won.[7]

Abner appealed again, to the state's highest court of appeals. In 1872 (court delays are not a uniquely modern phenomenon) Abner lost again. The attorneys presented the same arguments. Perhaps surprisingly, however, the highest court did not mention *Lyman*. Instead it seemed to say that *Waterman* does correctly state the law, but

[6]*Lyman v. Hale*, pp. 183–184.
[7]*Hoffman v. Armstrong*, 46 Barbour 337 (1866).

Abner's lawyer forgot to prove that the cherry tree's roots actually extended across the property line:

> We have not been referred to any case showing that where no part of a tree stood on the land of a party, and it did not receive any nourishment therefrom, that he had any right therein, and it is laid down in Bouvier's Institutes . . . that if the branches of a tree only overshadow the adjoining land and the roots do not enter into it, the tree wholly belongs to the estate where the roots grow.[8]

Therefore Abner lost.

This simple case, occupying only a few pages in the reports of the two New York appellate courts, richly illustrates many essential features of common law:

1. Note first that none of the judges either in *Hoffman* or in *Lyman* questioned their authority to decide these cases without reference to statutes. The laws, both of assault and battery and of the more fundamental problem of ownership, come from the common law heritage of cases, commentaries, and treatises. The judges automatically assumed the power to make law governing a very common human conflict—overlapping claims to physical space on this planet. Surely a legislature could legislate on the subject, but judges have no guilt about doing so themselves in the face of legislative silence.

In this connection, recall that legislatures pass statutes addressing general problems. How likely is it that a legislature would ever pass a statute regulating tree ownership on or near property lines? Is it not better that our government contains a mechanism, the courts, that must create some law on this subject once the problem turns out to be a real one?

2. The general common law definitions of battery and of property ownership do not resolve this case. Neither do specific precedents. Instead, both sides cite conflicting principles and inconsistent precedents and urge from them contradictory conclusions. The judge must find some justification or reason for choosing, but nothing in either side's argument, at least in this case, compels the judge to choose one way rather than another. Judges possess the freedom to say that either *Lyman* or *Waterman* expresses the right law for resolving this problem.

Consider specifically the matter of the Connecticut precedent, *Lyman*. Judges possess the freedom to say, as the first appellate court said, "We find the facts of *Lyman* much like those in Abner's conflict with Sarah. We also find *Lyman*'s reasoning persuasive; therefore we apply the rule of *Lyman* to this case and rule for Sarah." But judges also possess the freedom to say, as did the second court, "Connecticut precedents do not govern New York. Older common law precedents and principles from England conflict with Connecticut's law. We choose the older tradition. Abner would win if only he could show that the roots really grew on his property."

The New York courts in *Hoffman* had other options. The second court could have easily assumed that, since roots underground grow about the same distances as do branches above ground, that the roots did cross the line and that their nourishment probably supported the cherries Sarah tried to pick. Or they could take judicial notice of the fact that any reasonably sized tree grows roots in all directions more than two feet from its base. But they didn't.

---

[8] *Hoffman v. Armstrong*, 48 N.Y. 201 (1872), pp. 203–204.

Judges must decide which facts in the case before them matter and what they mean. They must simultaneously decide what the facts in the often inconsistent precedents mean in order to reach their legal conclusion. The two appellate courts reached the same conclusion but by emphasizing different facts. The first court found that roots shouldn't matter. Even though legal authorities sometimes mention them, the court believed the location of roots should have no legal significance. To give root location legal significance suddenly makes our knowledge of what we own more uncertain. Before we can cut down a tree we must trespass on our neighbor's land and dig a series of holes in his yard looking for roots. And what if the neighbor has flowers growing in a bed that he doesn't want dug up? The root rule leaves us out on a limb.

3. To understand how these two courts choose differently to reach the same result, examine the difference in their basic approach to the problem. The first appellate court seems eager to assume the responsibility to shape law, to acknowledge relevant background facts, and hence to make laws that promote human cooperation in daily affairs. The second court approaches the problem much more cautiously. It seems to say: "We admit the precedents conflict. Fortunately we do not really need to choose between them. As long as Abner failed to prove the roots grow on his side of the fence, he loses either way. Therefore we choose the path that disturbs common law the least. The lower appellate court explicitly chose to reject *Waterman,* but we don't have to do that, so we won't."

This judicial caution is very common, but it is not particularly wise. Without realizing it, the highest New York court (whose opinion therefore overrides the precedential value of the better opinion of the court below) has made new law. Now we have New York precedent endorsing *Waterman.* Future courts will have to wrestle with the problem of overruling it, or blindly follow it and produce all the practical problems against which *Lyman* rightly warned.

The reason these two sets of judges ruled differently, therefore, rests precisely on the fact that they are different people with different values and beliefs about what judges ought to do. Their values help determine the law they create.

4. At a deeper level, the difference reflects much more than a difference in judicial beliefs. These two approaches illustrate two common law styles. The final higher court opinion in *Hoffman* views common law as fixed, stable, and true. It wants to avoid upsetting Bouvier's *Institutes* and Blackstone's maxims if it possibly can. The court thinks these are the common law. The lower court's *Lyman* approach, while predating *Hoffman* by nearly 40 years, observes the spirit rather than the letter of common law. It views common law as a tradition in which judges seek to adapt law so that it improves our capacity to live together peacefully and to plan our affairs more effectively. It retains the capacity to change with changing conditions. This more modern style comes closer to helping law foster social cooperation—our legal system's most fundamental goal.

5. Finally, the case of the cherry tree illustrates a fundamental difference between statutory interpretation and common law. In statutory interpretation we saw that many judges often try to determine the intent of the legislature. Since in practice legislative intent proves slippery at best, we prefer interpretation based on determinations of statutory purpose. In either case of statutory interpretation, however, we saw that judges must attempt to see the legal problem through the eye of the lawgiver. Once the court determines a statute's purpose, it has no need to second-guess the wisdom of that purpose.

In common law, on the other hand, the judge who reasons from a precedent does not care about what the prior judge intended or about the purpose of the announced rule of law. In common law, the judge is always free to decide on his own what the law ought to say. The prior judge's intent or purpose does not dictate how his opinion will bind as precedent. Put another way, the legislature's classification of what does and does not belong in its legal category, a classification created by the words of the statute, does bind the judge. In common law, the judge deciding the case creates the classification. He sets his own goals.

This goal-setting occurred in both the first and second *Hoffman* opinions. The first court wanted to make workable and practical law, not because *Lyman* or any other precedent commanded it to but because the court wanted to achieve that goal. The second court ruled as it did not because Bouvier's *Institutes* or *Waterman* commanded it to do so but because that court preferred the goal of changing past formal statements of law as little as possible.[9]

The Pit

Five years after Sarah's final victory, New York's highest court faced a related common law problem. A Mr. Carter, along with several other citizens of the town of Bath, maintained an alley running between their properties: "Exchange Alley," people called it. The public had used the alley for 20 years as a convenient way to travel from one long block to another, but the town never acknowledged Exchange Alley as a public street nor attempted to maintain it. In May 1872, Carter began excavating to erect a building on his land. The construction went slowly, so slowly in fact that on a gloomy night the next November an open pit still remained on Carter's property. That night a Mr. Beck passed through the alley on his customary way to supper when, rather suddenly, a carriage turned down the alley and rushed toward him. Beck stepped rapidly to his left to avoid the carriage, tripped, and fell headlong into the pit, injuring himself. Although the evidence was never completely clear, since the alley had no marked border, it appeared that the pit began no less than 7 feet away from the outermost possible edge of the "public" alley.

The lawsuit that followed brought much the same kind of problem to the court as had Sarah's problem. Lawyers for Carter cited the common law rule that landowners have the right to use their property as they please. They have no duty to avoid harming trespassers negligently. The lawyers cited English cases to show that travelers who were hurt falling into pits 5, 20, and 30 feet from a public way could not recover damages because the danger must "adjoin" the public way.

Despite these arguments the court held for Beck. It had no difficulty whatsoever determining that, even though Carter and others together privately owned Exchange Alley, allowing the public to use the property over time created a duty to the users not to hurt them negligently."[10]

---

[9]By contrast, the words of the Mann Act do command the courts to include at least the transportation of willing prostitutes, and the courts should not ignore that command.

[10]As an aside, you might try at this point to define "property." You should observe from this example that, legally speaking, property is not so much what people hold title to as it is what the law says they can and cannot do with a thing, whether they hold title to it or not.

But the pit excavated truly private property. Is a 7-foot distance from a public alley sufficient to exempt the owner from liability to the public, or does the pit legally "adjoin" the alley, thereby creating a duty of care?

The court ruled that the alley did adjoin. It held Carter negligently responsible for Beck's injuries. It approved the idea that if the hole was "so situated that a person lawfully using the thoroughfare, and, in a reasonable manner, was liable to fall into it, the defendant was liable."[11]

The court did not have to rule this way. It could have defined adjoining pits as pits that literally border on public land. Or it could have said that 7 feet was simply too far away to make a landowner liable. But the court offered a better decision. As in *Lyman*, it produced a workable distinction between injuries to deliberate trespassers and to those who reasonably attempt to use either their own space or the public's space. Just as in the *Lyman* and *Hoffman* decisions, the judges in *Beck v. Carter* chose as they did because their values—their beliefs about desirable and undesirable social relations—led them to this conclusion. If they deeply believed in the absolute sanctity of private property, ambiguity in common law would certainly have given them freedom to say, "Landowners must be free to do what they wish with their land. Carter's pit was entirely on his private land, separated from the thoroughfare. Therefore Carter owed Beck no duty of care."

The Diving Board

Before you proceed, note how these two principal cases, reduced to their simplest terms, combine to form a seemingly comprehensive statement of law: When the plaintiff's deliberate act is not proved a trespass on the defendant's property, then the defendant owes the plaintiff a duty of care (*Hoffman*). Furthermore, when the plaintiff accidentally but conclusively does trespass on the defendant's property, but the defendant should have foreseen the injury from such accidental trespass, the defendant is also liable (*Beck*). Thus arises the final question: What result should a court reach when the plaintiff deliberately and unambiguously trespasses on the defendant's property and is injured?

On another summer day in New York, July 8, 1916, Harvey Hynes and two friends had gone swimming at a favorite spot along the Bronx bank of the then relatively unpolluted Harlem River. For five years they and other swimmers had dived from a makeshift plank nailed to the wooden bulkhead along the river.

The electrified line of the New York Central Railroad ran along the river. The power line was suspended over the track between poles—half of which ran between the track and the river. Legally the railroad owned the strip of river bank containing track, poles, wires, and bulkhead. Hence, about half of the 16-foot diving board touched or extended over the railroad's land while the rest reached out, at a height of about 3 feet, over the surface of the public river.

---

[11]*Beck v. Carter*, 68 N.Y. 283 (1876), p. 293. If you are dubious, measure off 7 feet from your standing place in a very dark room and mark the spot. Then imagine you suddenly must get out of the way of a carriage by moving toward your mark in the dark. If you pass the mark, you've fallen in the pit. In 1996, in a case evaluating the free speech rights of anti-abortion protesters at abortion clinics, the Supreme Court debated during oral argument the "meaning" of 15 feet. See "Court Hears Challenge to Anti-Abortion Curb," *New York Times*, October 17, 1996, p. A8.

As Harvey prepared to dive, one of the railroad's overhead supports for the power line suddenly broke loose from the pole, bringing down with it the writhing electric line that powered the trains. The wires struck Harvey, throwing him from the board. His friends pulled him dead from the waters of the Harlem River.

Harvey's mother sued the railroad for the damages caused by its alleged negligence in maintaining the supports for the wire. Conceding that New York Central's maintenance of the supports failed to meet the "reasonable man" standard of care, the trial court and the intermediate appellate court nevertheless denied her claim. Harvey was a trespasser, a deliberate trespasser, and property owners have no duty to protect such trespassers from harm.

Before proceeding further, reflect on the cases of the cherry tree and the pit because you are about to see these rather distantly related cases, two cases among thousands that had tried to thrash out the borderline between property and tort, merge as key precedents in the final *Hynes* decision.

The lawyers for the railroad presented a battery of cases in their favor. They cited *Hoffman* to show that, while perched on the board, even if he was over the river, Harvey trespassed, because the board was attached to the railroad's land. They also cited cases, *Beck* among them, to establish the point that the trespass was not a temporary and involuntary move from a public space but a sustained series of deliberate trespasses onto the defendant's land.

Three of the justices on New York's highest court agreed. The railroad had no duty of care to this trespasser. But a majority of four, led by Cardozo, supported Harvey's mother and reversed.

Cardozo cited relatively few precedents. He did, however, cite *Hoffman* and *Beck*, but not in the way the railroad's lawyers had hoped. The lawyers tried to convince the judges that a mechanical rule commanded a decision for the railroad. Anything, a cherry tree or a diving board, belongs to the railroad if it is affixed to the railroad's land, regardless of what it overhangs. Therefore, Harvey, at the time the wires struck him, trespassed. Since the trespass was deliberate, *Beck* commands a decision for the railroad.

Cardozo, however, appealed to the deeper spirit of these cases, a spirit that rejects mechanical rules like the root rule for determining ownership of cherry trees. He cited *Hoffman* not for its reasoning but for its result: There was no real trespass. The spirit requires enunciating policy—law–that corresponds to a deeper sense of how society ought to regulate rights and responsibilities in this legal, as well as physical, borderland. He wrote:

> This case is a striking instance of the dangers of "a jurisprudence of conceptions" (Pound, "Mechanical Jurisprudence," 8 *Columbia Law Review,* 605, 608, 610), the extension of a maxim or a definition with relentless disregard of consequences to . . . "a dryly logical extreme." The approximate and relative become the definite and absolute. Landowners are not bound to regulate their conduct in contemplation of the presence of trespassers intruding upon private structures. Landowners *are* bound to regulate their conduct in contemplation of the presence of travelers upon the adjacent public ways. There are times when there is little trouble in marking off the field of exemption and immunity from that of liability and duty. Here structures and ways are so united and commingled, superimposed upon each other, that the fields are brought

together. In such circumstances, there is little help in pursuing general maxims to ultimate conclusions. They have been framed *alio intuitu*. They must be reformulated and readapted to meet exceptional conditions. Rules appropriate to spheres which are conceived of as separate and distinct cannot, both, be enforced when the spheres become concentric. There must then be readjustment or collision. In one sense, and that a highly technical and artificial one, the diver at the end of the springboard is an intruder on the adjoining lands. In another sense, and one that realists will accept more readily, he is still on public waters in the exercise of public rights. The law must say whether it will subject him to the rule of the one field or of the other, of this sphere or of that. We think that considerations of analogy, of convenience, of policy, and of justice, exclude him from the field of the defendant's immunity and exemption, and place him in the field of liability and duty. . . .[12]

Note again the effect of fact freedom on judicial choices. Although they wrote no dissenting opinion, we can make an intelligent guess that the dissenters in *Hynes* reasoned from *Hoffman* this way: "The fact is that the diving board grew from the railroad's land. If the cherry tree growing from *Hoffman*'s land belongs to him, then the board belongs to the railroad. Therefore Harvey trespassed." But Cardozo in effect responds, "The important fact is that Sarah didn't really trespass. Just as she used what didn't clearly belong to Abner, so these boys diving into the river from a board over the river didn't really interfere with the railroad's property." Reason in law does not allow us to call one approach legally right and the other legally wrong. After all, with a switch in one vote, *Hynes* would produce a very different legal precedent. However, by recognizing that judges' values determine choices, we do free ourselves to say that one choice is better, another worse, and to justify why we feel that way.

These cases reveal the inevitability of ambiguity, fact freedom, and choice in the legal process. They teach at least three additional lessons about the analysis of cases, about changing judicial styles, and about the way common law itself changes.

Analyzing Cases

For the better part of a century, students of law, both in law schools and in college courses, have paid special attention to the opinions of appellate courts. In 1930 Professor Arthur L. Goodhart published what has turned out to be one of the more popular methods for reading an opinion and discerning its meaning. I shall paraphrase his statement of the method for locating what he calls the principle or *ratio decidendi* of the case. Think about the preceding cases as you read, and you will see why Goodhart's well-known method gives a very misleading view of legal reasoning. I shall explain why in a moment. Here is the paraphrase of Goodhart:

1. We cannot determine the principle, the essential legal meaning of a case, simply by examining the reasons the judge gives in the opinion. Sometimes judges state reasons that don't logically relate on close examination to the legal issue; sometimes judges never state the reasons that produce the result.

---

[12]*Hynes v. New York Central R.R.*, 231 N.Y. 229 (1921), pp. 235–236. How should a judge, following *Hynes,* rule in a case identical to *Hoffman* except that Abner picks cherries from the branches overhanging his yard and that, to stop him, Sarah shoots him in the leg with a .22 pistol?

2. We cannot determine the principle only by articulating the rule of law set forth in the case. This is because judges often state legal rules in very general terms—landowners have no duty to trespassers—when the facts of the case raise a much more precise and delimited question.

3. We cannot, moreover, find the principle by looking at all the facts in the case, for some of the facts have no legal significance. Had Sarah Hoffman's parents instead christened her Griselda or if Harvey had been a girl, the result, we devoutly hope, would not have been different.

4. We *can* find the principle of a case by examining the facts that the deciding judge treats as material and his rulings of law based on these material facts.

5. In doing so we must also take account of the facts the judge determines do not matter, facts the judge determines to be immaterial.[13]

Think about how Cardozo treated *Hoffman* and *Beck*. Does Goodhart's method accurately describe how Cardozo found the meaning, the precedential value, in these cases? The basic problem with Goodhart's method is that it asks us to determine the principle of a case in the abstract, by reading it. But a judge starts from a very different place. The judge starts always with a new case—a legal conflict to be resolved. Judges inevitably look at any precedent from the frame of reference provided by the new facts before them. By Goodhart's method the principle of the final *Hoffman* opinion would look something like this: To collect the fruit of a tree overhanging your property you must introduce evidence that the roots also intrude into your land. Neither Cardozo nor the dissenters, confronted with the problem of liability for Harvey's death, saw the case that way at all. The meaning of cases, then, emerges only as judges compare them and use them.

Changing Judicial Styles

We can detect a shift in style—the basic sense of what common law is all about—in these cases. We might label this style change with the question, "Whatever happened to Bouvier's *Institutes?*" Judges are today more conscious of their responsibility to shape the law so as to promote cooperation, and they are more conscious of the importance of social background facts. They are less likely to hide behind a formal statement of law in a treatise, a commentary, or a common law principle. Do they indeed carry this style too far in the discretionary direction? We shall return to this question in the final section of this chapter.

Change in Law Itself

Before reading further in this subsection, consider the general change in the borderline law of property and tort the preceding cases describe.

Do they not narrow the freedom one has for doing as one pleases with one's land and expand our obligation to avoid hurting others? In the last 50 years, the shift from a legal philosophy whose principles emphasize property rights and individualism to a system

---

[13]Arthur L. Goodhart, "Determining the *Ratio Decidenci* of a Case," 40 *Yale Law Journal* 161 (1930).

that promotes social caring and cooperation is as major a change as our legal system has ever experienced, at least in so short a time. The case at the end of this chapter will illustrate this trend further. Do you believe that, if such a change is occurring in our law, it corresponds to a more fundamental shift in public sentiments recognizing interdependence and acknowledging our collective obligation to share and help rather than compete? If so, then common law here has passed at least the minimal test of changing to reflect changing social values.

But how, over a period of time, does change in law occur? Some legal scholars say that law changes in a circular way. Basic concepts, much less crisp and precise than legal rules, build up in law as cases accumulate. But then these concepts disappear when, as they become rigid, they prove too inflexible to accommodate new ideas. Edward Levi describes it this way:

> In the long run a circular motion can be seen. The first stage is the creation of the legal concept which is built up as cases are compared. The period is one in which the court fumbles for a phrase. Several phrases may be tried out; the misuse or misunderstanding of words itself may have an effect. The concept sounds like another, and the jump to the second is made. The second stage is the period when the concept is more or less fixed, although reasoning by example continues to classify items inside and out of the concept. The third stage is the breakdown of the concept, as reasoning by example has moved so far ahead as to make it clear that the suggestive influence of the word is no longer desired.[14]

Levi illustrates the point by describing the emergence and later decay of the legal concept known as the "inherently dangerous" rule. The courts had, for several decades in the beginning of this century, held manufacturers of products legally liable to people who were hurt by *negligently* manufactured items only if (1) the injured person was the one who actually contracted the purchase of the product or (2) the product was "inherently dangerous." The effect was to insulate corporate wealth from liability for damages when the corporation did behave negligently.

No doubt, legal concepts do move in and out of law in much the way Levi describes. The history of the inherently dangerous rule, studied carefully, makes fascinating reading.[15] Many texts in legal process have reprinted it. I must, however, voice two related cautionary notes.

First, the neatness of Levi's thesis and illustration that makes it such an appealing addition to textbooks also makes the model seem universal when it is not. The more typical model of legal change must accommodate the fact that common law can evolve by a process of fumbling from one half-formed concept to another without ever moving through Levi's crystallized stage. The second *Hoffman* opinion's deliberate ignoring of *Lyman* and Cardozo's creative use of *Hoffman* in *Hynes* to recover the spirit of *Lyman* illustrate my point.

---

[14]Edward H. Levi, *An Introduction to Legal Reasoning* (Chicago: University of Chicago Press, 1949), pp. 8–9.

[15]Not too surprisingly, the hero in the dispatch of the inherently dangerous rule was Benjamin Cardozo, writing in *MacPherson v. Buick,* decided in the year of Harvey's death, 217 N.Y. 382 (1916). Cardozo's principal tactic for discrediting the concept was to deny that it ever really existed in the first place.

Second, do not lose sight of Levi's own qualification of the model. Even when concepts in law do crystallize, they do not automatically resolve cases. The facts of the case, as we have seen, may permit the judge to invoke a variety of different concepts, some of them crystallized and some of them created spontaneously. Which one she chooses, and hence the impact of her decision on change in law, is still very much a function of fact freedom.

In summary, concepts do exist in law. Often they turn out to be sufficiently fixed and stable so that lawyers can engineer from them secure plans for their clients. At any given time for any given problem, however, lawyers must initially be prepared to contend with changing, uncertain, or competing concepts rather than fixed law.

KEEPING THE COMMON LAW TRADITION ALIVE

The preceding section introduces the most typical common law judicial problem, one in which precedents provide some guidance but do not automatically resolve problems. In the typical situation, the judge faces an array of precedents—some of which may seem inconsistent, some seem imaginative, and others wedded to past "truths" in common law. None of them necessarily controls, so the judge must make a choice. Sometimes the precedent or principle gives the judge no more than a point of departure from which to justify the unexpressed beliefs and values that determine the result. Precedents in many cases are vehicles for rationalizations.

Sometimes, however, a genuinely new problem arises, one to which precedents prove so remote, so factually different, that the judge cannot build his rationalizations on them. He must then realize that a decision for either party in the case will create not a new variation on older law but a new and different law—a new and different definition of how people should relate to one another. In other situations, the reverse happens. The judge faces a precedent so factually similar to the one before him that he cannot distinguish or ignore it. If he chooses to reach a new result, he must overrule the precedent.

This section answers questions involving these less typical judicial problems: How should judges proceed when they cannot find common law cases that seem to apply to the case before them? When should they make common law from whole cloth? Conversely, in what circumstances should courts choose deliberately to reject a case or principle that controls the case before it? How, in other words, does stare decisis operate in common law?

Answers to these questions depend, as did much of the analysis in Chapter 3, on what we think about the proper balance between judicial and legislative lawmaking. What kinds of problems require the kind of fact-gathering and value-balancing techniques available to legislatures but not courts? What types of problems require, for their solution, the creation of complex administrative planning and enforcement apparatus that only legislatures can create, fund, and supervise?

You may have already discerned my own general approach to the problem of judicial-legislative balance. Let me make it explicit here. Courts and legislatures have much in common. They both gather evidence in a systematic way, courts through witnesses at trial and through the briefs of the parties on appeal, and legislatures through committee hearings and the many other efforts of lobbyists. Both institutions do so, at least formally, in an open-minded way. Courts hear both sides. Our adversary system requires it. Legislatures also hear competing arguments in committee hearings and in the vying efforts of lobbies. Furthermore, we acknowledge that both courts and legislatures possess lawmaking power. People who look to law to plan their affairs know they should look to both institutions to find final answers. Finally, politics influences both branches of government. Many state judges win office by election. Politicians appoint federal judges and those state judges in nonelective posts, so political restraints affect both.

In Chapter 5, we will address some important political differences. Nevertheless, *judges should always presume themselves competent to take the lawmaking initiative when the legislature has not spoken clearly to them.* In other words, because as a general matter courts and legislatures have a similar authority and competence, the burden of proof always rests on the party that argues for the court to remain silent because the legislature is better qualified to speak.

Making Common Law Without Close Precedents

In early March 1928, two seagoing tugboats towing barges of coal set out in good weather from Norfolk, Virginia, bound for New York. About midnight on March 8, under fair skies but with the barometer falling slightly, the tugs passed the Delaware Breakwater, a safe haven for tugs and barges caught in bad weather. The next morning, however, the wind began to freshen. By noon, gale force winds blew up heavy seas. Early in the afternoon two barges sprung leaks. Their crews signaled the tugs that they would proceed to anchor the barges and ride out the storm. They did so, but conditions steadily worsened. The Coast Guard heroically rescued the crews of both barges late in the day. The dawn light on March 10 revealed no trace of the barges. By then, both the barges and their cargoes rested on the ocean floor.

The coal owners sued the barge company alleging both that the company had breached its contract of carriage and that the unseaworthiness of the barges made it liable for the loss of the coal. The barge company in turn sued the tugboat owners for the loss of both the coal and the two barges. The barge owners claimed that the two tugs had not properly handled the cargo. More precisely, they claimed that the tug owners should bear the total loss because they had not provided their tugs with conventional AM radio receivers.

At trial, the barge owners established several critical facts. On March 8 the Arlington weather bureau broadcast a 10:00 A.M. prediction calling for shifting and increasing winds the following day. Another ship in the vicinity of the tugs and barges had received this report on its AM radio. At 10:00 P.M. on the same day, the Arlington bureau predicted "increasing east and southeast winds, becoming fresh to strong Friday night and increasing cloudiness followed by rain on Friday." On the basis of the morning report, one tug owner towing cargo in the vicinity had anchored at the Delaware Breakwater. Even the captain of the defendant tug conceded at trial that, had he heard the evening report, he would have done the same.

Place yourself in the position of a judge resolving this case. In your first step, aided by the arguments of the lawyers, you try to discover how much, if any, of this problem the law already makes clear. You soon find that the law of admiralty—a branch of common law for our purposes—imposes an absolute liability on shipowners for the loss of cargoes in their ships if unseaworthiness of the ship caused the loss. Note that this unseaworthiness doctrine does not simply extend the law of negligence to the sea. The shipowner may have no knowledge of the faulty condition. It may have been impossible even for a reasonable and prudent man to prevent the unseaworthy condition—hidden rot in some of a hull's wooden planking, for example. The rule creates a guarantee of seaworthiness.

But is a ship that does not carry a radio in 1928 therefore unseaworthy because it won't receive weather reports? On this point the law gives no help. You find that Congress has passed a statute requiring steamers carrying more than 50 passengers to carry two-way radios so that they can call for help and receive information, but the statute does not include tugs and barges. You find no precedents whatsoever linking seaworthiness with possession of radios or any other new invention. At this point you have several choices.

Choice One:
Congress in its wisdom chose not to require two-way shortwave radios of tugs and barges. Furthermore, Congress has made no law requiring AM radios. Therefore, Congress has intended that tugs without AM radios are seaworthy and the tug owners are not liable for the loss.

Choice Two:
I find no law requiring receiving sets. Since legislatures, not the courts, are the lawmakers in our democratic nation, I have no legal authority to find the tug owners liable. Therefore they are not liable.

You can, I trust, reject both these choices immediately. Choice one possesses many of the evils described in Chapter 3. We have no evidence whatsoever that Congress thought about AM receivers, much less intended or decided to pass a statute calling tugs without them nevertheless seaworthy. We could just as easily conclude that the statute recognizes the general importance of radios in improving navigation safety. Therefore, the statute gives shipowners a positive signal that they should seriously examine whether radios can help them navigate better. If you have any further doubts about the weakness of the first choice, consider the fact that no congressional statute required tugs to carry compasses.

The second choice conflicts with the common law tradition. Courts do continue to make law as conditions change; over the years, courts have specifically fashioned the principles of admiralty and of seaworthiness within admiralty law.

Choice Three:
I admit that judges retain their general lawmaking power in admiralty. In this case, however, only a legislature can decide whether ships must carry radios. Only through legislative hearings could we learn, for example, how common it was in 1928 for people to own radios. It would hardly be fair to hold the tug owners liable if, in 1928, radios were only novel. Similarly, only legislative hearings can learn whether shipowners themselves carry radios and think it wise or necessary to do so. If they do, then the fact dictates a new policy of seaworthiness, but we can't tell. As in ancient common law, custom may hold the key to justice, but only a legislature today is equipped to find the key.

The third choice may sound like an improvement, but it's not. Its major premise, that courts can't obtain the facts, is false. The actual case, from which this example is derived, shows that the courts were able to make the necessary factual determinations.[16] The brief for the cargo owners documented the phenomenal growth in the sales of radios, over 1000 percent between 1922 and 1928. It quoted Frederick Lewis Allen's *Only Yesterday* (1931): "At the age of three and a half years, radio broadcasting had attained its majority. Behind those figures of radio sales lies a whole chapter of the life of the Postwar Decade: radio penetrating every third home in the country; giant broadcasting stations with nation-wide hook-ups."[17] The cargo owners also elicited testimony on the witness stand from one tug captain to the effect that, although only one tug line required radios, at least 90 percent of the tugs had them, if only for entertainment.

The lesson here is critically important. As a rule, courts can find background facts as effectively as can legislatures. We applaud the adversary system in courts precisely because we believe it gives lawyers the incentive to present the fullest possible range of facts to support their position. Legislatures may be superior lawmakers where complex problems require a simultaneous set of solutions and the means to coordinate them, but well-established judicial practices allow courts in cases like this one to determine the background facts that determine whether a given legal choice is wise and fair.

Choices Four and Five:

Custom is a time-honored source of common law. In this case it has been convincingly shown that tugs customarily carry radios. Radio has become a part of our everyday lives. The absence of the radios in this case caused the loss.

Custom is a time-honored source of common law. In this case it has been convincingly shown that a majority of tug owners do not customarily require radios. Since we cannot say that the customs of the sea require radios, we cannot conclude that the absence of a radio in this case caused the loss.

Choices four and five are improvements over earlier choices; they are better judicial choices because they do not shrink from judicial responsibility for lawmaking. They succeed where the other choices failed in that they create a clear rule to guide future conduct. But, of course, you should still feel unsatisfied, for custom appears to produce two contradictory results. How should you choose between them?

Choice Six:

Is it then a final answer that the business had not yet generally adopted receiving sets? There are, no doubt, cases where courts seem to make the general practice of the calling the standard of proper diligence. . . . Indeed, in most cases reasonable prudence is in fact common prudence; but strictly it is never its measure; a whole calling may have unduly lagged in the adoption of new and available devices. It may never set its own tests, however persuasive be its usages.

---

[16]*The T. J. Hooper*, 60 F.2d 737 (2nd Cir. 1932). As is customary in admiralty law, the name of the ship whose seaworthiness is questioned provides the name of the case.

[17]Quoted in Henry M. Hart and Albert M. Sacks, *The Legal Process* (Cambridge: Harvard Law School, 1958), pp. 432–433, My selection of illustrative cases in this section draws heavily upon the much larger variety of cases that Hart and Sacks provide. Although I use these cases for somewhat different purposes, I cannot improve upon their choice of working materials; here, as elsewhere, I am much indebted to them.

Courts must in the end say what is required; there are precautions so imperative that even their universal disregard will not excuse their omission. . . . We
hold the tugs . . . had they been properly equipped . . . would have got the
Arlington reports. The injury was a direct consequence of this unseaworthiness.

The language of choice six speaks with a power and persuasiveness the other choices
lack because it is Judge Learned Hand's, taken from his opinion finally disposing of the
case.[18] Hand's choice sets a clear standard, one that, anticipating the certain further
growth of the radio industry, would occur sooner or later. Note, however, that with the
exception of choice four, any other choice could well have created a precedent that
would delay considerably any judicial decision requiring tugs to carry radios. These
choices say tugs don't need to carry radios. Judicial change would require overruling any
of these alternative decisions. In short, the timid and deferential judge potentially creates a common law precedent with just as much policy impact as does the active judge.

Above all, Hand's choice avoids the problem of lawmaking by default. Judges can
never know whether or when or how Congress will act on any but dramatic national
issues. Courts that wait for better legislative solutions may wait for a solution that never
comes. Do you disagree with Hand's choice? Is it not the court's proven capacity to
establish the facts about the use of radios—coupled with Hand's sound ethical judgment that tugs ought to carry radios—that makes his opinion persuasive?

The problem illustrated in this case is a perennial one in law. It has recently
appeared in a case in which the victim of a nighttime mugging in the parking lot of a private shopping center sued the owners, claiming the parking lot was not adequately illuminated. Also consider whether Johnson & Johnson, the makers of Tylenol, should have
been held liable for the deaths caused in the first known "tampering" case (in 1982)
because Tylenol was not packaged in tamper-proof containers. Tamper-proof technology had been available for many years. The simple paper tax seal on a liquor bottle,
although it served a different purpose initially, is such a technology.

At the trial of the Tylenol case in 1988, the judge dismissed the case and stressed
that manufacturers and retailers have no duty to customers to prevent tampering. In
1991, pending decisions on appeal in several such lawsuits, Johnson & Johnson settled
the suits out of court for undisclosed sums with the victims' families. At the same time
the company issued a statement strongly denying that it made these payments under any
legal obligation.[19]

Horizontal Stare Decisis in Common Law

We now move to the other end of the spectrum, horizontal stare decisis. How should
judges respond to precedents that seem to state outdated or "bad" social policy, but at
the same time seem completely to cover and control the outcomes of cases before them?
Lawyers label these precedents "precisely on point" or "on all fours with the case at
bar." The existence of these precedents does not, however, contradict the concept that
law remains ambiguous. Judges always choose the results. Some judges, faced with a

---

[18]*The T. J. Hooper*, p. 740.
[19]See "Tylenol Tampering Ruling Is Seen Affecting Corporate Liability Issue," *Wall Street Journal*,
November 18, 1988, p. B8; "Maker of Tylenol Settles Lawsuits," *New York Times*, May 14, 1991, p. A12.

precedent that produces an unwanted conclusion, will choose to ignore it, much to the anger of the losing lawyer. A judge always retains the choice to overrule or to refuse deliberately to follow a precedent, even when she doesn't choose to ignore it. Choices remain. However, they no longer resemble choices reasoned by example. Instead, ideally, they rest on choices of purpose much like those discussed in Chapter 3. The purposes of stare decisis, as we have seen, are to promote legal stability, to protect honest reliance, to preserve efficient judicial administration, to maintain similar treatment of persons similarly situated, and to promote public confidence in courts. The judge must always decide whether adherence to a precedent will accomplish any of these goals.

Here are two sample cases, one where stare decisis theory was used persuasively and one where the court mindlessly botched the job.

Rightly Adhering to Precedent Because the Need for Stability and Reliance Is Present   The law of tort, especially the law of negligence, creates enticing moral questions because, almost by definition in the case of negligence, courts apply the law only when it has in fact failed to control how people behave. The negligent driver simply does not plan to have or avoid an accident based on his knowledge of negligence law, even if he has some understanding of it. As a result, negligence law does not, unless the expectations expressed in an insurance contract are thwarted, confront a judge with the problem of upsetting someone's expectations if he changes the law. Negligence law defines when someone owes someone else a remedy for a past wrong, and this focus leads inevitably to the moral question of how we ought to relate to others, be they friends or strangers.

The need for stability in law more often exists with respect to laws that deal with people's business and contractual relations and with their related planning of the use and disposition of their property. Here we may not reach ultimate moral questions so quickly. When plans depend on law, the law's philosophical shortcomings may not justify changing it. We therefore temporarily abandon tort law and turn to one very small problem in a very complicated subject—the law of business contracts.

Contracts, among many other items, are agreements among businesspeople that allow them to formalize their buying and selling of each other's goods and services. Plans involving millions or even billions of dollars can rest on such agreements. For example, a construction company specializing in high-rise office buildings may conditionally contract with a supplier of steel to buy steel at a given price in order to know what to bid on a construction project. If the company receives the award, its entire profit margin could disappear if its steel supplier at the last minute insisted on a higher price for the steel.

But what legal rules convert an ordinary agreement—He: "Can you come to dinner at my place at 8:00?" She: "I'd love to! See you then."—into a legally binding contract? In early common law, if a written agreement contained the impression of a promise-making person's seal in wax, then the beneficiary of the promise could hold him to his promise. Men wore signet rings etched with their sign (their seal) with which to impress the wax. The only exception for a time was the king. He sealed the wax on his agreements with the impression of his front teeth. Gradually the use of wax, seals, and front teeth declined, to the point where printing the word "seal" or the letters "L.S." (for the Latin *locus sigilli*) created the contractual tie.

Today, seals do not make agreements legally binding: half the American states have passed statutes abolishing the seal. But, in many jurisdictions in the past and in some today, when people have sealed their contract (perhaps simply by adding at the end "Seal" or "L.S."), the law has made it very difficult for the contracting parties to dispute it. The law has rendered it difficult if not impossible to argue that the contract has been made fraudulently or to prove that the promisor has already performed the act he promised.

Long after agreements became enforceable in law without a seal, the law preserved some of the special rigidities for those contracts with seals. In one specific example, unlike an unsealed contract, only the person named in a sealed contract can be held to it. When, for example, a buyer seeks to disguise his interest by having another contract for him, using the agent's name but remaining the interested party, he along with the agent may find himself bound, but only if the contract of sale bears no seal. The sealed purchase contract, on the other hand, would only bind the agent named in it, not the interested party.

Businesspeople regularly transact business through agents. Sometimes, and this is particularly true in commercial real estate transactions, a businessperson will fund another to buy or sell property for him. He will fund the agent but insist that the agent assume all the responsibilities of the contract. The legal name for such a backer is "undisclosed principal." This technique of preserving anonymity is not necessarily unfair to the other side. If someone buys up various lots in an area in order to build a factory in his own name, the owners approached last may insist on a highly inflated price, knowing that if the buyer fails to get the last lot in order to proceed, all his other purchases will become meaningless.

Beginning in the nineteenth century, by both statute and judicial decision, the legal gap between the protections of sealed and unsealed contracts began to narrow. However, in the 1920s, this New York case arose. In a contract under seal, an agent agreed to buy land without naming an undisclosed principal. The seller agreed, but the agent shortly thereafter withdrew from the agreement. The seller, having learned the name of the principal, sued the principal. He asked the judge to order the principal to pay for the land and accept the deed.

The court ruled for the defendant. It noted many New York precedents limiting the significance of a seal on a contract. Nevertheless it concluded:

> We find no authority for the proposition that a contract under seal may be turned into the simple contract of a person not in any way appearing on its face to be a party to or interested in it, . . . and we do not feel at liberty to extend the doctrine applied to simple contracts executed by an agent for an unnamed principal so as to embrace this case. . . .
>
> Neither do we find any authority since 1876 in this court for the proposition. *Briggs v. Partridge*[20] has been cited by us many times with no hint of disapproval. . . . We repeat that we do not feel at liberty to change a rule so well understood and so often enforced. If such a change is to be made it must be by legislative fiat. . . .

[20]*Briggs v. Partridge*, 64 N.Y. 357 (1876).

. . . Thousands of sealed instruments must have been executed in reliance upon the authority of *Briggs v. Partridge.* Many times the seal must have been used for the express purpose of relieving the undisclosed principal from personal liability. It may not be unwise to preserve the distinction for this especial purpose. But whether wise or unwise the distinction now exists.[21]

Any doctrine, stare decisis included, has impact only when it leads to action not likely otherwise. Stare decisis affects judicial choices when, because of judges' commitment to it, they reach decisions they might in general terms think to be poor social policy.

In many respects it is inequitable to allow the undisclosed principal to avoid contractual responsibility because of a seal. New York's Justice Crane, who did not participate in the *Crowley* decision, wrote:

> Thus, if an unsealed contract to sell real estate is signed by the agent in his own name, and the fact that he is acting for another and not for himself appears nowhere upon the face of it, the real principal can always sue and be sued upon the instrument. But if it should happen that the printed letters "L.S." appear after the agent's name, all would be different. The principal could neither sue nor be sued. The absurdity of this is apparent upon the face of the statement, and the danger and pitfall of such a doctrine in business transactions is realized when we pause to consider how many printed forms of agreements have the letters "L.S." stamped upon them, or how easy it is to make the scroll.[22]

But another justice who joined the *Crowley* opinion, Benjamin Cardozo, later praised the result:

> The rule was settled at common law that an undisclosed principal might not be held to liability upon a contract which had been executed under seal. Much of the law as to seals has small relation in society as now organized to present-day realities. The question came up whether we would adhere to the rule that I have mentioned, or hold it to have faded away with the fading significance of seals. The decision was that the old rule would be enforced. Precedents of recent date made departure difficult if *stare decisis* was not to be abandoned altogether, but there were other and deeper grounds of policy. Contracts had been made and transactions closed on the faith of the law as it had been theretofore declared. Men had taken title in the names of "dummies," and through them executed deeds and mortgages with the understanding, shared by the covenantees, that liability on the covenant would be confined to the apparent principal. They had done this honestly and without concealment. Something might be said, too, in favor of the social utility of a device by which the liability of the apparent principal could be substituted without elaborate forms for the liability of another back of him who was to reap the profits of the transaction. The law has like devices for limiting liability in other situations, as *e.g.*, in joint stock associations, corporations, and limited partnerships. In any

---

[21]*Crowley v. Lewis,* 239 N.Y. 264 (1925), pp. 265–267.
[22]Frederick E. Crane, "The Magic of the Private Seal," 15 *Columbia Law Review* 24 (1915), pp. 34–35.

event retrospective change would be unjust. The evil, if it was one, was to be eradicated by statute.[23]

Both Crane and Cardozo are in a sense correct. The rule may work to an unfair advantage, and it is the place of courts, not just legislatures, to minimize unfair advantages in law. However, the court rightly left legal change to the legislature because it understood that many businessmen, without acting unfairly, regularly employed that legal technique in planning their affairs. Judicial action would upset existing plans made by fair men, but the legislature would make law for the future. This difference, not a difference in lawmaking authority, gives the *Crowley* decision its wisdom.

Wrongly Adhering to Precedent when Stability Is Unnecessary   I hope I have not left the impression that courts should always follow precedents in business, contract, and property matters but never in the case of negligence. It is not that simple. Tort law can, for example, influence a person's decision to insure against loss. In this final illustration, however, let us look at a property problem in which a court, in a thoughtless opinion, followed precedent when the reasons for stare decisis did not support adherence. This case involves the laws of wills and of trusts, areas in which stability and reliance normally deserve great respect.

The case involved a section of the will of a New Jersey resident. In it the deceased, Rosa E. Green, stated: "I give and bequeath unto my husband, William L. Green, all of the money which I have on deposit at the Paterson Savings and Trust Company, Paterson, New Jersey, however, any money which is in the said account at the time of my said husband's death, the said sum shall be held by my niece, Catherine King Fox, absolutely and forever." William died without removing the money.

Naturally Ms. Fox attempted to withdraw the money from the bank. However, heirs of William claimed that the conditional gift to Ms. Fox was invalid. Lawyers for the heirs cited many New Jersey precedents stating that an unconditional bequest in a will, like the one to William, gave him unconditional ownership. Any conditional gift of the same property would have to be invalid; otherwise, the first gift would not be absolute. William's heirs won. The court said:

> Appellants ask this Court to explicitly and expressly overrule the long estab-
> lished law of this state. This we decline to do. Such action would be fraught with
> great danger in this type of case where titles to property, held by bequests and
> devises, are involved. A change of the established law by judicial decision is
> retrospective. It makes the law at the time of prior decisions as it is declared in
> the last decision, as to all transactions that can be reached by it. On the other
> hand a change in the settled law by statute is prospective only.[24]

Think briefly about this result in terms of the reasons for stare decisis. For whom should this law remain stable? Who could plan on the basis of this rule? Certainly not Rosa. She intended to make a conditional gift to Catherine but failed. William, if he

---

[23]Benjamin N. Cardozo, *The Paradoxes of Legal Science* (New York: Columbia University Press, 1928), pp. 70–71. More recently, the development of a new golf course by golfer Jack Nicklaus almost failed because land prices surged when news of the development leaked out. See "A Golfer Becomes an Executive," *Wall Street Journal,* January 27, 1987, p. 33.

[24]*Fox v. Snow,* 6 N.J. 12 (1950), p. 14.

wanted the money, had only to withdraw it. Until the moment of his death (or legal incapacitation), no one but William could make any plans based on what might happen to "Catherine's" money. For William to plan, we must suppose some reasoning like this: "I am going to die. I don't want the money, but I don't want Catherine to obtain the money, either. I could prevent her from receiving it by depositing it in another bank, but, since the clause is invalid, I'll leave it there." Such planning is possible, but is it probable? Is it the sort of planning that the law needs to preserve at the expense of carrying out the wishes of the deceased? Many people do not know rules of law of this kind. Is it not more probable that William also intended the money to go to Catherine? Is it plausible that, once William died leaving the money in the bank, Catherine made plans on the assumption that she did have the money?

Consider the other purposes of stare decisis: Is the image of justice improved by defeating Rosa's wishes? How important is equality of treatment in this kind of situation? How important is it to say that because courts have refused to carry out the wishes of past testators (the creators of wills) they must treat current testators in the same way for equality's sake?

Finally, efficiency in the judicial process does matter. Judges should not have to question the wisdom of every point of law that arises, but that hardly means they can never do so.

One judge disagreed with the majority in *Fox*. Chief Justice Vanderbilt's dissent is one of the finest essays from the bench on the subject of stare decisis. It provides a fitting summary of this section:

VANDERBILT, C. J. (dissenting):

I am constrained to dissent from the views of the majority of the court, first, because they apply to the case a technical rule of law to defeat the plain intent of the testatrix without serving any public policy whatever in so doing and, secondly—and this seems to me to be even more important—because their opinion involves a view of the judicial process, which, if it had been followed consistently in the past, would have checked irrevocably centuries ago the growth of the common law to meet changing conditions and which, if pursued now, will spell the ultimate ossification and death of the common law by depriving it of one of its most essential attributes—its inherent capacity constantly to renew its vitality and usefulness by adapting itself gradually and piecemeal to meeting the demonstrated needs of the times. . . .

By the words in the third paragraph, "any money which is in said account at the time of my said husband's death, the said sum shall be held by my niece, Catherine King Fox, absolutely and forever," the testatrix beyond any doubt intended that her husband could use up the bank account but that if he did not, the plaintiff should take what was left of it on his death. To hold otherwise is to proceed on the untenable assumption that the quoted words are meaningless and to ignore the elementary principle that the provisions of a will are not to be construed as meaningless except on the failure of every attempt to render them effective. . . . This principle is an integral part of the most fundamental rule of testamentary construction, *i.e.*, the duty of the court is to ascertain what the intent of the testator was and, then, having ascertained it, to give it effect. . . .

The opinion of the majority of the court, like every other decision in this State on the subject, makes no attempt to justify the rule it perpetuates either in reason or on grounds of public policy. Despite the deleterious effects of the rule and the lack of any sound principle to support it, the majority maintains that it should not be overthrown, because it has been the long established law of this State and because over-ruling it "would be fraught with great danger in this type of case where titles to property, held by bequests and devises, are involved" by reason of the retroactive effect of all judicial decisions. This view, if it had been consistently applied in the past, would have prevented any change whatever in property law by judicial decisions. . . . Every change in the law by judicial decision necessarily creates rights in one party to the litigation and imposes corresponding duties on the other party. This is the process by which the law grows and adjusts itself to the changing needs of the times.

The process is necessarily used not only to create new rights and corresponding duties but, where necessary, to strike down old ones. . . . "It is revolting," says Mr. Justice Holmes, "to have no better reason for a rule of law than that so it was laid down in the time of Henry IV. It is still more revolting if the grounds upon which it was laid down have vanished long since, and the rule simply persists from blind imitation of the past," and "To rest upon a formula is a slumber that, prolonged, means death." *Collected Legal Papers* (1920) 187, 306. . . .

To hold, as the majority opinion implies, that the only way to overcome the unfortunate rule of law that plagues us here is by legislation, is to put the common law in a self-imposed strait jacket. Such a theory, if followed consistently, would inevitably lead to the ultimate codification of all of our law for sheer lack of capacity in the courts to adapt the law to the needs of the living present. The doctrine of *stare decisis* neither renders the courts impotent to correct their past errors nor requires them to adhere blindly to rules that have lost their reason for being. The common law would be sapped of its life blood if *stare decisis* were to become a god instead of a guide. The doctrine when properly applied operates only to control change, not to prevent it. As Mr. Justice Cardozo has put it, "Few rules in our time are so well established that they may not be called upon any day to justify their existence as means adapted to an end. If they do not function they are diseased, . . . they must not propagate their kind. Sometimes they are cut out and extirpated altogether. Sometimes they are left with the shadow of continued life, but sterilized, truncated, impotent for harm." *Nature of the Judicial Process* (1921) 98. All lawyers as well as laymen have a perfectly natural longing to think of the law as being as steadfast and immutable as the everlasting hills, but when we face the realities, we must agree with Dean Pound when he says. "Law must be stable, and yet it cannot stand still," *Interpretations of Legal History* (1923) . . . , and with Professor Williston when he tells us, "Uniform decisions of 300 years on a particular question may, and sometimes have been overthrown in a day, and the single decision at the end of the series may establish a rule of law at variance with all that has gone before." *Some Modern Tendencies in the Law* (1929) 125. . . .

The dangers that the majority fear, it is submitted, are more apparent than real. The doctrine of *stare decisis* tends to produce certainty in our law, but it is important to realize that certainty *per se* is but a means to an end, and not an end in itself. Certainty is desirable only insofar as it operates to produce the maximum good and the minimum harm and thereby to advance justice. The courts have been reluctant to overthrow established rules when property rights are involved for the simple reason that persons in arranging their affairs have relied upon the rules as established, though outmoded or erroneous, and so to abandon them would result sometimes in greater harm than to observe them. The question whether the doctrine of *stare decisis* should be adhered to in such cases is always a choice between relative evils. When it appears that the evil resulting from a continuation of the accepted rule must be productive of greater mischief to the community than can possibly ensue from disregarding the previous adjudications on the subject, courts have frequently and wisely departed from precedent, 14 Am. Jur., Courts, Section 126.

What then, are the relative evils in the instant case? First, we should consider the evils that will result from a perpetuation of the rule here involved. It has already been demonstrated that the rule, in each and every instance in which it is applied, results in a complete frustration of the legitimate intention of the testator. It can only operate to take property from one to whom the testator intended to give it and to bestow it upon another. . . .

Having considered the evils flowing from continuing to follow the rule, let us now inquire into the evils, if any, which might result from its rejection. It is pertinent at this point to recall the words of Mr. Justice Cardozo minimizing the effect of overruling a decision: "The picture of the bewildered litigant lured into a course of action by the false light of a decision, only to meet ruin when the light is extinguished and the decision is overruled, is for the most part a figment of excited brains." *The Nature of the Judicial Process* (1921) 122 [sic.]. The rule in question by its very nature is never relied upon by those who are seeking to make a testamentary disposition of their property, for if the rule were known to a person at the time of the drawing of his will, its operation would and could be guarded against by the choice of words appropriate to accomplish the result desired. This rule is truly subversive of the testator's intent. It is relied upon only after the testator's decease by those who seek, solely on the basis of its technical and arbitrary requirements, to profit from the testator's ignorance and to take his property contrary to his expressed desires. Certainly it is not unjust or inequitable to deny such persons resort to this rule. . . .[25]

THE COMMON LAW TRADITION TODAY

Chief Justice Vanderbilt's dissent in *Fox* does more than state a sound theory of stare decisis. It also describes the essence of the common law tradition. Judicial choices continue to change common law today. Indeed, only within the past one hundred years have judges recognized the inevitability and desirability of choice and change. Thus the full political consequences of choice and change have just come sharply into focus.

[25]*Fox v. Snow*, pp. 14–15, 21–27.

By this I mean that understanding the nature of judicial choice has more than academic consequences in law. Common law has in the past changed even when judges believed they merely chose the one applicable statute or line of precedents that "correctly" resolved the conflict before them. When judges think they solve problems by mechanically finding the one right solution from the past, the slow and erratic developments in law do not occur deliberately. Judges do not grapple with moral and economic aspects of policy choices when judges do not believe they choose policies.

But, when the point of view shifts, when judges begin believing they do make policy choices, this consciousness changes the kind and quality of law that judges make in several ways.

The first of these changes we have already studied and condemned. It occurs when judges throw up their hands and say, "In a democracy only the legislature can make new law, not the courts. We must, therefore, deliberately avoid making changes." These decisions, in spite of themselves, do make changes, of course, just as the *Fox* decision, by rejecting Vanderbilt's powerful arguments, more deeply embedded a mechanical view of stare decisis as well as the rule against conditional gifts, in New Jersey's law.

A second modern view of the consequences of acknowledged judicial discretion can avoid this evil. Judges, acknowledging that they can and do make law, pay closer attention, as we are about to see, to the facts and values that help them (and us) decide that some policy choices are wiser than others. Modern decisions do tend to be less mechanistic and more concerned with the consequences for the future of various alternative choices of policy. This quality, after all, gave the *Lyman* case its modern flavor.

There is, however, a third consequence of this shift in viewpoint. Judges may dramatically increase the speed of change and deliberately broaden the lengths of the legal jumps they take from old law to new. When judges realize they rightly possess authority to remake common law, they may overreact and enact what they believe are ideal legal solutions without properly honoring competing needs for stability. Similarly, they may ignore the possibility that, while both courts and legislatures share authority to make law, they do not necessarily possess identical institutional characteristics for making wise law.

The problem is so central to reasoning in constitutional law that a thorough canvass of the "judicial limits" territory must be postponed until the following chapter, which deals with reasoning in constitutional interpretation. This problem does, however, arise in common law and statutory interpretation.

In this perspective, consider the next case. It illustrates deliberate lawmaking. It exemplifies a dramatic expansion of common law, and it faces squarely the double problem of determining whether a given policy is wise and whether the courts were the wise place to make it. The case, *Tarasoff v. Regents of the University of California,* takes the law of negligence and duty on a substantial jump outward.[26]

Tatiana Tarasoff spent the summer of 1969 in Brazil. She had, with her parents' consent and assistance, left the United States, in part, to escape the almost fanatical affections of one Prosenjit Poddar. During her absence Poddar kept his contact alive. He persuaded Tatiana's brother to share an apartment with him near Tatiana's home in Berkeley, California.

---

[26]*Tarasoff v. Regents of the University of California,* 551 P.2d 334 (1976).

Tatiana returned from Brazil in October. On October 27, 1969, Poddar killed her.

In due course, Tatiana's parents learned that Poddar had, during the summer, received psychological therapy on an outpatient basis from Cowell Memorial Hospital at the University of California, Berkeley. Their further investigation uncovered these facts:

- On August 20, 1969, Poddar told his therapist, Dr. Moore, that he planned to kill his girlfriend when she returned from Brazil.
- When Poddar left, Dr. Moore felt Poddar should be committed for psychiatric examination in a mental hospital. He urgently consulted two of his colleagues at Cowell. They concurred.
- Moore then told two campus police officers that he would request commitment of Poddar. He followed up with a letter of request to the campus police chief.
- Three officers, in fact, took Poddar into custody. Poddar promised them he would leave Tatiana alone in the future. The officers believed Poddar was rational and released him.
- After, and presumably in part because the officers released Poddar, Dr. Moore's supervisor, Dr. Powelson, asked the police to return Moore's letter. Dr. Powelson also ordered destroyed all written evidence of the affair and prohibited any further action to commit Poddar for examination or observation.
- At no point did any members of the hospital staff or the campus police attempt to notify Tatiana, her brother, or her parents of Poddar's threat.
- The staff could easily have determined Tatiana's identity as well as her location and that of her family.

The Tarasoffs sued the doctors, the officers, and the university's board of regents, claiming damages for the loss of their daughter. Among other charges, they alleged that "defendants negligently permitted Poddar to be released from police custody without 'notifying the parents of Tatiana Tarasoff that their daughter was in grave danger from Prosenjit Poddar.'"[27] They claimed, in other words, that the defendants had a duty to use reasonable care to protect Tatiana.

The California Supreme Court upheld the legality of this claim, but only against the regents and the doctors. Reasoning by example played a major part in its result. The court cited precedents from California and elsewhere holding a doctor liable for the damage caused by illness contracted by people in contact with his patient if the doctor negligently failed to diagnose the disease as contagious and to isolate the patient. It also cited a case holding a doctor liable for damages where, following his negligent refusal to admit a mental patient to a hospital, the mental patient assaulted the plaintiff.

The directly relevant case law in California, however, imposed a duty only where the defendant already assumed some responsibility for the victim. If, for example, a mental hospital failed negligently to protect one patient from another's violence, the hospital became liable. In California, no law extended the duty further.

Using fact freedom, however, the court ignored the distinction. It said, "[W]e do not think that the duty should logically be constricted to such situations."[28] Let us review the majority's reasons for the conclusion.

---

[27]Ibid., p. 341.
[28]Ibid., p. 344.

The majority first stated a general framework for determining the existence or absence of a duty, a statement amply supported by recent California precedents. Note above all how different this statement is from earlier mechanical statements like "duty to invitees but no duty to trespassers or licensees." The court, quoting precedents, said the existence of a duty depends

> only upon the "balancing of a number of considerations"; major ones "are the foreseeability of harm to the plaintiff, the degree of certainty that the plaintiff suffered injury, the closeness of the connection between the defendant's conduct and the injury suffered, the moral blame attached to the defendant's conduct, the policy of preventing future harm, the extent of the burden to the defendant and consequences to the community of imposing a duty to exercise care with resulting liability for breach, and the availability, cost and prevalence of insurance for the risk involved."
>
> The most important of these considerations in establishing duty is foreseeability. As a general principle, a "defendant owes a duty of care to all persons who are foreseeably endangered by his conduct, with respect to all risks which make the conduct unreasonably dangerous."[29]

Having said this much, the majority then noted that at common law a duty to warn of foreseeable harm done by a dangerous person existed only when the defendant had a "special relationship" with either the source of danger or the potential victim. The court admitted that the doctors had no special relationship to Tatiana, but it asserted that because they did have such a relationship to Poddar, they therefore owed Tatiana a duty of care.

The court cited no convincing precedent or other authority for this expansion of law, but that did not seem to bother it. The court did pay attention to the arguments sustaining and attacking the practical wisdom and effect of the new policy.

The court had to deal first with the possibility that the harm was not foreseeable in the first place. The issue was made even more difficult because only a few years earlier the court had based an important mental health ruling on the fact that psychological and psychiatric predictions of future behavior are notoriously inaccurate.[30] To this the court responded:

> The role of the psychiatrist, who is indeed a practitioner of medicine, and that of the psychologist who performs an allied function, are like that of the physician who must conform to the standards of the profession and who must often make diagnoses and predictions based upon such evaluations. Thus the judgment of the therapist in diagnosing emotional disorders and in predicting whether a patient presents a serious danger of violence is comparable to the judgment which doctors and professionals must regularly render under accepted rules of responsibility.
>
> We recognize the difficulty that a therapist encounters in attempting to forecast whether a patient presents a serious danger of violence. Obviously we do

---

[29]Ibid., p. 342.

[30]In this particular case, *People v. Burnick,* 14 Cal. 3rd 306 (1975), the court held that a person could be committed to an institution for mentally disturbed sex offenders only after proof at trial beyond reasonable doubt that the defendant was, in fact, likely to repeat the offense.

not require that the therapist, in making that determination, render a perfect performance; the therapist need only exercise "that reasonable degree of skill, knowledge, and care ordinarily possessed and exercised by members of [that professional specialty] under similar circumstances." (*Bardessono v. Michels* (1970) 3 Cal.3d 780, 788 . . .) Within the broad range of reasonable practice and treatment in which professional opinion and judgment may differ, the therapist is free to exercise his or her own best judgment without liability; proof, aided by hindsight, that he or she judged wrongly is insufficient to establish negligence.

In the instant case, however, the pleadings do not raise any question as to failure of defendant therapists to predict that Poddar presented a serious danger of violence. On the contrary, the present complaints allege that defendant therapists did in fact predict that Poddar would kill, but were negligent in failing to warn.[31]

The court then turned to the most complex policy issue of all: Will imposition of the duty to warn discourage patients from seeking the psychiatric help they need, thus preventing not only their own improvement but perhaps increasing the actual incidence of violent harm to others because people don't get help? The court insisted that such a prediction is entirely speculative. It noted that both the California code of evidence and the Principles of Medical Ethics of the American Medical Association permit a doctor to reveal information about a dangerous person if doing so could protect the patient, other individuals, or the community. The court concluded that

the public policy favoring protection of the confidential character of patient-psychotherapist communications must yield to the extent to which disclosure is essential to avert danger to others. The protective privilege ends where the public peril begins.

Our current crowded and computerized society compels the interdependence of its members. In this risk-infested society we can hardly tolerate the further exposure to danger that would result from a concealed knowledge of the therapist that his patient was lethal. If the exercise of reasonable care to protect the threatened victim requires the therapist to warn the endangered party or those who can reasonably be expected to notify him, we see no sufficient societal interest that would protect and justify concealment. The containment of such risks lies in the public interest.[32]

Backed by powerful opposition communicated to the court in an amicus curiae ("friend of the court") brief from the American Psychiatric Association, Justice William Clark heatedly disputed the court's policy conclusion.[33] He began by noting that a California statute *prohibits* the release of "all" information about a patient once a person authorized to begin commitment proceedings does so. The majority had avoided that issue by insisting that the pleadings in the case did not state that Dr. Moore was

[31]*Tarasoff v. Regents,* p. 345.
[32]Ibid., pp. 347–348.
[33]William Clark later served President Ronald Reagan, first as National Security Advisor and then as U.S. Secretary of the Interior.

so authorized. Clark insisted he was and further argued that the purpose of the statute applied clearly in the *Tarasoff* case. "The Legislature," he wrote, "obviously is more capable than is this court to investigate, debate, and weigh potential harm through disclosure against the risk of public harm by nondisclosure. We should defer to its judgment."[34]

Clark then turned to common law analysis itself:

Assurance of confidentiality is important for three reasons. . . .

First, without substantial assurance of confidentiality, those requiring treatment will be deterred from seeking assistance. (See Sen. Judiciary Com. comment accompanying Sec. 1014 of Evid.Code; Slovenko, *supra,* 6 Wayne L.Rev. 175, 187–188; Goldstein & Katz, *Psychiatrist-Patient Privilege: The GAP Proposal and the Connecticut Statute* (1962) 36 Conn. Bar J. 175, 178.) It remains an unfortunate fact in our society that people seeking psychiatric guidance tend to become stigmatized. Apprehension of such stigma—apparently increased by the propensity of people considering treatment to see themselves in the worst possible light—creates a well-recognized reluctance to seek aid. (Fisher, *The Psychotherapeutic Professions and the Law of Privileged Communications* (1964) 10 Wayne L.Rev. 609, 617; Slovenko, *supra,* 6 Wayne L.Rev. 175, 188; see also Rappeport, *Psychiatrist-Patient Privilege* (1963) 23 Md.L.J. 39, 46–47.) This reluctance is alleviated by the psychiatrist's assurance of confidentiality. . . .

Second, the guarantee of confidentiality is essential in eliciting the full disclosure necessary for effective treatment. (*In re Lifschutz, supra,* 2 Cal.3d 415, 431, 85 Cal.Rptr. 829, 467 P.2d 557; *Taylor v. United States* (1955), 95 U.S. App.D.C. 373, 222 F.2d 398, 401; Goldstein & Katz, *supra,* 36 Conn.Bar.J. 175, 178; Heller, *Some Comments to Lawyers on the Practice of Psychiatry* (1957) 30 Temp.L.Q. 401; Guttmacher & Weihofen, *Privileged Communications between Psychiatrist and Patient* (1952) 28 Ind.L.J. 32, 34.° The psychiatric patient approaches treatment with conscious and unconscious inhibitions against revealing his innermost thoughts. "Every person, however well-motivated, has to overcome resistances to therapeutic exploration. These resistances seek support from every possible source and the possibility of disclosure would easily be employed in the service of resistance." (Goldstein & Katz, *supra,* 36 Conn. Bar J. 175, 179; see also, 118 Am. J.Psych 734, 735.) Until a patient can trust his psychiatrist not to violate their confidential relationship, "the unconscious psychological control mechanism of repression will prevent the recall of past experiences." (Butler, *Psychotherapy and Griswold: Is Confidentiality a Privilege or a Right?* (1971) 3 Conn.L.Rev. 599, 604). . . .

Third, even if the patient fully discloses his thoughts, assurance that the confidential relationship will not be breached is necessary to maintain his trust in

---

[34]*Op. cit.,* p. 358.

°One survey indicated that five of every seven people interviewed said they would be less likely to make full disclosure to a psychiatrist in the absence of assurance of confidentiality. (See Comment, *Functional Overlap Between the Lawyer and Other Professionals: Its Implications for the Doctrine of Privileged Communications* (1962) 71 Yale L.J. 1226, 1255). [Asterisk note in original.]

his psychiatrist—the very means by which treatment is effected. "[T]he essence of much psychotherapy is the contribution of trust in the external world and ultimately in the self, modelled upon the trusting relationship established during therapy." (Dawidoff, *The Malpractice of Psychiatrists*, 1966 Duke L.J. 696, 704). Patients will be helped only if they can form a trusting relationship with the psychiatrist. (*Id.* at 704, fn. 34; Burham, *Separation Anxiety* (1965) 13 Arch.Gen. Psychiatry 346, 356; Heller, *supra,* 30 Temp. L.Q. 401, 406.) All authorities appear to agree that if the trust relationship cannot be developed because of collusive communication between the psychiatrist and others, treatment will be frustrated. (See, e.g., Slovenko (1973) *Psychiatry and Law*, p. 61; Cross, *Privileged Communications between Participants in Group Psychotherapy* (1970) Law and Social Order, 191, 199. . . .)

Given the importance of confidentiality to the practice of psychiatry, it becomes clear the duty to warn imposed by the majority will cripple the use and effectiveness of psychiatry. Many people, potentially violent—yet susceptible to treatment—will be deterred from seeking it; those seeking it will be inhibited from making revelations necessary to effective treatment; and, forcing the psychiatrist to violate the patient's trust will destroy the interpersonal relationship by which treatment is effected.[35]

Is Justice Clark correct? Should the court defer here to the legislature's fact-finding abilities? Or is he only using the timeworn argument, condemned by Chief Justice Vanderbilt's powerful dissent in *Fox v. Snow*, that legislatures, not courts, should make policy? Consider two possibilities. First, the court did in fact hear a wide variety of points of view on the policy questions. The American Psychiatric Association did file an amicus brief. Interest groups lobby courts much as they do legislatures. Is there any reason to believe that a legislature facing this issue would hear substantially more or different or better policy arguments? Does not Justice Clark's dissent tend to undercut his position? He appears to have digested and incorporated into his thinking a wide range of literature bearing on the subject. Second, if Clark's analysis is so compellingly correct, nothing in the common law prevents the California legislature from amending the statute Clark cites to include within its scope the type of situation that occurred in *Tarasoff*.

The *Tarasoff* case, like the *Hynes* case, took the common law of duty in negligence cases a large step forward. As I pointed out after the discussion of *Hynes*, the common law does not, however, move smoothly forward in rational increments. True to its nature, the common law did much backing and filling after *Tarasoff;* indeed the false starts,

---

[35]Ibid., pp. 358–360. In 1984, Daniel Givelber, William Bowers, and Carolyn Blitch published the results of their survey of over 2000 therapists nationwide. They concluded that most therapists found the *Tarasoff* ruling was consistent with their sense of professional ethics and that the ruling did not significantly impair their ability to treat their patients. See "*Tarasoff* Myth and Reality," 1984 *Wisconsin Law Review* 443 (1984). See also Kathleen Quinn's "The Impact of Tarasoff on Clinical Practice," 2 *Behavioral Sciences and the Law* 319 (1984). Quinn, a doctor of medicine, goes so far as to say that the physician may encourage a potentially violent patient voluntarily to commit himself by reminding the patient that in the absence of voluntary commitment, the law may require the psychiatrist to warn potential victims. Compare "More Psychotherapists Held Liable for the Actions of Violent Patients," *Wall Street Journal* 2 March, 1987, p. 23.

contradictions, and inconsistencies, generated in the 1970s, only began ironing themselves out in the 1990s.

For example, in *Thompson v. County of Alameda* (614 P.2d 728, 1980), the California Supreme Court reaffirmed *Tarasoff*'s holding that one has a duty to warn only specific victims who were actually identified or were easily identifiable, as was Tatiana herself. However, the facts were different. A juvenile offender in detention told a parole officer that if he were released on furlough he would murder a child chosen at random. He was in fact released, and he did just as he predicted, but the family of the victim child lost because no specific or identifiable victim was named. Similarly in 1984, a federal appellate court affirmed that the therapist of John Hinckley, who attempted to assassinate President Reagan, was not liable for the injuries Brady and others suffered in the attempt because Hinckley had identified no specific or identifiable victim.[36]

The difficulty, as you may already have noted, is that such rulings contradicted California common law as it existed before *Tarasoff*. Recall that California law previously held physicians liable for the damage done by contagious patients that spread disease because they were misdiagnosed. The third-party victims in such cases were not specifically identifiable beforehand. The reality is that in some cases we cannot reasonably expect the doctor to prevent harm to a victim unless she can identify a specific victim, but in other cases we can. As the Wisconsin Supreme Court more recently put it:

> [I]f a patient announces an intention to, for example, leave the psychotherapist's office and commit random acts of violence, the psychotherapist would be unable to warn victims of potential danger. . . . Nevertheless, notwithstanding the absence of a readily identifiable victim, warnings could, in certain instances, effectively be made to, perhaps, the patient's family or police. . . . Society must not become the victim of a dangerous patient's ambiguity.[37]

Over time new and unanticipated problems will inevitably arise and reasoning by example will apply such precedents in new and not entirely predictable ways. Indeed this is happening with respect to potential responsibility and liability for the spread of HIV and AIDS. The author of an article reviewing the case developments I've just summarized represents a client injured in the following way. He had received a number of blood transfusions before anyone tested blood for HIV. He had no other risk factor. At the time of treatment for a kidney stone condition he asked for a blood test. The physicians at the hospital told him if he didn't hear anything, it meant the tests came out negative. In fact the client tested positive but out of sheer oversight no one at the hospital notified him. Thinking he was HIV negative, he then had a number of sexual encounters without using barrier protection. If he has infected a partner, does the partner have a cause of action against the negligent hospital? Was the patient negligent for not asking for the test results? For not using condoms?[38] Or suppose a family practitioner treats a husband and wife and discovers that one of the two is HIV positive. Does she have a duty to warn the other, who is also her patient? Does any physician treating any mar-

---

[36]And see *DeShaney v. Winnebago County Dept. of Social Services*, 109 S.Ct. 998 (1989).

[37]*Schuster v. Altenberg*, 424 N.W.2d 159 (1988), 172–173.

[38]See Kenneth Labowitz, "Beyond *Tarasoff*: AIDS and the Obligation to Breach Confidentiality," 9 *Saint Louis University Public Law Review* 495 (1990).

ried patient have an obligation to warn a spouse, even when the spouse is *not* her patient? Any doctor who knows her patient is married can identify the spouse at least as easily as the psychiatrists at the University of California could have identified Tatiana. Reasoning by example in common law marches on.[39]

ILLUSTRATIVE CASE

Like *Tarasoff,* the following case went to the court of appeals on a question of law before any trial occurred to test the actual facts. Thus the court's holding here does not mean that defendant O'Daniels is liable to the plaintiff for damages. In a telephone conversation with Judge Andreen in July of 1983, I learned that the defendants had chosen not to appeal this ruling to the California Supreme Court.

Soldano v. O'Daniels
California Court of Appeals, Fifth District 190
California Reporter 310 (1983)

ANDREEN, Associate justice.

Does a business establishment incur liability for wrongful death if it denies use of its telephone to a good samaritan who explains an emergency situation occurring without and wishes to call the police?. . .

Both briefs on appeal adopt the defense averments:

"This action arises out of a shooting death occurring on August 9, 1977. Plaintiff's father [Darrell Soldano] was shot and killed by one Rudolph Villanueva on that date at defendant's Happy Jack's Saloon. This defendant owns and operates the Circle Inn which is an eating establishment located across the street from Happy Jack's. Plaintiff's second cause of action against this defendant is one for negligence."

"Plaintiff alleges that on the date of the shooting, a patron of Happy Jack's Saloon came into the Circle Inn and informed a Circle Inn [bartender] that a man had been threatened at Happy Jack's. He requested the [bartender] either call the police or allow him to use the Circle Inn phone to call the police. That [bartender] allegedly refused to call the police and allegedly refused to allow the patron to use the phone to make his own call. Plaintiff alleges that the actions of the Circle Inn [bartender] were a breach of the legal duty that the Circle Inn owed to the decedent." . . .

There is a distinction, well rooted in the common law, between action and nonaction. (*Weirum v. RKO General, Inc.* (1975) 15 Cal. 3d 40, 49). It has found its way into the prestigious Restatement Second of Torts (hereafter cited as "Restatement"), which provides in Section 314:

The fact that the actor realizes or should realize that action on his part is necessary for another's aid or protection does not of itself impose upon him a duty to take such action.

The distinction between malfeasance and nonfeasance, between active misconduct working positive injury and failure to act to prevent mischief not brought on by the defendant, is founded

[39]See "Asking AIDS Victims to Name Past Partners Stirs Debate on Privacy," *Wall Street Journal,* January 29, 1987, A1.

on "that attitude of extreme individualism so typical of Anglo-Saxon legal thought." (Bohlen, *The Moral Duty to Aid Others as a Basis of Tort Liability*, part I, (1908) 56 U.Pa.L.Rev. 217, 219–220.). . . .

The refusal of the law to recognize the moral obligation of one to aid another when he is in peril and when such aid may be given without danger and at little cost in effort has been roundly criticized. Prosser describes the case law sanctioning such inaction as a "refus[al] to recognize the moral obligation of common decency and common humanity" and characterizes some of these decisions as "shocking in the extreme. . . . Such decisions are revolting to any moral sense. They have been denounced with vigor by legal writers." [Prosser, *Law of Torts* (4th ed. 1971) §56, pp. 340–341, fn. omitted.] A similar rule has been termed "morally questionable" by our Supreme Court. [*Tarasoff v. Regents of University of California* 551 P.2d 334 (1976).]

Francis H. Bohlen, in his article "The Moral Duty to Aid Others as a Basis of Tort Liability," commented:

> Nor does it follow that because the law has not as yet recognized the duty to repair harm innocently wrought, that it will continue indefinitely to refuse it recognition. While it is true that the common law does not attempt to enforce all moral, ethical, or human-itarian duties, it is, it is submitted, equally true that all ethical and moral conceptions, which are not the mere temporary manifestations of a passing wave of sentimentalism or puritanism, but on the contrary, find a real and permanent place in the settled con-victions of a race and become part of the normal habit of thought thereof, of necessity do in time color the judicial conception of legal obligation. . . .

As noted in *Tarasoff v. Regents of University of California, supra,* the courts have increased the instances in which affirmative duties are imposed not by direct rejection of the common law rule, but by expanding the list of special relationships which will justify departure from that rule. . . .

Here there was no special relationship between the defendant and the deceased. It would be stretching the concept beyond recognition to assert there was a relationship between the defen-dant and the patron from Happy Jack's Saloon who wished to summon aid. But this does not end the matter.

It is time to reexamine the common law rule of nonliability for nonfeasance in the special cir-cumstances of the instant case.

The Legislature has recognized the importance of the telephone system in reporting crime and in summoning emergency aid. Penal Code section 384 makes it a misdemeanor to refuse to relinquish a party line when informed that it is needed to call a police department or obtain other specified emergency services. This requirement, which the Legislature has mandated to be printed in virtually every telephone book in this state, may have wider printed distribution in this state than even the Ten Commandments. It creates an affirmative duty to do something—to clear the line for another user of the party line—in certain circumstances.

In 1972 the Legislature enacted the Warren-911-Emergency Assistance Act. This act expressly recognizes the importance of the telephone system in procuring emergency aid. . . .

The above statutes are cited without the suggestion that the defendant violated a statute which would result in a presumption of a failure to use due care under Evidence Code section 669. Instead, they, and the quotations from the prestigious national commissions, demonstrate that "that attitude of extreme individualism so typical of Anglo-Saxon legal thought" may need limited reexamination in the light of current societal conditions and the facts of this case to determine whether the defendant owed a duty to the deceased to permit the use of the telephone.

We turn now to the concept of duty in a tort case. The Supreme Court has identified certain factors to be considered in determining whether a duty is owed to third persons. These factors include:

> The foreseeability of harm to the plaintiff, the degree of certainty that the plaintiff suffered injury, the closeness of the connection between the defendant's conduct and the injury suffered, the moral blame attached to the defendant's conduct, the policy of preventing future harm, the extent of the burden to the defendant and consequences to the community of imposing a duty to exercise care with resulting liability for breach, and the availability, cost, and prevalence of insurance for the risk involved. (*Rowland v. Christian* [1968] 443 P.2d 561.)

We examine those factors in reference to this case. (1) The harm to the decedent was abundantly foreseeable; it was imminent. The employee was expressly told that a man had been threatened. The employee was a bartender. As such he knew it is foreseeable that some people who drink alcohol in the milieu of a bar setting are prone to violence. (2) The certainty of decedent's injury is undisputed. (3) There is arguably a close connection between the employee's conduct and the injury: the patron wanted to use the phone to summon the police to intervene. The employee's refusal to allow the use of the phone prevented this anticipated intervention. If permitted to go to trial, the plaintiff may be able to show that the probable response time of the police would have been shorter than the time between the prohibited telephone call and the fatal shot. (4) The employee's conduct displayed a disregard for human life that can be characterized as morally wrong: he was callously indifferent to the possibility that Darrell Soldano would die as the result of his refusal to allow a person to use the telephone. Under the circumstances before us the bartender's burden was minimal and exposed him to no risk: all he had to do was allow the use of the telephone. It would have cost him or his employer nothing. It could have saved a life. (5) Finding a duty in these circumstances would promote a policy of preventing future harm. A citizen would not be required to summon the police but would be required, in circumstances such as those before us, not to impede another who has chosen to summon aid. (6) We have no information on the question of the availability, cost, and prevalence of insurance for the risk, but note that the liability which sought to be imposed here is that of employee negligence, which is covered by many insurance policies. (7) The extent of the burden on the defendant was minimal, as noted.

The consequences to the community of imposing a duty, the remaining factor mentioned in *Rowland v. Christian, supra,* is termed "the administrative factor" by Professor Green in his analysis of determining whether a duty exists in a given case. (Green, *The Duty Problem in Negligence Cases,* I [1929] 28 Colum.L.Rev. 1014, 1035–1045. . . .) The administrative factor is simply the pragmatic concern of fashioning a workable rule and the impact of such a rule on the judicial machinery. It is the policy of major concern in this case.

As the Supreme Court has noted, the reluctance of the law to impose liability for nonfeasance, as distinguished from misfeasance, is in part due to the difficulties in setting standards and of making rules workable. (*Tarasoff v. Regents of University of California, supra.* . . .)

Many citizens simply "don't want to get involved." No rule should be adopted which would require a citizen to open up his or her house to a stranger so that the latter may use the telephone to call for emergency assistance. As Mrs. Alexander in Anthony Burgess's *A Clockwork Orange* learned to her horror, such an action may be fraught with danger. It does not follow, however, that use of a telephone in a public portion of a business should be refused for a legitimate emergency call. Imposing liability for such a refusal would not subject innocent citizens to possible attack by the "good samaritan," for it would be limited to an establishment open to the public during times when it is open to business, and to places within the establishment ordinarily accessible to the public. . . .

We conclude that the bartender owed a duty to the plaintiff's decedent to permit the patron from Happy Jack's to place a call to the police or to place the call himself. . . .

The creative and regenerative power of the law has been strong enough to break chains imposed by outmoded former decisions. What the courts have power to create, they also have power to modify, reject and re-create in response to the needs of a dynamic society. The exercise of this power is an imperative function of the courts and is the strength of the common law. It cannot be surrendered to legislative inaction.

Prosser puts it this way:

> New and nameless torts are being recognized constantly, and the progress of the common law is marked by many cases of first impression, in which the court has struck out boldly to create a new cause of action, where none had been recognized before. . . . The law of torts is anything but static, and the limits of its development are never set. When it becomes clear that the plaintiff's interests are entitled to legal protection against the conduct of the defendant, the mere fact that the claim is novel will not of itself operate as a bar to the remedy." (Prosser, *op. cit. supra,* at pp. 3–4, fns. omitted.)

The possible imposition of liability on the defendant in this case is not a global change in the law. It is but a slight departure from the "morally questionable" rule of nonliability for inaction absent a special relationship. . . . It is a logical extension of Restatement section 327 which imposes liability for negligent interference with a third person who the defendant knows is attempting to render necessary aid. However small it may be, it is a step which should be taken.

We conclude there are sufficient justiciable issues to permit the case to go to trial and therefore reverse.

FRANSON, Acting P. J., and STANTON, J., concur.

QUESTIONS ABOUT THE CASE

1. *Soldano* overrules a long-standing common law rule. Do you agree that the old rule was "bad law"? (Remember that for the doctrine of stare decisis to come into play, you must believe that the old rule states unwise public policy.) If you so agree, do the principles of stare decisis permit overruling in this instance? Why or why not?
2. Note Judge Andreen's citation of *Tarasoff.* Is *Tarasoff* really a precedent for the *Soldano* holding? In what sense? In what sense is it no precedent at all?
3. Do you believe this case is only a "slight departure" from prior law? Why or why not?
4. Judge Andreen sent me copies of the parties' briefs in this case. The large majority of Judge Andreen's reasoning appears nowhere in either brief. That is, despite our adversary system, this judge felt no hesitation to go beyond the parties' arguments to decide on the basis that he and a unanimous court felt best. Are you comfortable with this practice?

FOR FURTHER THOUGHT

Here are four legal problems that appeared recently in the news. How would you apply materials covered in this chapter to answer the questions these cases pose?

1. In late 1995, following the tragic bombing of the federal building in Oklahoma City, a group of plaintiffs filed a lawsuit against ICI Explosives USA, Inc., the manufacturer of the ammonium nitrate fertilizer that prosecutors in the criminal case claimed was mixed with diesel fuel and used in the bombing. The plaintiffs alleged that ICI, and indeed the whole fertilizer industry, "should have known" that the fertilizer could fall into the hands of bombers. Johnnie L. Cochran, who represented O. J. Simpson at the same time, was among the plaintiffs' lawyers. The defendant manufactured two grades of fertilizer, "fertilizer grade," which is not porous enough to mix with diesel fuel, and "industrial grade." "Industrial grade" is made and sold with the specific knowledge that it can be legally used as an explosive. (In fact, an explosive mixture of ammonium nitrate and diesel oil has replaced 95 percent of the world's sale of dynamite.) The federal government does not classify the fertilizer alone as an explosive. Consider what social background facts might make your reasoning in this case similar to or different from the tugboat case. What if bombers could easily grind down the "fertilizer grade" into "industrial grade" if they wished? What if there is no known additive that could be mixed with industrial grade fertilizer to prevent it from exploding when combined with diesel fuel, but still function as an effective fertilizer?[40]

   Would you analyze differently the lawsuit filed by the victims of Colin Ferguson, who shot 6 and wounded 19 strangers on a Long Island Rail Road commuter train in December of 1993? Plaintiffs sued the makers of the gun, the magazine, and the ammunition Ferguson used in the shootings.[41]

2. In Virginia, on December 5, 1990, George Edwards held a gun to the head of Angela Nasser Lemon and threatened to kill her. Ms. Lemon later filed a successful complaint leading to his arrest, and then went into hiding. Dr. Charles E. Parker, who had treated Mr. Edwards for 17 years, then saw Edwards and convinced him to commit himself to a mental hospital for long-term intensive therapy. Believing she was then safe, Ms. Lemon came out of hiding. Unfortunately, Edwards legally left the hospital only a day after he had checked in. He saw Dr. Parker a few days later, and the doctor prescribed medication for Edwards. Three days later, Edwards killed Ms. Lemon and then himself. Heirs of Ms. Lemon sued both the hospital and Dr. Parker, claiming that they had a duty to warn Ms. Lemon that Edwards had left the hospital. Do you see any basis for distinguishing this case from *Tarasoff?* In March of 1995, the Virginia Supreme Court held that neither the hospital nor the doctor had a duty to warn the victim. What is the easiest way to explain the seeming inconsistency with *Tarasoff?*[42]

3. On June 16, 1996, the U.S. Supreme Court resolved a case brought by a licensed clinical social worker and her patient, a police officer. The officer had received therapy after killing a man in the line of duty. Both plaintiffs sought an injunction to prohibit release of the records of and notes from therapy from being admitted in a lawsuit brought by the victim's family against the officer. The Supreme Court, voting 7–2, declared for the first time that, as in the case of physicians and patients, lawyers and clients, and ministers and parishioners, the therapist-client relationship was privileged, so that the therapeutic notes and records could not be introduced without the

---

[40]"Lawsuit Filed in Bombing Now Includes 384 Plaintiffs," *New York Times,* November 2, 1995, p. A12. A federal trial judge dismissed the case against ICI on July 2, 1996.

[41]"Arms Makers Sued Over L.I.R.R. Shootings," *New York Times,* October 27, 1994, p. A15.

[42]"Hospital Had No Duty to Warn Victim, Court Says," *Richmond Times-Dispatch,* March 4, 1995, p. B5. See also "Whose Fault When the Medicated Run Amok?", *New York Times,* October 28, 1994, p. A16, and "Doctors Failed to Monitor Train Suspect," *New York Times,* February 21, 1996, p. A13.

patient's permission in court proceedings. Is this result inconsistent with *Tarasoff*? Why or why not?[43]

4. The *New York Times* of September 15, 1994 (C19) printed an article headlined "Officer Says Groping Devastated Woman." The article described a lawsuit brought by Paula Coughlin, a former Navy lieutenant, against the Hilton Hotels Corporation. Ms. Coughlin had been a victim of sexual harassment by male officers in the infamous "tailhook" convention in 1991. She claimed that the Las Vegas Hilton, the host of the Tailhook convention (and the host of 19 "boisterous and drunken" such conventions in previous years) negligently failed to provide adequate security to prevent the sexual harassment of a guest at the hotel. Ms. Coughlin had resigned from the Navy on May 31, 1994, saying at the time that "she felt harassed by other officers because she had taken the convention misconduct public." How would you apply the principles articulated in *Soldano* to resolve this case? What social background facts in such a case might bear on your decision? What widely shared cultural values might influence you were you the judge in this case? Is it not clear that courts adjudicating this and all the cases covered in this chapter inevitably must decide where moral responsibility lies for the loss of careers, property, health and lives?

5. The late Professor Robert Cover once condemned what he called the "static and simplistic" model of law. If this model were true:

> [T]he judge caught between law and morality has only four choices. He may apply the law against his conscience. He may apply conscience and be faithless to the law. He may resign. Or he may cheat. . . .[44]

Do not the cases described in this chapter, and throughout this book, suggest that the task of judging is dramatically more complicated and dynamic than the "static" model suggests?

---

[43]See "Justices Uphold Psychotherapy Privacy Rights," *New York Times,* June 14, 1996, p. A1. See also "Questions of Privacy Roil Arena of Psychotherapy," *New York Times,* May 22, 1996, p. A1.

[44]Robert M. Cover, *Justice Accused: Antislavery and the Judicial Process* (New Haven: Yale University Press, 1975), p. 6. My thanks to Professor L.H. LaRue for bringing this quote to my attention.

CHAPTER 5

Interpreting the United States Constitution

We are under a Constitution—but the Constitution is what the Judges say it is.

—Charles Evans Hughes

I look forward to seeing my plays staged so that I can find out what they mean.

—Tom Stoppard, playwright

At the beginning of the book, I discussed *legal reasoning* as a shorthand term for evaluating the fairness by which courts and judges exercise political power. Let me review why this term is used. First, because we believe in something called the *rule of law*, we care that people act consistently with the law. Second, because we have inherited a common law tradition, we give courts power to interpret what the law means in legal cases. (This is not true, for example, in France, where judges do not give extensive justifications for their decisions.) Third, rules of law are often unclear when applied to specific cases, so cases constantly get appealed on points of law, and judges must choose what the law means. Fourth, liberal democracy requires judges to *justify* these choices because they exert judicial power. We expect judges to do so through the medium of legal reasoning, which requires them to render decisions that fit together or harmonize rules of law, facts of cases, social background facts, and widespread social values.

In constitutional law, the third and final type of law this text examines, we encounter what we conventionally think of as the most truly political part of law. Common and statutory law have never been the political science staple that constitutional law has traditionally been. Indeed, all 50 states have constitutions, but it is only the Constitution of the United States that we conventionally teach. Why should this be so?

The Constitution does two important things. First, it allocates specific powers. It allocates powers both among the branches of the national government and between national and state governments. (Only the national government may coin money; the states have primary but not exclusive power over alcohol regulation.) Second, the Constitution declares rights that no branch of government at any level can exert power over—freedom of speech or the free exercise of religion for example. But state constitutions also simultaneously convey powers and provide rights to resist power. The question remains, why is the U.S. Constitution uniquely important?[1]

"THE SUPREME LAW OF THE LAND"

The short answer is that the Constitution of the United States is "the supreme law of the land," as stated in Article VI. If the Constitution is supreme, it presumably overrides all state constitutions and all statutes and common law rulings. In other words, when one rule of law is inconsistent with a constitutional rule, the other rule has got to go. Furthermore, the Constitution in Article III gives the U.S. Supreme Court, and all federal courts, jurisdiction to hear cases "arising under this Constitution." In the famous case of *Marbury v. Madison* in 1803, Chief Justice John Marshall, a lifetime appointee from the repudiated Federalist government of John Adams, put the jurisdiction clause and the supremacy clause together and declared that the federal courts could declare the acts of democratically elected Congress—in 1803 a very Republican Congress—null and void. We call this process "judicial review."

Judicial review of constitutionality puts the courts in a uniquely strong position. Legislatures can, as Chapter 3 showed, overturn statutory interpretations, and they can overturn common law decisions. In constitutional interpretation, no such democratic backstopping exists.

The Constitution is the law that defines and limits the powers of government, and the U.S. Supreme Court's applications of the Constitution limit by definition what the government can do. Short of holding a constitutional convention, those who dislike a constitutional ruling must either persuade the Court to change its mind or amend the Constitution. But a constitutional amendment requires approval of two-thirds of both houses of Congress *and* three-fourths of the states. Therefore, relatively small minorities can block a proposed amendment's passage. Only 2 of the 11 amendments ratified in the twentieth century (the Sixteenth Amendment, authorizing a federal income tax, and the Nineteenth, granting women's suffrage) can be said to have corrected controversial Supreme Court readings of the Constitution.

Furthermore, the issues themselves are often fundamentally important. Courts strike down laws prohibiting abortions in the first trimester of pregnancy. Courts tell

---

[1]Particularly in the area of education reform, however, some state supreme courts have interpreted state constitutions to require radical reorganization of public education. The Texas Supreme Court has interpreted the Texas constitution's guarantee of "an efficient system" for "the general diffusion of knowledge" to require a complete redesign of state school funding. See *Carrollton-Farmers Branch Independent School District v. Edgewood*, 826 S.W.2d 489 (1992). And see "Texas Meets School-Financing Deadline," *New York Times*, June 1, 1993, p. A8.

states what property they can and cannot tax. Courts order busing to integrate schools. Courts order legislatures to reapportion. Courts reverse the convictions of killers because of what some critics call "technicalities." The Court's calls for ending racial discrimination, for permitting abortions in the first trimester of pregnancy, and for creating a qualified right to die in the 1990 *Cruzan* case have impacts far greater than routine statutory decisions have. On June 26, 1997, the Court denied the existence of a broad constitutional right to physician-assisted suicide. At the same time, however, the majority opinion strongly suggested that the government could not interfere with a person's right to receive medication sufficient to relieve the pain and suffering of a terminal illness.[2]

Congressional opponents of the proposed amendment to require the Congress to balance the federal budget cited the federal courts' specific responsibility for enforcing the Constitution as supreme law. They pointed out that no constitutional clause works automatically and that the courts would be dragged into an endless array of lawsuits to decide what counted as a balanced budget. As Harvard Law Professor Laurence Tribe put it to the Senate Budget Committee, if the idea was "not stealing from our children," then "[w]hat are we doing if we cheapen the most precious legacy we have to leave to our children, the Constitution?"[3]

There are three more reasons why constitutional interpretation is politically so important. First, the Constitution speaks in some instances with considerable clarity and in other instances with much generality, ambiguity, and vagueness. For example, the president must be 35 years old, and while we can imagine hypothetical cases—an 18-year-old guru claims to be reincarnated and "really" 105—in fact no case has ever litigated that clause. But the Constitution's most frequently litigated clauses do little more than command the courts to *care* about basic political and governmental values without specifying with any precision the values or the problems to which the provisions apply.

- "Care," says the First Amendment to the courts, "that government not take sides on religious matters. Care that it not constrain religious freedom, or speech, or the press, unduly. But it's up to you to define religion, speech, and press and to decide when government action and those values simply cannot stand together."
- "Care," say the Fourth, Fifth, Sixth, and Eighth Amendments, "that government not become too zealous in fighting crime. Respect people's homes and property. Give them a fair chance to prove their innocence in court and do not punish the guilty too harshly. In short, be fair. But it's up to you to decide what's fair."
- "Men must be able to trade effectively," say the commerce clause and the contract clause. "Work it out so they can."

The Constitution omits references to some rights that the structure of our government seems to require. For example, the Constitution contains no guarantee of a right to vote. Obviously the Constitution's words could not anticipate some violations of liberty and privacy, such as wiretapping and other forms of electronic surveillance. On the other hand, it does omit reference to some rights that we assume the Constitution's

---

[2]*Washington v. Glucksberg*, 65 U.S.L.W. 4669 (1997), and *Vacco v. Ouill*, 65 U.S.L.W. 4695 (1997).

[3]"Starring Role in Budget Act: Fear of Voters," *New York Times*, June 5, 1992, p. A9. More recently, a judge used the Constitution to strike down a law granting the president the line-item veto. See "Judge Voids Law Giving President Line-Item Vetos," *New York Times*, April 11, 1997, p. A1.

authors knew about and took for granted—rights that are so much a part of our "liberty" as to "go without saying." The right to marry may well fall in this category. Thus to interpret the Constitution only according to what its words actually say seems to defeat its purpose. Once a constitutional right is established, we have no definitive rule for drawing constitutional lines so as to exclude other more controversial liberties.[4]

The Supreme Court has declared the right to choose whether to carry a fetus to term to be such a liberty. The right, articulated in the *Cruzan* case, to have a "living will" honored so that one will die with dignity is another such liberty. Gay and lesbian rights fall within the basic concept of liberty. Several state courts have struck down state sodomy laws. In 1990, in a rare public statement, retired Justice Lewis Powell admitted regret for his vote supporting the constitutionality of Georgia's sodomy law in the 1986 case, *Bowers v. Hardwick*. Hardwick, a gay male, had been the victim of overt police harassment.[5]

Second, if we could assume that every governmental representative—whether a legislator before voting for a statute or a policeman before deciding to arrest—stopped and made a conscientious determination of the constitutionality of a decision, under our Constitution, we would still need a constitution-interpreting organization like the courts. The Constitution is so vague, general, and ambiguous that people with the best of intentions do not necessarily reach the same interpretation.

Third, federalism compounds the problem. We have one national constitution but many state constitutions. If we take its legal status seriously, then the Constitution should mean the same everywhere, just as the Mann Act should not have one meaning in Utah and another in the District of Columbia. If we lived under a unitary government, then maybe (but only maybe) we could count on a conscientious Congress to determine uniform constitutional applications. Under our Constitution, however, Congress is neither structured nor empowered to review the constitutionality of the actions of state and local governments.

For all these reasons—the finality of the Supreme Court, the importance of constitutional issues, the inconclusiveness of the Constitution's text, and the need for constitutional uniformity—we might expect the Supreme Court to take particular care to honor the conventional formulas for good legal reasoning in order to persuade us that justice is done. The bulk of this chapter explains why just the opposite happens, and why the practice of justification in constitutional law differs from the practices of legal reasoning described in previous chapters.

Readers will have to put up with a higher level of abstraction in this chapter than the two that precede it. In part, one must move toward the general and the abstract in order to say anything at all about such an immense subject—one on which books about the Rehnquist Court, the Bork and Thomas nominations, or constitutional

---

[4]See Judge Richard Posner's case against strict constructionism aptly titled, "What Am I? A Potted Plant?" *New Republic,* September 28, 1987, pp. 23–25.

[5]See Peter Irons, *The Courage of Their Convictions* (New York: Penguin Books, 1990), Chapter 16, and "Powell Regrets Backing Sodomy Law," *Washington Post,* October 26, 1990, p. A3.

[6]Here is a small sampling of recent books on the subject. Bruce Ackerman, *We the People: Foundations* (Cambridge: Belknap Press of Harvard University Press, 1991); H. W. Perry, *Deciding to Decide* (Cambridge: Harvard University Press, 1991); Bernard Schwartz, *Decision: How the Supreme Court Decides Cases* (New York: Oxford University Press, 1996). John Maltese, *The Selling of Supreme Court Nominees* (Baltimore: The Johns Hopkins University Press, 1995); Stephen Griffin, *American Constitutionalism: From Theory to Politics* (Princeton, N.J.: Princeton University Press, 1996).

interpretation itself—flow steadily forth.[6] But there is a much more profound reason for the abstraction to follow, and the reason itself will seem difficult and abstract at first: Because the Constitution is supreme and because we believe we should follow it, we have throughout the many turbulent changes in our history worked very hard to make the Constitution fit and harmonize with what we do and what we believe. Bruce Ackerman's *We the People: Foundations* emphasizes that the United States has had—under one written document—two profound constitutional revolutions since the original revolutionary period: the Civil War and the New Deal.

Constitutional law, in other words, gets abstract because most of the Constitution's meaning is purely symbolic. We need the security of believing we are one political community with a continuous history, so we say we are living under one Constitution when in fact we work hard to change our interpretations of it to legitimate contemporary realities. Recall, however, that common law systems do work just this way.

CONVENTIONAL LEGAL REASONING IN CONSTITUTIONAL INTERPRETATION

The Court's unique political position, we shall now see, makes it unwise to use the conventional techniques of legal reasoning that might be appropriate in statutory and common law. You might well think that factors described in the last section—the inconclusiveness of the Constitutional text, the interpretation of the courts, the need for uniform constitutional meaning both within the national government and among all the states—call for especially stable and clear patterns of legal reasoning and justification. However, this is precisely what 200 years of constitutional interpretation has *never* achieved, and for good reason. Precisely because "the Constitution is what the Judges say it is" (as stated in the Hughes epigraph at the beginning of the chapter), the "construction of the Constitution is always open. . . ." (Chief Justice Taney). Therefore we must next explore why conventional legal reasoning in constitutional interpretation fails.

In 1985 Attorney General Edwin Meese called for a style of constitutional interpretation derived from the original understandings of the framers of the Constitution.[7] In this section, I suggest that Meese's call was unrealistic. Neither the words of the Constitution, the intent of the framers, nor the purposes served by clauses separately or in combination provide uncontroversial methods of resolving cases.

Words as Channels of Meaning

Article I, Section 10 of the Constitution prohibits the states from engaging in certain activities altogether. It prohibits them from making treaties, coining money, or keeping a state militia during times of peace without Congressional permission. The section also includes these words: "No state shall . . . pass any . . . law impairing the obligation of contracts."

Debts provide the best example of the kind of contract the state may not impair under the contract clause. In the typical case of such a contract—"executory" contracts

[7]Edwin Meese III, "Toward a Jurisprudence of Original Intention," 45 *Public Administration Review* 701 (1985).

in legal language—Pauline borrows money, say from a bank, and promises to pay the money back some time in the future. Until she pays the money back (and at the stated time), she has a contractual obligation to do so. The contract clause prevents the state from impairing Pauline's "obligation" to repay. In short, the state can't pass a law saying people don't have to pay back what they owe, even if a popularly elected legislature voted to do so. Thus the word "impairing" would seem to prevent the state from allowing Pauline to forget about paying the interest or to pay back years later than she promised.

During the Great Depression, a number of states passed laws allowing owners of homes and land to postpone paying their mortgage payments as the mortgage contracts required. These statutes forbade banks and other mortgage holders from foreclosing. The Depression, of course, destroyed the financial ability of hundreds of thousands of "Paulines" to repay mortgages on time, but these mortgage moratorium laws spared the "Paulines" from this peril. These laws spared the "Paulines" because they impaired the bank's ability to recover the debt; yet the Supreme Court ruled, in *Home Building and Loan Association v. Blaisdell,* that these laws did not violate the contract clause.[8]

The political context of Minnesota's moratorium statute was volatile. In Brest and Levinson's words, "angry farmers denounced and in some instances forcibly stopped foreclosure of their farms. In Iowa, a local judge who refused to suspend foreclosure proceedings was dragged from a courtroom and had a rope put around his neck before the crowd let him go."[9] Yet surely the Supreme Court should not decide cases simply to minimize violence. That only invites constitutional blackmail.

We *can* defend such a result. Just as in nature, survival of economic and political values depends on adaptation, on change, and on the ability to reevaluate policies in light of new information. The Supreme Court rejected the contract clause's words and upheld the Depression's mortgage moratorium laws because these laws were based on economic knowledge not fully available to the framers. In the forced panic sale of land following massive numbers of foreclosures of mortgages, what would happen to the price of land? Supply and demand analysis predicted that the price would drastically decline, quite possibly to the point where creditors as well as debtors would lose because the land could be sold for only a fraction of what the banks had originally loaned on it. The Court upheld the law as a defensible method for attempting to prevent the further collapse of the economy.

A decision in the monumental school desegregation cases provides another example of prudent judicial flight from constitutional words. In its celebrated decision, *Brown v. Board of Education,* the Court held that the equal protection clause of the Fourteenth Amendment prohibited laws and policies designed to maintain segregation in public schools of the then 48 states.[10] The issue concerned the problem of segregation of schools in the nation's capital. The Fourteenth Amendment's sentence containing the equal protection clause begins with the words "no state shall." It does not govern the District of Columbia. The original Bill of Rights does govern the national government and hence the district, but it contains no equal protection clause. The Court forbade segregation in the

[8]*Home Building and Loan Association v. Blaisdell,* 290 U.S. 398 (1934). See also *East New York Savings Bank v. Hahn,* 326 U.S. 230 (1945) and *El Paso v. Simmons,* 379 U.S. 497 (1965).

[9]Paul Brest and Sanford Levinson, *Processes of Constitutional Decisionmaking* (Boston: Little, Brown & Co., 3rd ed., 1992), p. 352.

[10]*Brown v. Board of Education,* 347 U.S. 483 (1954).

District's public schools by invoking the due process clause of the Fifth Amendment.[11] Unfortunately, the due process clause does not address the problem of equality. Its words—"No person shall . . . be deprived of life, liberty, or property, without due process of law . . ."—seem to address the problem of the fairness of procedures, the "due process," in the courts. The Fourteenth Amendment contains both due process and equal protection clauses, which further suggests that they convey different messages.

Nevertheless, the Court prohibited segregation in the district. If the Constitution denies government the power to segregate schools by race, it is proper to avoid the absurdity of permitting segregation only in the national capital. It is proper to say in this instance that the due process clause of the Fifth Amendment does address this problem of equality despite its words.[12]

The Intent of the Framers and the Purpose of Constitutional Provisions

Searching for the actual intent of the framers of the original Constitution (or of its later amendments) proves just as frustrating as the search for legislative intent. The processes of constitution and statute making are equally political. People make arguments they don't fully believe in order to win support. Others do not express what they do believe in order to avoid offending. The painful process of negotiation and accommodation that produced the Constitution in 1787 left many questions unresolved. Most confounding of all, the authors could have had no intent in relation to the new facts that have surfaced since their work concluded.[13]

Thus, the Court ignored the original purpose of the Sixth Amendment's command when it expanded the right to counsel. This amendment states in part that "In all criminal prosecutions, the accused shall enjoy the right . . . to have the assistance of counsel for his defense." The framers who drafted it sought to alter the common law rule that prohibited accused felons from having any lawyer at all. They wanted to stop the government from preventing the accused from bringing his lawyer to court with him. It

---

[11]*Bolling v. Sharpe,* 347 U.S. 497 (1954). See also *Hirabayashi v. United States,* 320 U.S. 81 (1943).

[12]Some of the Court's creative manipulations of words in constitutional law come disguised as statutory interpretations. For example Section 6(j) of the old draft law stated, "Nothing contained in this title shall be construed to require any person to be subject to combatant training and service . . . who, by reason of religious training and belief, is conscientiously opposed to participation in war in any form. Religious training and belief, in this connection, mean an individual's belief in a relation to a Supreme Being involving duties superior to those arising from any human relation, but do not include essentially political, sociological, or philosophical views or a merely personal moral code." In 1966, one Elliott A. Welsh, II, was convicted for refusing to submit to induction. He had applied for an exemption as a conscientious objector under Section 6(j), but he insisted that his feelings were not religious but moral, based upon "reading in the fields of history and sociology," he said. He believed that taking any life was "morally wrong" and "totally repugnant." The Court reversed Welsh's conviction. Hugo Black, speaking for himself and three other Justices (Blackmun did not sit; Harlan concurred on other grounds), said that Section 6(j) exempted all those who held moral and philosophical beliefs "with the strength of more traditional religious convictions." To avoid invalidating Section 6(j), Black made it say precisely what the words in Section 6(j) take pains to avoid. *Welsh v. United States,* 398 U.S. 333 (1970).

[13]For further elaboration see my *Contemporary Constitutional Lawmaking: The Supreme Court and the Art of Politics* (Elmsford, N.Y.: Pergamon Press, 1985), pp. 52–55. For a very thorough recent review of the intellectual history of the founding period, see Jack N. Rakove, *Original Meanings* (New York: Alfred A. Knopf, 1996).

makes no reference to the problem that a man's poverty may stop him from hiring a lawyer. Yet in 1938 the Court held that these words required the federal government to provide lawyers for the poor and the court has since expanded the right to protect those accused of felonies and misdemeanors in state and local courts.[14]

And consider again the mortgage moratorium laws of the Depression. If we examine the purpose of the contract clause from the framers' viewpoint, we discover that they feared excessive democracy—feared that popularly elected legislators would enact the "selfish" interests of the masses. The masses contain more debtors than creditors, and it was in economically difficult times that the framers most feared that debtors would put irresistible pressure on legislators to ease their debts. Hence the Court in *Home Building and Loan* rejected more than constitutional words; it rejected the purpose of the provision. But it did so wisely because it understood, as presumably the framers did not, how postponing mortgage foreclosures could benefit creditors and debtors alike.

Finally, H. Jefferson Powell has recently shown two reasons why the leading figures of the founding period repeatedly and expressly rejected the idea that their own actual hopes and expectations of the Constitution would dictate legal conclusions in the future. First, at common law, the reading of texts like wills and contracts rejected actual intent in favor of giving words their "reasonable," "grammatical," or "popular" meaning. Second, the framers, as members of the Protestant tradition, believed that texts ought to speak for themselves, unmediated by church or scholarly authority. They believed each person should be free to interpret biblical texts for himself and that complex scholarly interpretations—interpretations imposed by "experts"—had no presumptive authority.

Powell describes how George Washington required in his will the nonlegal arbitration of any ambiguity in administering its provisions precisely in order that the decision maker might consider Washington's actual intent in the matter. None of the debaters in Philadelphia acknowledged that their words might shape the future, and James Madison believed that usage ("usus") and the lessons learned from political practice should override any "abstract opinion of the text." Thus, as president he signed the Second Bank Bill. He thought the First U. S. Bank had been unconstitutional, but he approved the successor because the people had approved it and it had worked.[15]

In this historical evidence we find the beginnings of America's major contribution to Western philosophy—pragmatism. Pragmatism does not refer to a selfish attempt to "do whatever it takes to win." Pragmatism holds that our attitudes and choices should follow primarily from what experience tells us is good, not from abstract rules or theories. The "radicalism of the American revolution," as Gordon Wood calls it, succeeded in implanting a democracy that made a pragmatic move away from the values and beliefs of the framers inevitable. Wood's conclusion holds:

> "We cannot rely on the views of the founding fathers anymore," Martin Van Buren told the New York convention in 1820. "We have to rely on our own

---

[14]*Johnson v. Zerbst,* 304 U.S. 458 (1938), *Gideon v. Wainwright,* 372 U.S. 335 (1963), *Argersinger v. Hamlin,* 407 U.S. 25 (1972). For a persuasive defense of this trend see Anthony Lewis's classic, *Gideon's Trumpet* (New York: Random House, 1964).

[15]H. Jefferson Powell, "The Original Understanding of Original Intent," 98 *Harvard Law Review* 885 (1985). Compare Richard Kay, "Adherence to the Original Intentions in Constitutional Adjudication: Three Objections and Responses," 82 *Northwestern University Law Review* 226 (1987).

experience, not on what they said or thought." "They had many fears," said Van Buren, "fears of democracy, that American experience had not borne out."[16]

Stare Decisis

In 1940 the Supreme Court held that a public school could require all children—including Jehovah's Witnesses, whose religious convictions forbade it—to salute the flag each day. In 1943 the Court overruled itself and held the opposite.[17] In 1946 the Court refused to require state legislatures to make electoral districts roughly equal, but in 1962 the Court began to do just that.[18]

The justices themselves have from time to time recognized the reasons to ignore stare decisis in constitutional law. After all, no legislature sits mainly to update constitutional policy in light of new conditions. It is not simply that the Court should correct its own mistakes—that, as indicated in Chapter 3, is always wise policy. It is rather that wise policy at one time is not necessarily wise policy at another. If we take seriously the idea that the Constitution is law—ought to have teeth—then the courts must do the updating. As Justice William O. Douglas once said:

> The place of *stare decisis* in constitutional law is . . . tenuous. A judge looking at a constitutional decision may have compulsions to revere past history and accept what was once written. But he remembers above all else that it is the Constitution which he swore to support and defend, not the gloss which his predecessors may have put on it. So he comes to formulate his own views, rejecting some earlier ones as false and embracing others. He cannot do otherwise unless he lets men long dead and unaware of the problems of the age in which he lives do his thinking for him.[19]

Of course people rely on constitutional decisions. Teachers in 1943 believed they could require all students—regardless of their individual beliefs—to salute the flag. State judges in 1963 did not believe they had to appoint counsel in all felonies. Candidates for political office and their parties in the early 1960s may have created their election strategies assuming malapportionment in voting districts. The point is that constitutional values may be important enough to override reliance on past policy.

TWO ALTERNATIVE APPROACHES TO CONSTITUTIONAL REASONING

If neither the conventions of legal justification nor the backstop of legislative correction of judicial decisions limits the Supreme Court's power and discretion, then what does? This question has preoccupied constitutional scholarship for nearly a century.

---

[16]*The Radicalism of the American Revolution* (New York: Alfred A. Knopf, 1992), pp. 368–369.

[17]*Minersville School District v. Gobitis*, 310 U.S. 586 (1940), and *West Virginia State Board of Education v. Barnette*, 319 U.S. 624 (1943).

[18]*Colegrove v. Green*, 328 U.S. 549 (1946), and *Baker v. Carr*, 369 U.S. 186 (1962).

[19]William O. Douglas, "Stare Decisis," 4 *Record of the Association of the Bar of the City of New York* 152 (1949), pp. 153-154.

This section reviews two possible answers: Perhaps a theory of constitutional justification exists but the justices have not yet learned to practice it. Or perhaps the political system imposes sufficient practical and informal checks on the court to compensate for the fact that judges aren't themselves elected.

Theories About Constitutional Justification

The search for limits on the Supreme Court's power and discretion is not driven merely by the sometimes obsessive need of scholars to make the world neat and tidy. In the late nineteenth and early twentieth centuries the Supreme Court did try to proclaim itself the final arbiter of social and economic policy and of political morality. It actively thwarted economic and social reforms at all levels of government for the sake of then-popular beliefs in Social Darwinism, which seemed to many judges to equate unregulated private business activity with the improvement of the human race. So in *U.S. v. E.C. Knight* (1895) the Court aggressively reduced national power over commerce by defining the commerce power (contrary to precedents going back to John Marshall) to cover only the physical movement of goods among the states.[20] In 1905, in *Lochner v. New York*, the Court struck down statutory amelioration of harsh working conditions in bakeries by creating, under the Fourteenth Amendment's due process clause, a constitutional right to individuals' freedom to make any contracts they chose subject only to the "reasonable" exercise of the state's police power. The Court decided what was "reasonable."[21] In 1918, Congress forbade the shipment in interstate commerce of goods made with child labor. Although the statute seemed to honor restrictions on the commerce power set in *E.C. Knight*, the Court struck down this statute because there was nothing inherently harmful about the goods shipped.[22]

The Court's official version of Social Darwinism mistook the absence of regulation for free competition. Social Darwinism promised the improvement of the species through free competition, but such government regulations as the antitrust laws (which *E.C. Knight* curtailed) actually encouraged the sort of competition that Social Darwinism required; that is, the Court claimed the power to review and reverse social policy on the basis of a theory that contradicted itself. Thus, Justice David Brewer in 1893 told the New York Bar Association that strengthening the judiciary was necessary to protect the country "against the tumultuous ocean of democracy!" He believed that

> the permanence of government of and by the people . . . rests upon the independence and vigor of the judiciary, . . . to restrain the greedy hand of the many from filching from the few that which they have honestly acquired. . . .[23]

This claim to unlimited judicial power prompted a search for theories that would limit judicial power, a search that has continued to this day.

The first of these theories, authored by James B. Thayer of the Harvard Law School, tried to reaffirm the representative nature of American constitutional government. All acts of elected bodies carry a heavy presumption of constitutionality. The

---

[20]156 U.S. 1.
[21]198 U.S. 45.
[22]*Hammer v. Dagenhart*, 247 U.S. 251.
[23]*Proceedings of the New York State Bar Association* (1893), p. 37.

courts may properly overturn legislation only on a showing that the legislature has made a very clear mistake.[24]

Thayer's antithesis proved unsatisfactory for two reasons. First, like the "golden rule" of statutory interpretation, it contained no standards for determining what counted as a clear mistake. From the perspective of David Brewer (and Justice Field, who thought the income tax marked the beginning of a war waged by the poor against the rich), economic regulation *was* a clear mistake. Thayer's position left to courts the responsibility for doing the extra-legal analysis necessary to decide what counts as a clear mistake: "The ultimate arbiter of what is rational and permissible is indeed always the courts, so far as litigated cases bring the question before them."

Second, if Thayer's theory did nudge the court into a posture of judicial self-restraint, the Court would then lack power to protect violations of civil liberties. Yet before the final collapse of the Court's economic activism in 1937, it had begun to move into the civil liberties area. In 1931 the Court struck down a Minnesota law permitting prior censorship of the press.[25] In 1932 it reversed the death sentences of six black defendants sentenced to death after a one-day trial in Scottsboro, Alabama, in which the six were denied adequate representation of counsel.[26]

The synthesis of the two extremes—the theory that justified judicial abstinence from evaluating the rationality of economic policy without curtailing its power to protect civil liberties—appeared quietly (and in the obscurest possible legalese) in the fourth footnote to a 1938 case in which the Court upheld congressional authority to regulate the ingredients in milk products processed for interstate commerce. This now famous "Carolene footnote four" reads:

> There may be narrower scope for operation of the presumption of constitutionality when legislation appears on its face to be within a specific prohibition of the Constitution, such as those of the first ten amendments, which are deemed equally specific when held to be embraced within the Fourteenth. . . .
>
> It is unnecessary to consider now whether legislation which restricts those political processes which can ordinarily be expected to bring about a repeal of undesirable legislation, is to be subjected to more exacting judicial scrutiny under the general prohibitions of the Fourteenth Amendment than are most other types of legislation. . . .
>
> Nor need we inquire whether similar consideration enter into the review of statutes directed at particular religious . . . or national . . . or racial minorities . . . whether prejudice against discrete and insular minorities may be a special condition, which tends seriously to curtail the operation of those political processes ordinarily to be relied upon to protect minorities, and which may call for a correspondingly more searching judicial inquiry. . . .[27]

The first paragraph justified cases like *Near* because the First Amendment guarantees a free press—and *Powell* because the Fifth and Sixth Amendments guarantee a

---

[24]"The Origin and Scope of the American Doctrine of Constitutional Law," 7 *Harvard Law Review* 129 (1893).

[25]*Near v. Minnesota*, 283 U.S. 697.

[26]*Powell v. Alabama*, 287 U.S. 45.

[27]*United States v. Carolene Products Co.*, 304 U.S. 114, pp. 152–153.

fair trial. In such cases the Court deemed that the Fourteenth Amendment's due process clause applied these federal restrictions to state and local governmental actions.

The note's second paragraph explained why the Court need not intervene in economic policy: Fights over allocation of economic resources—like the debate over the working conditions in bakeries in *Lochner*—are usually waged by well-organized groups on various sides of the issue. The political compromises among those interests may not equate with a professional economist's definition of rationality, but they are legally acceptable because all sides participate in the process. But if the electoral machinery itself breaks down so as to bias the messages policy makers receive, the Court may intervene, for example, as in the reapportionment cases.[28]

The footnote's third paragraph suggests that even when the machinery of electoral politics works properly, prejudice against racial, religious, or other minorities (including people accused of serious crimes like murder, rape, and robbery) may prevent them from being heard. The Court's leadership regarding racial segregation took place at a time when blacks in the deep South were systematically denied the chance to organize and vote. These racist policies arguably violated all three parts of the *Carolene* theory.

In 1980, John Hart Ely and Jesse Choper developed the details of these theories.[29] To the three *Carolene Products* points Choper added a fourth: The Court should avoid upsetting political decisions about the balance of power between national and local government. The fact that state and local parties and elections select the members of Congress and that reelection depends on satisfying local demands ensures a rough balance of state and local power without help from the Supreme Court. (Indeed, a common modern complaint about Congress, particularly regarding its seeming inability to reduce the national budget deficit, holds that congressmen's outlooks are excessively parochial and local.)

Many more scholarly theories of the Court's role have emerged since 1937. Herbert Wechsler has advocated that the Court decide cases only on the basis of "neutral principles," on the basis of rules that future courts can apply in cases with very different partisan or political alignments. A principle protecting those who demonstrate for racial justice must be articulated in such a way as to protect demonstrating members of the American Nazi Party.[30] Alexander Bickel believed that, to preserve its capacity to announce such principles without endangering the Court's political support, the Court should exploit its many technical procedures by which it can avoid deciding at all.[31] This book's appendix describes some of these techniques.

Despite the scholarly elegance of each of these theories, they do not answer our fundamental question. We seek legal and political dynamics that actually do limit the constitutional power of the Supreme Court—not merely a resolution of an academic debate about what might, in theory, limit the Court. We seek an understanding of the Court's actual practices that can assure us that its justifications are good, and the fact of the matter is that, in practice, the Court does not consistently follow these theories any better than it follows more conventional methods of legal reasoning.

[28]*Baker v. Carr*, 369 U.S. 186 (1962), and see *Reynolds v. Sims*, 377 U.S. 533 (1964).
[29]John Hart Ely, *Democracy and Distrust: A Theory of Judicial Review* (Cambridge: Harvard University Press, 1980), and Jesse Choper, *Judicial Review and the National Political Process: A Functional Reconsideration of the Role of the Supreme Court* (Chicago: University of Chicago Press, 1980).
[30]Herbert Wechsler, "Toward Neutral Principles of Constitutional Law," 73 *Harvard Law Review* 1 (1959).
[31]Alexander Bickel, *The Least Dangerous Branch* (Indianapolis: Bobbs-Merrill, 1962).

Consider the Court's decision in *Griswold v. Connecticut*, in which the Court struck down state laws prohibiting the distribution of contraceptives. The "right of privacy" created by the Court to justify the result is hardly a "specific prohibition" in the Bill of Rights, and the people it protects—women and men both—are as far from an insular and discrete minority as we could imagine.[32] The Court's extension of the principle of privacy in the abortion case—including the right of a single female—might seem to practice Wechsler's neutral principles concept but for the fact that the Court also ruled that the Constitution permits government to deny funds for abortion to the indigent who are otherwise qualified to receive them.[33] Indeed Justice Stone, the coauthor of *Carolene Products'* footnote four voted (perhaps for Bickelian reasons) *against* allowing the Court to intervene in legislative reapportionment, in direct contradiction to his note's second paragraph.[34]

We have already seen that a precedent does not dictate how a judge applies it. (If it did, the case would usually not reach the appellate courts in the first place.) Just as "fact freedom" allows different judges to apply the same precedents in opposite ways, so each constitutional theory does not dictate or constrain. The history of judicial review, starting with *Marbury v. Madison*,[35] more resembles a tool bench where the judge decides how the case ought to come out and then chooses whatever tool seems handiest to get the job done. All academic theories about the Supreme Court's role fail to answer our question. Perhaps the political role of the Supreme Court makes theoretical consistency both impossible and unnecessary. We explore that possibility next.

Political Constraints on the Court

One school of thought, which political scientists have called "political jurisprudence," supplies constraints on the Supreme Court not through political theory or legal doctrine but from the practical operation of politics itself. This resolution of the constitutional paradox was expressed most pithily by Mr. Dooley's conclusion that "th' Supreme Court follows th' iliction returns." Martin Shapiro, a leading figure in political jurisprudence for a quarter of a century, put it this way:

> No regime is likely to allow significant political power to be wielded by an isolated judicial corps free of political restraints. To the extent that courts make law, judges will be incorporated into the governing coalition, the ruling elite, responsible representatives of the people, or however else the political regime may be expressed.[36]

Subject to a few historical exceptions, particularly the Court's advocacy of Social Darwinism and laissez-faire economics, the theory holds that the Court rarely strays far enough from dominant popular opinion to worry about checking it through legal doctrine or theories of judicial review.[37] This approach combines historical observations of

---

[32]*Griswold v. Connecticut*, 381 U.S. 479 (1965).

[33]*Roe v. Wade*, 410 U.S. 113 (1973), but *Harris v. McRae*, 448 U.S. 297 (1980).

[34]*Colegrove v. Green*, 328 U.S. 549 (1946).

[35]*Marbury v. Madison*, 5 U.S. 87 (1803).

[36]Martin Shapiro, *Courts: A Comparative Political Analysis* (Chicago: University of Chicago Press, 1981), p. 34.

[37]See Robert Dahl, "Decision-Making in a Democracy: The Supreme Court as National Policy Maker, 6 *Journal of Public Law* 294 (1958).

instances in which presidential selections of justices have steered the Court onto more popular courses with analyses of the structural and procedural characteristics of the Court's work that make it politically responsive. Here are the major threads this perspective weaves together.

Many constitutional decisions do not invalidate the work of popularly elected legislators in the first place. They set aside—as in the decisions regarding search and seizure of criminal evidence and of interrogation of suspects—decisions of nonelected administrative personnel who are, like judges, only indirectly affected by electoral politics. In less than one-half of 1 percent of all statutes passed by Congress since World War II the Court has found a point to invalidate. In nearly all of these instances, the Court has invalidated not an entire statutory scheme or policy but only an offending clause or provision.[38] The most activist of courts touches only a tiny fraction of the democratic work of Congress.

Elected officials do not vote according to the "majority will" because on most policy issues before a legislature the public has no opinion whatsoever. The benefit of elections in the daily operation of politics comes from the fact that elected politicians listen to interest groups and individual citizens because they need as many votes from as many different sources as possible. Elections tend to overcome the natural inertia of all organized human effort. The legal process has a different but equally effective method for forcing judges to listen: Anyone can file a lawsuit about anything, and judges must listen to it at least long enough to determine that the lawsuit alleges no legal injury.

The president fills a vacancy on the Supreme Court on the average of slightly less often than once every two years. Even before Ronald Reagan's appointments of Sandra Day O'Connor and Antonin Scalia, the Nixon-Ford presidencies had named a majority of the Supreme Court bench, and this Burger Court very much slowed the expansion of the Warren Court's protection of the rights of the accused, just as President Nixon's "law and order" campaign had pledged.[39] Except for the failed nomination of Robert Bork—a nomination that President Reagan probably could have saved by aggressive campaigning on the Hill—the Republican nominations (of Anthony Kennedy and David Souter) met no serious opposition. Even when Clarence Thomas was publically charged with sexual harassment at the time he headed an agency responsible for preventing such abuses, the Senate confirmed his nomination, 52–48. The political jurisprudence solution becomes more persuasive when, in spite of predictions to the contrary, Souter and Kennedy voted to follow the *Roe v. Wade* abortion precedent at a time (1992) when popular opinion seemed to favor just that result.

As we saw regarding the case of the sunken barges in Chapter 4, courts process information very much as other decision makers do. Various sides present positions. Lawyers file briefs containing abundant factual as well as legal assertions. They criticize the positions their opponents take. The capacity of judges to understand information depends on two things. First, does the issue really depend on the intelligent digestion and interpretation of a complex body of facts at all? Many of the most dramatic civil

---

[38]Through the year 1978, the Supreme Court had invalidated portions of about 100 Acts of Congress, 900 State Statutes, and 124 local ordinances. My thanks to Professor Sam Krislov for calling these tabulations to my attention.

[39]For a recent argument favoring independent Senate screening of the President's judicial appointments, see Laurence Tribe, *God Save This Honorable Court* (New York: Random House, 1985).

rights questions are so fundamentally normative and depend so extensively on moral rather than factual reasoning that the technical competence of judges really does not seem relevant. The decision to forbid mandatory flag salutes does not depend on scientific analysis of data revealing the beneficial and harmful consequences of such practices. Second, when the issue does depend on an understanding of facts, then we should really expect judges to have the capacity to understand the facts before they proceed. Judges must understand the language through which the problem expresses itself. Most judges are well equipped to understand the dimensions of a right-to-counsel issue. Most judges are not equipped to understand the econometric analysis on which the Federal Reserve Board determines its national monetary policy. The problem must not be of the sort in which part of the information is necessarily hidden from judges, as it is in many foreign policy matters because the information is secret or because the only people who possess it do not live or work within the reach of the court's jurisdiction. Finally, if a given decision generates feedback information that will produce improved policy, the courts should have access to that information in the course of further litigation.[40]

Constitutional decisions possess all the characteristics of the common law tradition. No one decision permanently sets the course of law. The process is a thoroughly incremental one in which, case by case, new facts and new arguments pro and con repeatedly come before the courts. The law can change and adjust to new facts and conditions. A judicial commitment to protecting liberties does not require the courts to articulate a complete theory of equal protection or due process.[41]

In the twentieth century the Court has avoided creating legal doctrine that appears to "take sides" along popular partisan lines. Decisions defending the freedom of civil rights activists to organize and demonstrate also protect neo-Nazis and Klansmen. The Burger Court voted without dissent against President Nixon's claim of executive privilege in the Watergate crisis. The Court steered a middle course regarding affirmative action when it ruled that race alone could not determine admissions policies.[42]

Although the Burger Court sometimes forgot the lesson, particularly in the legislative veto case, the structural core of American government is not and has never been the idea that power is separated. The main thrust of the Madisonian constitutional scheme was to prevent too much power from accumulating in one place. The dispersion of power takes place more through the sharing than the separating of power. Different institutions must compromise because none can act effectively without cooperating with the others. Perhaps therefore the indeterminacy of constitutional theory is a blessing in disguise, a measure of the success of Madison's vision.[43]

---

[40]Lief H. Carter, "When Courts Should Make Policy: An Institutional Approach," in *Public Law and Public Policy*, John A. Gardiner, ed. (New York: Praeger, 1977), pp. 141–157; Donald L. Horowitz, *The Courts and Social Policy* (Washington, D.C.: The Brookings Institution, 1977); Gerald Rosenberg, *The Hollow Hope* (Chicago: University of Chicago Press, 1991); David Schultz, ed. *Leveraging the Law* (New York: Peter Lang, 1997).

[41]Felix Cohen, "Transcendental Nonsense and the Functional Approach," 35 *Columbia Law Review* 809 (1935). See also Martin Shapiro, "Stability and Change in Judicial Decision Making: Incrementalism or Stare Decisis?" 2 *Law in Transition Quarterly* 134 (1964). And see Janet S. Lindgren, "Beyond Cases: Reconsidering Judicial Review," 1983 *Wisconsin Law Review* 583 (1983).

[42]*Regents of the University of California v. Bakke*, 438 U.S. 265 (1978).

[43]See Walter Murphy, James Fleming, and Will Harris, *American Constitutional Interpretation* (Mineola, N.Y.: Foundation Press, 1986), Chap. 1–3, esp. pp. 48–55.

Do these indisputable characteristics of American politics provide an acceptable substitute for persuasive legal justification? Two lines of reasoning indicate that they do not. First, although these factors do suggest no cause for immediate alarm about the Supreme Court's political role, they completely sidestep the original question. Legal reasoning ought to provide standards of satisfactory justification for specific case decisions. The political factors do not guide judges in the crafting of actual opinions. The political environment may provide some macroscopic reassurance, but it will hardly satisfy a losing litigant in a concrete case to learn that the president might appoint a more sympathetic justice a year or two later.

Second, the reassuring argument may prove too much. The Constitution is in some respects an antimajoritarian document. The Constitution in part seeks to protect individuals from what Tocqueville called "the tyranny of the majority." It protects individuals, not demographically defined groups. The unpopular speaker and the deviant religious belief may thrive only if the courts are not politically too responsive. If we must sustain the belief that the Constitution is a central source of political structure and communal values—if we need to believe in *it*—then conventional political jurisprudence provides no satisfying solution to our problem.

The neo-Marxist wing of political jurisprudence—the "Critical Legal Studies" movement—recognizes the two reservations I just described. Beginning in the mid-1970s, Duncan Kennedy, Roberto Unger, Mark Tushnet, Robert Gordon, Paul Brest, John Henry Schlagel, and other law professors who came of professional age during the antiwar movement of the 1960s began in their publications to assert that the political culture constrains court and legislature alike from protecting individual dignity adequately. But they also recognized that the solution lay in changing not legal doctrine but the political culture itself. The negative side of the movement has articulated a powerful case for abandoning the search for any doctrinal solution to constitutional interpretation.[44]

The positive contribution of critical legal studies is less clear or convincing, in part because the very success of the movement's critique of doctrine makes a case that no doctrinal solution is possible. Nevertheless, critical legal studies seems to move toward endorsing the idea that constitutional goodness depends on the Court's enhancing our capacity to converse about the moral or normative quality of our communal life. To accomplish this, the Court must do more than protect First Amendment freedoms or individual privacy. It must protect individual integrity and dignity so that people feel empowered to participate in political life. To accomplish that task, the Court must in turn model good conversation. It must speak candidly about the world that law, politics, science, economics, and religion all inhabit.

The critical legal studies movement has retained the radical and neo-Marxist orientation of its antiwar origins, but its substantive conclusions do not differ substantially from those reached by the more mainstream liberal philosophy of Ronald Dworkin, Walter Murphy, and Sotirios Barber.[45] Although mainstream liberalism persists in searching for a coherent constitutional philosophy, its approach emphasizes not legal

---

[44]I have treated the critical movement in my *Contemporary Constitutional Lawmaking*, especially pp. 98–101 and 127–133.

[45]Dworkin, *Taking Rights Seriously* (Cambridge: Harvard University Press, 1978), and *A Matter of Principle* (Cambridge: Harvard University Press, 1985); Murphy, "The Art of Constitutional Interpretation: A Preliminary Showing," in M. Judd Harmon, ed., *Essays on the Constitution of the United States* (Port

solutions but the process by which we arrive at them. The Constitution reminds us that we aspire to achieve political goodness. We, being imperfect, will never achieve it, but it is essential that we not abandon our effort to combine the lessons of the past with our experience in the present to define what is politically good.

The final chapter presents my own theory of justification in all areas of law and will elaborate on this approach. For now, the lesson is that a preoccupation with doctrine may do more harm than good. The judge or scholar who insists on a doctrinally elegant legal resolution of a case may shut herself off from the cares and aspirations of the litigants themselves. The people whose lives the courts shape will not likely have doctrinal elegance at the top of their list of priorities. Perhaps this is what Justice Harry Blackmun meant when quoted in a 1983 interview:

> The notion of humility is central to an understanding of Justice Blackmun's place on the Court. He believes he is there to do justice, not merely to oblige its doctrinal demands, and his unprepossessing style serves to remind him of the constituency he has been sent there to serve. "Maybe I'm oversensitive," Justice Blackmun says, "But these are very personal cases. We're dealing with *people*— the life, liberty and property of *people*. And because I grew up in poor surroundings, I know there's another world out there we sometimes forget about."[46]

ILLUSTRATIVE CASE

To understand the legal issues in the following case you need to know that the "equal protection clause" of the Fourteenth Amendment potentially invalidates any state law that classifies or differentiates people by sex. This body of law is complex and unsettled, but let us make several assumptions. First, assume that all legislation must pass some minimal test of rationality to be upheld. If, to use John Ely's example, someone were to invent a new, highly effective, "deadstop" brake for trucks, it might be rational for the legislature by law to require only trucks weighing more than five tons to install them, but it would not be rational for the legislature by law to require only blue trucks to install them.[47] That kind of irrationality would strongly imply that a corrupt under-the-table deal had taken place. Second, assume that all laws that treat people unequally on the basis of their race must meet a much higher test of necessity known as "strict scrutiny." Third, assume that for laws that discriminate on the basis of gender—laws that treat men more or less favorably than women, and vice versa—the law must meet a "higher" test of rationality than the minimum rationality test but not as severe as the "strict scruting" test for

Washington, N.Y.: Kennikat Press, 1980); Barber, *On What the Constitution Means* (Baltimore: Johns Hopkins University Press, 1984).

[46]John Jenkins, "A Candid Talk with Justice Blackmun," *New York Times Magazine*, February 20, 1983, p. 20, at pp. 23–24.

[47]See Ely's "Legislative and Administrative Motivation in Constitutional Law," 79 *Yale Law Journal* 1205 (1970) and the particularly lucid discussion of rationality analysis generally in Brest and Levinson, *Processes of Constitutional Decisionmaking*, 3rd ed., supra, pp. 559–579.

racial classifications. In *Craig v. Boren,* 429 U.S. 190 (1976), the Supreme Court held that "classifications by gender must serve important governmental objectives and must be substantially related to achievement of these objectives." In *Craig* the Court struck down a law that forbade the sale of 3.2 beer to men (but not women) ages 18 to 20. The Court in *Craig* placed on the state the burden of proving that *allowing* the females to buy the beer somehow made life safer than would denying the right to buy beer to both sexes. The state failed to produce such evidence, so the Court invalidated the sex-based classification. Consider by contrast the Supreme Court's conclusions about what the background facts do and do not prove in the following case. Assume that both male and female in this case were about 17 years old and that at least a half-hour of fully consensual foreplay occurred before the act of statutory rape itself.

Michael M. v. Superior Court of Sonoma County
(California, Real Party in Interest)
460 U. S. 464 (1981)

Justice Rehnquist announced the judgment of the Court and delivered an opinion, in which The Chief Justice, Justice Stewart, and Justice Powell joined.

The question presented in this case is whether California's "statutory rape" law, Section 261.5 of the California Penal Code . . . violates the Equal Protection Clause of the Fourteenth Amendment. Section 261.5 defines unlawful sexual intercourse as "an act of sexual intercourse accomplished with a female not the wife of the perpetrator, where the female is under the age of 18 years." The statute thus makes men alone criminally liable for the act of sexual intercourse. . . .

We are satisfied not only that the prevention of illegitimate pregnancy is at least one of the "purposes" of the statute, but also that the State has a strong interest in preventing such pregnancy. At the risk of stating the obvious, teenage pregnancies, which have increased dramatically over the last two decades, have significant social, medical, and economic consequences for both the mother and her child, and the State.[a] Of particular concern to the State is that approximately half of all teenage pregnancies end in abortion. And of those children who are born, their illegitimacy makes them likely candidates to become wards of the State.

We need not be medical doctors to discern that young men and young women are not similarly situated with respect to the problems and the risks of sexual intercourse. Only women may become pregnant, and they suffer disproportionately the profound physical, emotional, and psychological consequences of sexual activity. The statute at issue here protects women from sexual intercourse at an age when those consequences are particularly severe.

The question thus boils down to whether a State may attack the problem of sexual intercourse and teenage pregnancy directly by prohibiting a male from having sexual intercourse with

---

[a]The risk of maternal death is 60 percent higher for a teenager under the age of 15 than for a woman in her early twenties. The risk is 13 percent higher for 15-to-19-year-olds. The statistics further show that most teenage mothers drop out of school and face a bleak economic future. See, e.g., *11 Million Teenagers,* supra, at 23, 25; Bennett & Bardon, "The Effects of a School Program on Teenager Mothers and Their Children," *47 Am. J. Orthopsychiatry* 671 (1977); Phipps-Yonas, "Teenage Pregnancy and Motherhood," *50 Am. J. Orthopsychiatry* 403, 414 (1980).

a minor female. We hold that such a statute is sufficiently related to the State's objectives to pass constitutional muster.

Because virtually all of the significant harmful and inescapably identifiable consequences of teenage pregnancy fall on the young female, a legislature acts well within its authority when it elects to punish only the participant who, by nature, suffers few of the consequences of his conduct. It is hardly unreasonable for a legislature acting to protect minor females to exclude them from punishment. Moreover, the risk of pregnancy itself constitutes a substantial deterrence to young females. No similar natural sanctions deter males. A criminal sanction imposed solely on males thus serves to roughly "equalize" the deterrents on the sexes. . . .

In any event, we cannot say that a gender-neutral statute would be as effective as the statute California has chosen to enact. The State persuasively contends that a gender-neutral statute would frustrate its interest in effective enforcement. Its view is that a female is surely less likely to report violations of the statute if she herself would be subject to criminal prosecution. In an area already fraught with prosecutorial difficulties, we decline to hold that the Equal Protection Clause requires a legislature to enact a statute so broad that it may well be incapable of enforcement. . . .

There remains only petitioner's contention that the statute is unconstitutional as it is applied to him because he, like Sharon, was under 18 at the time of sexual intercourse. Petitioner argues that the statute is flawed because it presumes that as between two persons under 18, the male is the culpable aggressor. We find petitioner's contentions unpersuasive. Contrary to his assertions, the statute does not rest on the assumption that males are generally the aggressors. It is instead an attempt by a legislature to prevent illegitimate teenage pregnancy by providing an additional deterrent for men. The age of the man is irrelevant since young men are as capable as older men of inflicting the harm sought to be prevented. . . .

Accordingly, the judgment of the California Supreme Court is affirmed.

Justice STEWART concurring. . . . Young women and men are not similarly situated with respect to the problems and risks associated with intercourse and pregnancy, and the statute is realistically related to the legitimate state purpose of reducing those problems and risks.

As the California Supreme Court's catalog shows, the pregnant unmarried female confronts problems more numerous and more severe than any faced by her male partner.[b] She alone endures the medical risks of pregnancy or abortion. She suffers disproportionately the social, educational, and emotional consequences of pregnancy. Recognizing this disproportion, California has attempted to protect teenage females by prohibiting males from participating in the act necessary for conception.

The fact that males and females are not similarly situated with respect to the risks of sexual intercourse applies with the same force to males under 18 as it does to older males. The risk of pregnancy is a significant deterrent for unwed young females that is not shared by unmarried males, regardless of their age. Experienced observation confirms the commonsense notion that adolescent males disregard the possibility of pregnancy far more than do adolescent females. And to the extent that Section 261.5 may punish males for intercourse with prepubescent females, that punishment is justifiable because of the substantial physical risks for prepubescent females that are not shared by their male counterparts. . . .

[Concurring opinion of Justice BLACKMUN omitted.]

[b]The court noted that from 1971 through 1976, 83.6 percent of the 4,860 children born to girls under 15 in California were illegitimate, as were 51 percent of those born to girls 15 to 17. The court also observed that while accounting for only 21 percent of California pregnancies in 1976, teenagers accounted for 34.7 percent of legal abortions.

Justice BRENNAN, with whom Justices WHITE and MARSHALL join, dissenting. . . .

The plurality assumes that a gender-neutral statute would be less effective than Section 261.5 in deterring sexual activity because a gender-neutral statute would create significant enforcement problems. The plurality thus accepts the State's assertion that

> a female is surely less likely to report violations of the statute if she herself would be sub-ject to criminal prosecution. In an area already fraught with prosecutorial difficulties, we decline to hold that the Equal Protection Clause requires a legislature to enact a statute so broad that it may well be incapable of enforcement. Ante, at 473–474. . . .

However, a State's bare assertion that its gender-based statutory classification substantially fur-thers an important governmental interest is not enough to meet its burden of proof under *Craig v. Boren.* Rather, the State must produce evidence that will persuade the court that its assertion is true. See *Craig v. Boren,* 429 U.S., at 200–204.

The State has not produced such evidence in this case. Moreover, there are at least two seri-ous flaws in the State's assertion that law enforcement problems created by a gender-neutral statutory rape law would make such a statute less effective than a gender-based statute in deter-ring sexual activity.

First, the experience of other jurisdictions, and California itself, belies the plurality's conclu-sion that a gender-neutral statutory rape law "may well be incapable of enforcement." There are now at least 37 States that have enacted gender-neutral statutory rape laws. Although most of these laws protect young persons (of either sex) from the sexual exploitation of older individuals, the laws of Arizona, Florida, and Illinois permit prosecution of both minor females and minor males for engag-ing in mutual sexual conduct. California has introduced no evidence that those States have been handicapped by the enforcement problems the plurality finds so persuasive. Surely, if those [S]tates could provide such evidence, we might expect that California would have introduced it.

In addition, the California Legislature in recent years has revised other sections of the Penal Code to make them gender-neutral. For example, Cal. Penal Code Ann. Sections 286(b)(1) and 288a(b)(1), prohibiting sodomy and oral copulation with a "person who is under 18 years of age," could cause two minor homosexuals to be subjected to criminal sanctions for engaging in mutu-ally consensual conduct. Again, the State has introduced no evidence to explain why a gender-neu-tral statutory rape law would be any more difficult to enforce than those statutes.

The second flaw in the State's assertion is that even assuming that a gender-neutral statute would be more difficult to enforce, the State has still not shown that those enforcement problems would make such a statute less effective than a gender-based statute in deterring minor females from engaging in sexual intercourse. Common sense, however, suggests that a gender-neutral statutory rape law is potentially a *greater* deterrent of sexual activity than a gender-based law, for the simple reason that a gender-neutral law subjects both men and women to criminal sanctions and thus arguably has a deterrent effect on twice as many potential violators. Even if fewer per-sons were prosecuted under the gender-neutral law, as the State suggests, it would still be true that twice as many persons would be *subject* to arrest. The State's failure to prove that a gender-neutral law would be a less effective deterrent than a gender-based law, like the State's failure to prove that a gender-neutral law would be difficult to enforce, should have led this Court to inval-idate Section 261.5. . . .

Justice STEVENS, dissenting.

Local custom and belief rather than statutory laws of venerable but doubtful ancestry will determine the volume of sexual activity among unmarried teenagers. The empirical evidence cited by the plurality demonstrates the futility of the notion that a statutory prohibition will significantly affect the volume of that activity or provide a meaningful solution to the problems created by it . . . [T]he plurality surely cannot believe that the risk of pregnancy confronted by the female—any more than the risk of venereal disease confronted by males as well as females—has provided an effective deterrent to voluntary female participation in the risk-creating conduct. Yet the plurality's decision seems to rest on the assumption that the California Legislature acted on the basis of that rather fanciful notion.

In my judgment, the fact that a class of persons is especially vulnerable to a risk that a statute is designed to avoid is a reason for making the statute applicable to that class. The argument that a special need for protection provides a rational explanation for an exemption is one I simply do not comprehend.[c]

In this case, the fact that a female confronts a greater risk of harm than a male is a reason for applying the prohibition to her—not a reason for granting her a license to use her own judgment on whether or not to assume the risk. Surely, if we examine the problem from the point of view of society's interest in preventing the risk-creating conduct from occurring at all, it is irrational to exempt 50 percent of the potential violators. . . . And, if we view the government's interest as that of a *parens patriae* seeking to protect its subjects from harming themselves, the discrimination is actually perverse. Would a rational parent making rules for the conduct of twin children of opposite sex simultaneously forbid the son and authorize the daughter to engage in conduct that is especially harmful to the daughter? That is the effect of this statutory classification.

If pregnancy or some other special harm is suffered by one of the two participants in the prohibited act, that special harm no doubt would constitute a legitimate mitigating factor in deciding what, if any, punishment might be appropriate in a given case. But from the standpoint of fashioning a general preventive rule—or, indeed, in determining appropriate punishment when neither party in fact has suffered any special harm—I regard a total exemption for the members of the more endangered class as utterly irrational.

In my opinion, the only acceptable justification for a general rule requiring disparate treatment of the two participants in a joint act must be a legislative judgment that one is more guilty than the other. The risk-creating conduct that this statute is designed to prevent requires the participation of two persons—one male and one female.[d] In many situations it is probably true that one is the aggressor and the other is either an unwilling, or at least a less willing, participant in the joint act. If a statute authorized punishment of only one participant and required the prosecutor to prove that that participant had been the aggressor, I assume that the discrimination would be valid. Although the question is less clear, I also assume, for the purpose of deciding this case, that it would be permissible to punish only the male participant, if one element of the offense were proof that he had been the aggressor, or at least in some respects the more responsible participant in the joint act.

[c]A hypothetical racial classification will illustrate my point. Assume that skin pigmentation provides some measure of protection against cancer caused by exposure to certain chemicals in the atmosphere and, therefore, that white employees confront a greater risk than black employees in certain industrial settings. Would it be rational to require black employees to wear protective clothing but to exempt whites from that requirement? It seems to me that the greater risk of harm to white workers would be a reason for including them in the requirement—not for granting them an exemption.

[d]In light of this indisputable biological fact, I find somewhat puzzling the California Supreme Court's conclusion, quoted by the plurality, *ante,* at 467, that males "are the *only* persons who may physiologically cause the result which the law properly seeks to avoid." 25 Cal. 3d 608, 612, 601 p. 2d 572, 575 (1979) (emphasis in original). Presumably, the California Supreme Court was referring to the equally indisputable biological fact that only females may become pregnant. However, if pregnancy results from sexual intercourse between two willing participants and the California statute is directed at such conduct I would find it difficult to conclude that the pregnancy was "caused" solely by the male participant.

The statute at issue in this case, however, requires no such proof. The question raised by this statute is whether the State, consistently with the Federal Constitution, may always punish the male and never the female when they are equally responsible or when the female is the more responsible of the two.

It would seem to me that an impartial lawmaker could give only one answer to that question. The fact that the California Legislature has decided to apply its prohibition only to the male may reflect a legislative judgment that in the typical case the male is actually the more guilty party. Any such judgment must, in turn, assume that the decision to engage in the risk-creating conduct is always—or at least typically—a male decision. If that assumption is valid, the statutory classification should also be valid. But what is the support for the assumption? It is not contained in the record of this case or in any legislative history or scholarly study that has been called to our attention. I think it is supported to some extent by traditional attitudes toward male-female relationships. But the possibility that such a habitual attitude may reflect nothing more than an irrational prejudice makes it an insufficient justification for discriminatory treatment that is otherwise blatantly unfair. For, as I read this statute, it requires that one, and only one, of two equally guilty wrongdoers be stigmatized by a criminal conviction. . . .

Nor do I find at all persuasive the suggestion that this discrimination is adequately justified by the desire to encourage females to inform against their male partners. Even if the concept of a wholesale informant's exemption were an acceptable enforcement device, what is the justification for defining the exempt class entirely by reference to sex rather than by reference to a more neutral criterion such as relative innocence? Indeed, if the exempt class is to be composed entirely of members of one sex, what is there to support the view that the statutory purpose will be better served by granting the informing license to females rather than to males? If a discarded male partner informs on a promiscuous female, a timely threat of prosecution might well prevent the precise harm the statute is intended to minimize.

Finally, even if my logic is faulty and there actually is some speculative basis for treating equally guilty males and females differently, I still believe that any such speculative justification would be outweighed by the paramount interest in evenhanded enforcement of the law. A rule that authorizes punishment of only one of two equally guilty wrongdoers violates the essence of the constitutional requirement that the sovereign must govern impartially.

I respectfully dissent.

QUESTIONS ABOUT THE CASE

1. From the perspective of the average layman, does California's statutory rape statute treat men and women unequally? Why or why not? By what legal route does the Court conclude that there is no unconstitutional inequality here? On what assumptions about differences between male and female psychology and sexual behavior does the decision rest?
2. Is this decision consistent with the precedent of *Craig v. Boren?* If not, how much does the inconsistency bother you? Why should it, particularly if disregard for precedent is acceptable in constitutional law?
3. Males under the age of 18 are a group that lacks direct access to the normal electoral and legislative political processes. Why? How significant should that fact be in this case?
4. Do you think the authors of the Fourteenth Amendment intended the equal protection clause to cover sale of 3.2 beer to male versus female customers? To cover "statutory" rape statutes? To cover sex issues at all, given that women did not have the vote when the amendment was passed? How much attention do the opinions in this case pay to these questions?

For Further Thought

1. Professor Bradley C. Canon has recently analyzed the various forms judicial activism can take.[48] His analysis is particularly useful because it shows how a decision that appears highly active on one dimension may be inactive on another. His six dimensions are as follows:

   a. Majoritarianism—Does the decision nullify an act of an elected legislature?

   b. Interpretive stability—Does the decision overrule prior court precedent?

   c. Interpretive fidelity—Does the decision contradict the manifest intent of the framers?

   d. Substance—Does the decision make new basic policy for the society, e.g., public school desegregation?

   e. Specificity—Does the decision require people to follow specific, court-created rules?

   f. Availability of political alternatives—Are other political institutions equally able and willing to formulate effective policy in the area the decision touches?

   Is the majority opinion in *Michael M.* active in some respects and restrained in others?

2. In its 1995 term, the Supreme Court made a dramatic new move in the law of interstate commerce. Recall that under the commerce clause, Congress may regulate behaviors that look like "small potatoes." For example, we saw in Chapter 3 (p. 65) that Congress under the commerce clause could require Farmer Filburn not to plant extra acres in spite of the fact that he consumed all the extra acres produced on his own farm. And Congress could regulate Haviland's Dog and Pony Show. Recall also that the *Carolene Products* footnote doctrine, discussed previously in Chapter 5 (pp. 129–131), provides a theoretical basis for justifying why courts should not interfere in democratically made policies, like these regarding business regulation, when the positions on various sides of the issue presumably have been heard. However, in *United States v, Lopez,* the Court struck down, 5–4, the Guns-Free School Zones Act of 1990 provision making it a federal offense "for any individual knowingly to possess a firearm at a place that the individual knows, or has reasonable cause to believe, is a school zone." Chief Justice Rehnquist's majority opinion noted that such a law clearly did not either regulate the movement of things in interstate commerce (like the dog-and-pony show), or regulate intrastate or local activities with a cumulative effect on the interstate trading of goods (as would Farmer Filburn if he and all farmers were allowed to produce for themselves and their livestock instead of buying on the open market). Congress, the opinion reasoned, could therefore only regulate guns in school zones if this regulation had a substantial effect on interstate economic life. The government had argued that dangerous schools prevent the young from learning how to be economically productive members of a national workforce. The majority responded:

   > We pause to consider the implications of the Government's arguments. The Government admits, under its "costs of crime" reasoning, that Congress could regulate not only all violent crime, but all activities that might lead to violent crime, regardless of how tenuously they relate to interstate commerce. Similarly, under the Government's "national productivity" reasoning, Congress could regulate any

---

[48]"A Framework for the Analysis of Judicial Activism," in Halpern and Lamb, eds., *Supreme Court Activism and Restraint* (Lexington, Mass.: Lexington Books, 1982), Chapter 15.

activity that it found was related to the economic productivity of individual citizens: family law (including marriage, divorce, and child custody), for example. Under the theories that the Government presents in support of s922(q), it is difficult to perceive any limitation on federal power, even in areas such as criminal law enforcement or education where States historically have been sovereign. Thus, if we were to accept the Government's arguments, we are hard-pressed to posit any activity by an individual that Congress is without power to regulate.

For instance, if Congress can, pursuant to its Commerce Clause power, regulate activities that adversely affect the learning environment then, *a fortiori*, it also can regulate the educational process directly. Congress could determine that a school's curriculum has a "significant" effect on the extent of classroom learning. As a result, Congress could mandate a Federal curriculum for local elementary and secondary schools because what is taught in local schools has a significant "effect on classroom learning," cf. *post*, at 9, and that, in turn, has a substantial effect on interstate commerce. . . .

We do not doubt that Congress has authority under the Commerce Clause to regulate numerous commercial activities that substantially affect interstate commerce and also affect the educational process. That authority, though broad, does not include the authority to regulate each and every aspect of local schools. . . .

Justice Breyer's dissent, joined by Justices Souter, Stevens, and Ginsburg asserted by contrast:

The issue in this case is whether the Commerce Clause authorizes Congress to enact a statute that makes it a crime to possess a gun in, or near, a school. In my view, the statute falls well within the scope of the commerce power as this Court has understood that power over the last half-century. . . .

The Constitution requires us to judge the connection between a regulated activity and interstate commerce, not directly, but at one remove. Courts must give Congress a degree of leeway in determining the existence of a significant factual connection between the regulated activity and interstate commerce both because the Constitution delegates the commerce power directly to Congress and because the determination requires an empirical judgment of a kind that a legislature is more likely than a court to make with accuracy. The traditional words "rational basis" capture this leeway. Thus, the specific question before us, as the Court recognizes, is not whether the "regulated activity sufficiently affected interstate commerce," but, rather, whether Congress could have had *"a rational basis"* for so concluding. . . .

Applying these principles to the case at hand, we must ask whether Congress could have had a *rational basis* for finding a significant (or substantial) connection between gun-related school violence and interstate commerce. Or, to put the question in the language of the *explicit* finding that Congress made when it amended this law in 1994: Could Congress rationally have found that "violent crime in school zones," through its effect on the "quality of education," significantly (or substantially) affects "interstate" or "foreign commerce"? As long as one views the commerce connection, not as a "technical legal conception," but as "a practical one," *Swift & Co. v. United States,* the answer to this question must be yes. Numerous reports and studies generated both inside and outside government make clear that

Congress could reasonably have found the empirical connection that its law, implicitly or explicitly, asserts.

Having found that guns in schools significantly undermine the quality of education in our Nation's classrooms, Congress could also have found, given the effect of education upon interstate and foreign commerce, that gun-related violence in and around schools is a commercial, as well as a human, problem. Education, although far more than a matter of economics, has long been inextricably intertwined with the Nation's economy.

What position would you take on this case? Would you not, unless you simply wanted to play clever legal games with this issue, necessarily have to decide for yourself what kind of a political system the United States of the future ought to have, e.g., whether judicially active courts should carve out a space for state power that our democratically elected, nationwide representatives cannot touch?[49]

3. In its 1996 term, the Supreme Court decided a case in which a car owner, an Alabama physician named Ira Gore, bought a new BMW without being told by the dealer that the car had been damaged in shipment and repainted prior to sale. He sued BMW, claiming loss of resale value at $4000, plus punitive damages. An Alabama jury awarded him $4 million dollars in damages. The Alabama Supreme Court reduced the award to $2 million. BMW appealed, claiming that such disproportionate awards of punitive damages violated the due process clause. BMW won. The arguments on the facts of the case are fascinating. For example, the Alabama jury based its award on estimates of the number of repainted cars BMW had sold nationwide. But under the laws of most states, such repainting had been disclosed. And the justices debated the legal question of why our federal system allows one state's jury to protect the residents of other states through the award of punitive damages anyway. (We also learn that just a few months before Dr. Gore won his original $4 million, another BMW buyer had brought an identical suit before a different Alabama jury and won no punitive damages at all.) Again, which side would you take in this case, and why? What values do you think could support the principle that one plaintiff should pocket huge sums of money to deter defendants from conduct that would hurt others in the future? Refute it? To analyze the effectiveness of such punitive damage awards, do you not need first to have some clear model of human nature, or at least a model of how people trying to make a profit do or don't respond to such legal threats?[50]

4. Near the end of its 1996 term, the Supreme Court struck down a plan offered by Virginia to keep the state-funded Virginia Military Institute all male. Virginia had proposed to sponsor a comparable (but by no means identical) leadership program for women at Mary Baldwin College. How would you use fact freedom to apply the precedents of *Craig* and the more recent *Michel M.* cases to support or oppose Justice Ginsburg's majority opinion? Then ask yourself how well you think the legal

---

[49]*United States v. Lopez* 115 S.Ct. 1624 (1995). Note also how this constitutional argument completly sidesteps the implications of the Second Amendment, which guarantees to the people the right to keep and bear arms. See Sanford Levinson, "The Embarrassing Second Amendment," 99 *Yale Law Journal* 637 (1989).

[50]*BMW of North American, Inc., v, Gore*, 134 L. Ed. 2d 809 (1996). (You will see Justice Scalia referring disdainfully to this case in his dissent reprinted in part in the next problem.) And see "Supreme Court Examines, Gingerly, the Issue of Limits on Punitive Damages," Linda Greenhouse's coverage of the oral arguments in this case, *New York Times*, October 12, 1995, p. A12. To review more generally the extent to which free market forces rather than regulatory or judicial intervention should decide such problems as this, see the voluminous writings of Richard Epstein of the University of Chicago, e.g., his *Bargaining with the State* (Princeton: Princeton University Press, 1993).

reasoning arguments developed in this book support or undercut the arguments made by Justice Scalia, in dissent:

> Today the Court shuts down an institution that has served the people of the Commonwealth of Virginia with pride and distinction for over a century and a half. . . .
>
> " . . . The virtue of a democratic system with a First Amendment is that it readily enables the people, over time, to be persuaded that what they took for granted is not so, and to change their laws accordingly. That system is destroyed if the smug assurances of each age are removed from the democratic process and written into the Constitution. So to counterbalance the Court's criticism of our ancestors, let me say a word in their praise: they left us free to change. The same cannot be said of this most illiberal Court, which has embarked on a course of inscribing one after another of the current preferences of the society (and in some cases only the counter-majoritarian preferences of the society's law-trained elite) into our Basic Law. Today it enshrines the notion that no substantial educational value is to be served by an all-men's military academy—so that the decision by the people of Virginia to maintain such an institution denies equal protection to women who cannot attend that institution but can attend others. Since it is entirely clear that the Constitution of the United States—the old one—takes no sides in this educational debate, I dissent. . . .
>
> Justice Brandeis said it is "one of the happy incidents of the federal system that a single courageous State may, if its citizens choose, serve as a laboratory; and try novel social and economic experiments without risk to the rest of the country." *New State Ice Co. v. Lichmann,* 285 U.S. 262, 311, 52 S.Ct. 371, 386–387, 76 L.Ed. 747 (1932) (dissenting opinion). But it is one of the unhappy incidents of the federal system that a self-righteous Supreme Court, acting on its Members' personal view of what would make a "more perfect Union," *ante,* at 2288 (a criterion only slightly more restrictive than a "more perfect world"), can impose its own favored social and economic dispositions nationwide. As today's disposition, and others this single Term, show, this places it beyond the power of a "single courageous State," not only to introduce novel dispositions that the Court frowns upon, but to reintroduce, or indeed even adhere to, disfavored dispositions that are centuries old. See. *e.g., BMW of North America, Inc. v. Gore,* . . . 116 S.Ct. 1589, . . . (1996); *Romer v. Evans,* . . . , 116 S.Ct. 1620, . . . (1996). The sphere of self-government reserved to the people of the Republic is progressively narrowed. . . .
>
> In an odd sort of way, it is precisely VMI's attachment to such old-fashioned concepts as manly "honor" that has made it, and the system it represents, the target of those who today succeed in abolishing public single-sex education. The record contains a booklet that all first-year VMI students (the so-called "rats") were required to keep in their possession at all times. Near the end there appears the following period-piece, entitled "The Code of a Gentleman":
>
> > "Without a strict observance of the fundamental Code of Honor, no man, no matter how 'polished,' can be considered a gentleman. The honor of a gentleman demands the inviolability of his word, and the incorruptibility of his principles. He is the descendant of the knight, the crusader; he is the defender of the defenseless and the champion of justice . . . or he is not a Gentleman.

A Gentleman . . .

Does not discuss his family affairs in public or with acquaintances.

Does not speak more than casually about his girlfriend.

Does not go to a lady's house if he is affected by alcohol. He is temperate in the use of alcohol.

Does not lose his temper; nor exhibit anger, fear, hate, embarrassment, ardor or hilarity in public.

Does not hail a lady from a club window.

A gentleman never discusses the merits or demerits of a lady.

Does not mention names exactly as he avoids the mention of what things cost.

Does not borrow money from a friend, except in dire need. Money borrowed is a debt of honor, and must be repaid as promptly as possible. Debts incurred by a deceased parent, brother, sister or grown child are assumed by honorable men as a debt of honor.

Does not display his wealth, money or possessions.

Does not put his manners on and off, whether in the club or in a ballroom. He treats people with courtesy, no matter what their social position may be.

Does not slap strangers on the back nor so much as lay a finger on a lady.

Does not 'lick the boots of those above' nor 'kick the face of those below him on the social ladder.'

Does not take advantage of another's helplessness or ignorance and assumes that no gentleman will take advantage of him.

A Gentleman respects the reserves of others, but demands that others respect those which are his.

A Gentleman can become what he wills to be . . ."

I do not know whether the men of VMI lived by this Code; perhaps not. But it is powerfully impressive that a public institution of higher education still in existence sought to have them do so. I do not think any of us, women included, will be better off for its destruction.[51]

---

[51]*United States v. Virginia*, 116 S.Ct. 2264 (1996) at 2291–92 and 2308–09.

CHAPTER 6

Law and Politics

The ultimate goal is to break down the sense that legal argument is autonomous from moral, economic and political discourse.

—Duncan Kennedy

When judges make law and scholars propose rules of law, they necessarily rely on their vision of society as it is and as it ought to be. If law is to be made well, those visions must be accurate and attractive.

—Mark Tushnet

This book stated in the beginning that to study legal reasoning is to study politics. The discussion since has touched on many obviously political issues—the common law power of judges to make law; reasons why elected representatives so often make unclear statutes, to name just two. We have, however, focused principally on law and legal reasoning, on judicial "outputs" rather than political "inputs." The time has come to define politics and the connections between politics and law more precisely.

Let me begin by anticipating a potential source of confusion. We seem to live in an age where politics is a dirty word. H. Ross Perot's brief flirtation with the presidency in 1992 generated tremendous enthusiasm because he seemed ready to run against politics and politicians altogether. If we define *politics* as the sum of all our public grievances and shortcomings—declining economic competitiveness, declining rates of political participation, double-talk and self-serving double standards by elected representatives, the use of power to extract wealth from the less powerful, and so on—my proposal to connect legal reasoning and politics will surely confuse you. But politics is not inherently destructive. *Politics describes the many things we do in our public and collective lives to build and maintain communities.* Once we define *politics* this broadly, we begin to see that people do politics both well and badly, just as people can do "love" and "religion" and many other things either well or badly.

LEGAL REASONING AS LIBERAL JUSTIFICATION

A Recap

Communities are groups of people who seek to work and play cooperatively and productively together. Communities come in all sizes, from families and clusters of "good neighbors" to states and nations—communities of strangers. Sometimes, and particularly in small groups with long histories, cooperation comes easily. People know the customs that bind each other. They trust each other not to cheat, and so they trust the economic and social trades they make with each other. But as communities get larger, some people must rule others. Someone must use power to coerce those who have not cooperated either to become cooperative or to get out of the group. Here formal political institutions emerge—leaders with weapons, codes of rules and courts to enforce them, and so on.

Liberal political systems try to minimize the harm that rulers do to the ruled by imposing on the powerful the obligation to justify their use of power in terms of collective community good. No matter how shallow and uninformative the presidential debates between Bob Dole and Bill Clinton in the fall of 1996 may have seemed, these debates nevertheless illustrate the importance of justification in our political culture. In San Diego on October 16, 1996, swing voters got to ask the two candidates virtually any tough question they wanted, and we judged the candidates on the adequacy of their answers.

Here enters legal reasoning. Our political system generates an immense quantity of legal texts—statutes, regulations, constitutional provisions, and the prior judicial opinions that we call *precedents*. Cases come up in our political communities because cooperation has failed. Someone in desperation chloroforms a severely retarded child yet claims he has good moral character. A towing company loses its cargo because it didn't have a simple radio yet refuses to pay for the loss. An all male military academy refuses to admit fully qualified females in spite of a constitutional equal protection clause. Because we insist on justification in our legal culture, we do not simply permit judges who have political power to announce the legal solution to conflicts like these. Judges must justify their solutions. *Legal reasoning* is the name we use to describe judges' justifications. This book argues that when a judicial opinion makes the four elements of legal reasoning fit plausibly together, the judicial writer has met his or her obligation to use judicial power the way our political culture expects. By implication I have argued as well that when judges harmonize the four fundamentals—the facts of cases, the official legal texts, the social background facts we share about our world, and norms widely shared in our polity—they *necessarily* create an image of a viable community. This final chapter's job is to explain why you should believe this.

Impartiality and Trust

Governing a large community, a group of total strangers who happen to live, often by the millions, in one city, state, or nation, is a difficult business, more difficult than, say, running General Motors or the Seattle Symphony. This is because:

- The government's rules speak to the public, to the community, to everyone, in a way that General Motors' rules (or for that matter, the pope's rules) do not.
- The community is the greatest source of disruption and uncertainty in our lives because it exposes us to the work of strangers that we individually cannot control: crimes, nuclear wars, and changes in moral standards. The community is the place where people's psychological need for confidence in structure is greatest, for it is the one place that binds everyone and beyond which we will find no social structure at all. The rules that the *government* makes and enforces must maintain confidence in structure—confidence that even strangers can share values.
- People need to maintain this confidence even when they cannot express precisely the "right" limit or value by which to judge a concrete situation. They take most seriously the idea that the community has value in it.

The judicial process and legal reasoning therefore play a major part in preserving the confidence that the community can reconcile rules, facts of disputes, social conditions, and ethics. Our confidence does not rest entirely or immediately on the quality of legal reasoning, but the language of legal justification is one important means by which those who govern can reassure us that our communal life is "accurate and attractive." Unlike other social processes in and out of government, courts must make *some* decision—reach some closure on the problems litigants bring to them. Regardless of the wisdom of the solution, we need to believe that our community contains points where decisions and action replace indecision and drift. This book has criticized so many conventional practices, habits, and assumptions in legal reasoning precisely because legal reasoning is so important. Reason must "break down the sense that legal argument is autonomous from moral, economic, and political discourse" or it will ultimately destroy our confidence in community.

Thus, the ethical view of the legal process holds that, despite its potentially infinite complexity and uncertainty, law must contain a method of applying the abstractions of law to human affairs. This does not require finding the perfect solution. It is much more important that the process attempt to reach acceptable reconciliations of facts, social conditions, laws, and ethical values. For this process to succeed it is essential that we trust judges to speak for the community and not simply for the profession or for their personal gain. We must therefore shift our attention to the concepts of trust, impartiality, and judgment.

Impartial Judgment

Imagine yourself in each of these three situations:

1. *A midsummer afternoon in Wrigley Field.* The Cubs versus the Cardinals. You are calling balls and strikes behind home plate.
2. *A late Saturday night in Atlantic City in early September.* You are judging the finals of the Miss America Pageant.
3. *Eight-thirty in the evening, in the home of your young family.* The children are squabbling. They appeal to you for judgment.
   Laurie: "Mommie, Robbie bit me!"
   Robbie: "I did not!"
   Laurie: "You did too! Look! Tooth marks!"

Robbie: "But Mom! Laurie took my dime!"
Laurie: "I took your dime cuz you stepped on my doll and broke it."
Robbie: "But it was an accident, dum-dum."
Laurie: "I am not a dum-dum, you fathead!"

Each of these situations calls for judgment. Each judge makes decisions that affect the claims of others, and he decides before an audience that has some expectations about how the judge should decide. Without necessarily determining what the judge should conclude, the audience knows what the judge should look at and will test the judgment against these expectations. Even the children seeking justice from their mother do so.

To judge is to decide the claims of others with reference to the expectations of an audience that define the process of decision. We shall see shortly where this definition leads in law. For the moment, consider what these three nonlegal judging situations do and do not have in common.

First and most important, notice that the three are not equally reasoned. Reasoning—defined as a choice that depends on calculations about future consequences—influences the umpire calling balls and strikes only indirectly. Occasionally, he may reflect on the fact that if he calls a pitch wrong angry fans may pitch obscenities at him. Basically, however, he simply tries to fit physical—visual—evidence to a category, ball or strike, predetermined by the rule. He judges because the audience (baseball fans) has (have) specific expectations of how umpires should behave. In most households the mother, at the other extreme, cannot escape from making some calculation about the effects of her decision on the children, or at least on her own sanity.

The second difference is that rules do not equally affect all three situations. The umpire works with an elaborate set of written rules about baseball—most of which he commits to memory. He decides most questions literally in a second or less by applying the rules to the facts. In baseball, time is of the essence, which is why its rules are so elaborate. Additionally, baseball allows for precise rules because, as in most sports, we can pinpoint what matters to us in time and space.

On the other hand, we cannot define male or female beauty so precisely in time and space. Beauty contest judges exercise more discretion because their rules do not so precisely tell them what to seek.[1] Finally, the squabbling children may invoke no family rule at all. The family may have no regulation forbidding or punishing Robbie's toothy assault on his sister and his lie, and no conventions governing Laurie's theft or their gratuitous exchange of insults. Expectations, not precepts, create the need for judgment.

Third, these three kinds of judges have different opportunities to make rules for the future. The parent can explicitly respond to the squabble by announcing what is right and wrong and declaring her official policy for the future. Such a setting of limits may be precisely what the children hope the judge will do. But beauty contest judges

---

[1] There is another interesting difference: With rare exceptions, when he calls the game on account of rain or ejects an ornery manager or player, the umpire has minimal control over who wins. But the beauty contest judges *declare* the winner. This differential effect on the outcome explains why we have only one home plate umpire but several judges in contests of beauty and on our appellate courts. (Notice that when the umpire does make discretionary calls he is also more likely to consult other umpires than when he calls balls and strikes.) For a fascinating description of how one sport—competitive female body building—failed to grow precisely because the relevant audience could not agree on how such contests should be judged, see Charles Gaines and George Butler, "Iron Sisters," *Psychology Today,* November 1983, pp. 64–69.

may do so only informally and the umpires hardly at all, given audience expectations of their roles.

The definition and discussion of the nature of reason made clear that not all reasoning is legal reasoning. Legal reasoning involves judgment—deciding the claims of others in front of some audience, before a "public." We have also seen, from the example of the baseball umpire, that not all judgment involves reason. Law therefore employs reasoned judgment, and I shall develop that concept momentarily. First, however, we must pin down that quality inherent in all judging, whether reasoned or not: "impartiality."

Impartiality is not a mysterious concept. The *American Heritage Dictionary* defines "partial" as "pertaining to only part; not total; incomplete." To decide impartially is to leave the final decision open until all the relevant information is received. It means that the information—the placement of the pitch, the beauty contestant's stage performance, and the children's actual behavior—rather than a personal affection or preference for one "party" determines the result.[2]

While impartiality is not itself a difficult concept—we have all judged and been judged in our lives—it is often difficult for audiences to satisfy themselves that judges actually decide impartially. How can judges satisfy audiences that they decide impartially? Initially, a judge may succeed if her mistakes cancel out, if her errors favor both sides equally. But the loser, being the loser, will probably not take a balanced count of errors. The judge's only long-range security, therefore, is to care about and try as best she can to fulfill the expectations of judgment that the audience imposes.

To judge is to be judged. The argument assumes, of course, that audiences can, in fact, distinguish their expectations of the process of decision from their hopes that one side—their side!—will win. I am convinced that people can do so, though I rely more on my experience as a sports fan, employee, teacher, and parent than I do on psychological experimentation. Teams can lose championships, employees can receive poor assignments, students can receive disappointing grades, and children can be ordered to wash the dishes, all without doubting that the judges have decided impartially.

Professor Robert Cover has written:

> The critical dimension of the rule of law is not the degree of specificity with which an actor is constrained, but the very fact that the actor must look outside his own will for criteria of judgment. There is a difference—intelligible to most pre-adolescents—between the directions "Do what you want" and "Do what you think is right or just."[3]

---

[2]Recent empirical research on how jurors in trials think builds on a very similar definition of impartiality. These studies document the frequency with which jurors close their minds and refuse to admit new facts, sometimes long before a trial ends. These jurors don't come to court biased for one side. They simply jump to a conclusion and thereafter don't listen to the other parts of the argument. They are partial in just that sense. Effective trial lawyers know how to keep minds open: they tell stories. Jurors then have a framework for knowing what facts are missing, just as all of us do when we read or hear a story and stay alert waiting for the final clues to fall into place. See "Study Finds Jurors Often Hear Evidence with Closed Minds," *New York Times*, November 29, 1994, p. B5.

[3]Robert Cover, book review of R. Berger, *Government by Judiciary, New Republic,* January 14, 1978, p. 27. Two essays in which judges vigorously defended the impartiality of the appellate courts are Harry T. Edwards's "Public Misperceptions Concerning the Politics of Judging," 56 *Colorado Law Review* 619 (1985), and Patricia Wald's "Thoughts on Decisionmaking," 87 *West Virginia Law Review* 1 (1984). Compare the Australian film *Breaker Morant*.

To "look outside his own will for criteria of judgment": If we have any single key to legal judgment, it is here.

To judge is to decide the claims of others before an audience. The judgmental decision need not be reasoned, as the umpire's calling of pitches reveals. But judgmental decisions must be impartial, which means in the end they must, to appear impartial, conform to audience expectations of the process of decision.

Since appellate legal decisions are judgmental, we must determine the audience's expectations of that decision process. But the discussion of law's relationship to the state has already determined that. I believe that the audience of law expects the process to reassure it that society can reconcile and harmonize facts, rules, social conditions, and moral values; this is the test of judicial impartiality and hence of reason in law. When judges explain their results in judicial opinions, they must attempt to convince readers that the result does *not* depend on a fact at issue between the parties that we know is false, does *not* depend on false assumptions about social conditions, does not depend upon a tortured reading of a rule, and does not depend on an ethical judgment that the community of readers would reject. The result need not please everyone, but that is not the point. Judges cannot and need not discover one right solution that everyone somehow believes best. They convince us of their impartiality as long as they convince us that they have attempted to describe these four elements accurately. We expect law judges, unlike umpires, to engage in *reasoned* judgment when they do so.

Let me here anticipate and resolve two practical problems that often bother alert readers at this stage of the argument. The first problem arises because readers of judicial opinions, reading often many years after the litigation happened, never know even a small fraction of what the judges and attorneys actually know about a case. How, you may ask, can we ever know if judges who make a coherent and well-harmonized argument are in fact radically falsifying the key facts of the case, or deliberately ignoring a powerful set of legal texts that could justify a very different result?

Well, judges who disagree with a decision the majority of their colleagues make do write dissenting opinions. Judges must persuade each other that their reasoning is plausible. And in celebrated cases newspapers, magazines, radio, and television provide robust forums for criticism. But at a deeper level I think preoccupation with this problem misses the boat. The political good that good legal reasoning serves is not the same thing as "getting the right result," either in a technical legal sense or in a social justice sense. As you know by now, there is usually no technically correct legal result, and one person's social justice is another's social folly. As intelligent critical readers of judicial opinions, we have every right to demand that the writer spell out clearly what the four elements are in the case and how his or her solution harmonizes them. We have every right to protest that when judicial writers don't do this, they fail us politically. But here the work of legal reasoning ends and other criteria for evaluating results, criteria like our own political and ethical preferences, take over. We don't need to know a complete biography of an artist or composer to evaluate their paintings or symphonies. Judicial opinions stand on their own as do works of art like these.

The second practical problem is that only an infinitesimal number of people in a state or nation read appellate opinions. How can I argue that judges must build and maintain trust and impartiality by performing for an audience that is by definition very large and almost totally ignorant of the very performances I'm talking about? Doesn't history show us that the actual political reaction to controversial cases depends on whose ox got gored? I have three responses to this troublesome problem. First and foremost, judges must try to persuade the parties, and particularly the losers, that the results are impartial. But these parties do come from, and share understandings of facts and values in common with, the larger and ignorant audience. In writing for "the people," judges will more likely write justly for the parties than if judges write exclusively for legal professionals in obscure legalese. Second, over time on issues that concern many, the word tends, slowly, to get out. Anthony Lewis's now classic book, *Gideon's Trumpet* (p. 126n), did much to explain and justify the reasoning behind extending constitutional protections to the accused. Conversely, *Roe,* the first abortion case, which was widely criticized for its unconvincing reasoning, might have forestalled so much of the subsequent litigation had it constructed a clearer and more coherent statement of what the right of privacy did and did not entail and why. Finally, I think preoccupation with public ignorance also misses a mark. It's a free country, and cures for the problem of ignorance may be worse than the disease. Legal reasoning is not the most important thing in politics, but it should have integrity—it should communicate constructively—in its own political sphere, just as the Federal Reserve Board, whose secretive decisions profoundly affect all our economic lives, should act with integrity.

What Evidence Supports This Theory of Impartiality?

First, what evidence might confirm that lawyers and judges actually share these values of impartiality? In a fascinating assessment of the 1992 United States Supreme Court term, Linda Greenhouse of the *New York Times* identified the unassuming Justice David Souter as the emerging leader of the coalition of justices at the center of the Court. She explained his leadership this way:

> Court observers on both ends of the political spectrum have noted that Justice Souter, much more than most judges, tends to acknowledge the weight of opposing arguments and to discuss and defend his own choices from among competing rationales.[4]

According to Greenhouse, David Souter's trustworthiness, not the political acceptability of his results, accounts for his leadership. More importantly, this is just as it should be. If legal reasoning matters politically because it convinces us that we and the judge belong to the same community, then legal reasoning should build trust in the integrity of leaders, not conviction about the correctness of the outcome.

In contrast to Justice Souter, Ronald Dworkin argues that Justice Scalia's reasoning in *Casey* loses our trust precisely because he fails to harmonize the four elements of legal reasoning effectively.

> Scalia, in his own partial dissent, makes even plainer his contempt for the view that the Constitution creates a system of principle. He reaches the conclusion that abortion is not a liberty protected by the Constitution, he says, "not

---

[4]"Souter: Unlikely Anchor at Court's Center," *New York Times,* July 3, 1992, pp. A1 and A12. Souter's reclusive and scholarly lifestyle has been compared to that of Benjamin Cardozo. See Richard Posner, *Cardozo: A Study in Reputation* (Chicago: University of Chicago Press, 1990). Also linking candor and trustworthiness, see Shapiro, "In Defense of Judicial Candor," 100 *Harvard Law Review* 731 (1987) and Ginsburg, "Remarks on Writing Separately," 65 *Washington Law Review* 133 (1990).

because of anything so exalted as my views concerning the 'concept of existence, of meaning of the universe, and of the mystery of human life'" but "because of two simple facts: (1) The Constitution says absolutely nothing about it, and (2) the long-standing traditions of American society have permitted it to be legally proscribed." Scalia's flat assertion that the Constitution says nothing about abortion begs the question, of course. The Fourteenth Amendment does explicitly forbid states to abridge liberty without due process of law, and the question, in this case as in any other case involving that clause, is whether the state legislation in question does in fact do exactly that. If it does, then the Constitution does say something about it: the Constitution forbids it. The majority argues that if we accept the principles that underlie past Supreme Court decisions everyone accepts, we must also accept that forbidding abortion before viability denies liberty without due process. Scalia says nothing at all that undermines or even challenges that claim.

So Scalia's entire argument depends on his assertion that since a majority of states had outlawed abortion before the Fourteenth Amendment was adopted, it would be wrong to interpret the due process clause as denying them the power to do so now. He refuses to consider whether laws outlawing abortion, no matter how popular they were or are, offend other, more general principles of liberty that are embedded in the Constitution's abstract language and in the Court's past decisions. He disdains inquiries of that character because, he says, they involve "value judgments." Of course they do. How can any court enforce the abstract moral command of the Constitution that states may not violate fundamental liberties, without making judgments about "values"? Judges have had to make such judgments since law began.[5]

Here is a more recent example. Justice Stephen Breyer, appointed by President Clinton to the Supreme Court in the summer of 1994, has received very positive "reviews" from both the bar and the popular press. A self-described nonideological pragmatist, Breyer believes passionately in his responsibility to communicate clearly. Not long after he first took a lower position on the federal bench, he decided never to use footnotes in his opinions. In a 1995 interview he elaborated:

Sometimes it's awkward to use none at all, but if in fact you even use one, then you cannot make the point. And it is an important point to make if you believe, as I do, that the major function of an opinion is to explain to the audience of readers why it is that the Court has reached that decision.

It's not to prove that you're right: you can't prove you're right, there is no such proof. And it's not to create an authoritative law review on the subject. Others are better doing that than I.

It is to explain as clearly as possible and as simply as possible what the reasons are for reaching this decision. Others can then say those are good reasons or those are bad reasons. If you see the opinion in this way, either a point is sufficiently significant to make, in which case it should be in the text, or it is not, in which case, don't make it.[6]

[5]Ronald Dworkin, "The Center Holds," *The New York Review of Books*, August 13, 1992, pp. 29–33, p. 32.
[6]"In Justice Breyer's Opinion, A Footnote Has No Place," *New York Times*, July 28, 1995, p. B13.

Our culture reveals the same standard of integrity in many different settings beyond the law. In science, Richard Feynman has written that the ideal is

> a kind of scientific integrity, a principle of scientific thought that corresponds to a kind of utter honesty—a kind of leaning over backwards. For example, if you're doing an experiment, you should report everything that you think might make it invalid, not only what you think is right about it.[7]

Second, what evidence might confirm that people outside the legal system value these qualities? What evidence supports the position that trustworthiness (as opposed to, say, economic self-interest) influences political attitudes and behavior? In his book *Why People Obey the Law*, Professor Tom Tyler concludes that people obey the law primarily for noneconomic reasons. People do not comply because compliance costs them less. Rather, Tyler concludes they do so when they approve of the moral position the law takes and when they feel law is procedurally fair. The perception that the law is fair, and hence the willingness to comply, depends not on winning or losing, but on such moral factors as whether people trust the system to hear their arguments.[8]

Also, public-opinion polling done during both the 1988 and 1992 presidential elections found that most voters weighed the character and straightforwardness of candidates (or the lack of it) much more heavily than their ideologies or specific policy proposals. During his run for the governorship of Louisiana in November 1991, David Duke moderated nearly all of his ultraconservative policy positions. He nevertheless continued throughout the campaign to make statements that the news media and his opponent had proved false. He lost to a convicted felon, Edwin Edwards, who did not falsify his past.[9]

Applying the Theory

Let us now apply this theory of legal reasoning to some of the cases this book has applauded and some this book has criticized.

Consider first the *Prochnow* blood test case at the end of Chapter 1. We are tempted to condemn the case for flying in the face of science: the court reached a result that we all know couldn't be true. If so, we would be criticizing the case for its failure to harmonize the social background facts in the case. But the difficulties with the *Prochnow* opinion go deeper. If the opinion means to tell us that juries should be free to speculate on whether God or nature or some hidden force temporarily suspended the laws of science, the opinion should have addressed that claim head on. Such a principle would revolutionize our entire notion of how law works, for if a jury verdict based on

---

[7]Quoted by Philip J. Hilts, "The Science Mob," *The New Republic,* May 18, 1992, p. 24 at p. 31. And see Peggy Noonan's *Present at the Creation,* which links Ronald Reagan's political success to the public's trust in him. The trust was less in his philosophy than in his honesty—the belief that he *was* what he seemed: a modest actor of modest intelligence playing a part.

[8]Tom R. Tyler, *Why People Obey the Law* (New Haven: Yale University Press, 1990).

[9]"Duke Repeating Distorted Facts Despite Rebuttals," *New York Times,* November 12, 1991, p. C19. There is something slightly chilling in the prospect that, had he been truer to himself, Duke might have won. Villains in film and fiction who live consistently by an evil moral code, and thus stay true to their character, generally win more sympathy than villains who lack a moral anchor. Hannibal Lector, in the film *Silence of the Lambs* (1991), won considerable sympathy in spite of graphic filming of his crimes of cannibalism. (True to his code, at the film's end the escaped villain tells an F.B.I. agent by long-distance phone that he is "having someone for dinner.")

speculations about God's will can stand, a jury can find anything it wants, and no appellate court would ever overturn a jury verdict for being inconsistent with the weight of the evidence.

We have seen another less supernatural and more plausible explanation for the *Prochnow* result. Perhaps the legislature favored fatherhood so strongly that it authorized juries to disregard science for the sake of allowing children to grow up with fathers. But that possibility deserved an airing too, partly to give the legislature a chance to react if the court had misread the statute, and partly because the position makes so little intuitive sense. If the legislature in fact felt that way, why would it have authorized introducing blood test evidence at all? The majority opinion read the statute legalistically, that is, without attention to the other three elements in legal reasoning. It said the words of the statute make the tests admissible but not conclusive; therefore the law allows juries to disregard the tests. But an entirely plausible alternate reason exists for not making the tests conclusive: the laboratory might have gotten Robert's blood sample confused with another sample. If the plaintiff offers evidence that the blood tests were in error, or worse, corruptly falsified, then of course the test shouldn't be conclusive. But here the plaintiff introduced no such evidence.

In short, the Wisconsin Court majority might have reached the same result, in favor of Robert's paternity, if it had argued the value of fatherhood. It could have harmonized all four elements by saying, "We know all about science, and we know the blood tests in this case are incompatible. We admit that no evidence in the trial contradicted the blood tests, but we read the purpose of this law to favor paternity and we believe this value is a value widely shared in the community." That reasoning would give us a coherent vision of the community that we can discuss and seek to sustain or change. Instead the majority implies that we live in a confusing and unknowable world in which anything can happen, one in which we can't trust either science or God or the conventional trial court methods of fact finding.

The legal reasoning of *Repouille v. the United States* and *Michael M.* also fail. In both of these cases, a clear precedent stated law that seemed to apply directly to the case. The *Francioso* opinion said that the naturalization decision should rest on judgments about the person seeking naturalization, not on the nature of incest in the abstract. Yet in *Repouille* Learned Hand did quite the opposite. *Craig v. Boren* held that the state bears the burden of proving a substantial relationship between a law that classifies people by their gender and the achievement of an important public policy goal. Show us, said the *Craig* majority, that discriminating against young men (rather than banning alcohol to all young people) will actually reduce traffic accidents, and the Oklahoma beer policy can stand. But you can't just guess. Justice Rehnquist in *Michael M.* does the opposite. He's satisfied with California's guess that law enforcement will benefit from punishing only men for underage voluntary sex in the absence of any proof. Both *Repouille* and *Michael M.* lead us to believe that law doesn't matter. Both increase our mistrust.

I do not argue that *Repouille* and *Michael M.* "came out wrong." I argue that the results were not well reasoned or justified. A different opinion could have persuasively justified the result each case reached by giving reasons to overrule the precedent or distinguish the precedent through fact freedom, but the opinions we read fail to do so. They are incoherent. They only confuse lawyers who must advise future clients with similar cases—confuse and thereby perhaps encourage litigation when law should instead encourage cooperation. Worse, they leave lay readers with the suspicion that those with power over them have lied to them.

You should, I hope, be able to see in each of the cases that this book has criticized one or more of the four elements that were not harmonized. The evidence introduced in trial about baseball in *Toolson* made a strong case that baseball was a business in interstate commerce that monopolized. Why does the Court ignore that evidence? In *Lochner,* the bakers' hours case, the Court ignored the social background evidence that baking was unhealthy. *Repouille* and *Michael M.* ignore the law itself. The majority in *Fox v. Snow* ignored the ethical value of carrying out the hopes of those who write wills, and so on.

We should, of course, turn this analysis on the cases these pages have applauded. For example, *Hynes,* the diving board case, harmonizes (1) the fact in Harvey's case that the wire might have killed him had he been a swimmer lawfully using the river, and the fact that the railroad had not maintained the wires and poles; (2) the social background fact that property boundaries become increasingly hard to know and learn as life becomes more complex, urban, and interconnected; (3) a plausible reading of the thrust of the *Hoffman* and *Beck* precedents; (4) the deeply ethical value that law should promote cooperation—that the law of tort ought to encourage the railroad to prevent the dangerous wires it owns and controls from injuring others.

LEGAL REASONING AS A PUBLIC LANGUAGE

This book has emphasized the principle that law does not—and indeed cannot—provide objectively certain and correct answers to legal problems. For the same reasons, all inquiry—scientific and philosophical as well as legal—never gets to the true bottom of things. Near the beginning of this book I quoted a dust jacket description of *Inventing Reality,* which said that we do not discover the physical world, we invent good ways of talking about the world. "Reality" exists in this talk that we invent.

Our political language invents our communities in much the same ways that scientific language invents physical reality and religious language invents spiritual reality. The proposition that people find reality in and through their language is hardly a unique product of postmodernism. Aristotle's *Rhetoric* and *Poetics* hint in this direction. Shaw's play *Pygmalion*—from which *My Fair Lady* became one of the most successful musicals in the history of musical theater—starts with the same premise. The works of Murray Edelman have described how language constructs political reality with special clarity.[10]

Legal reasoning is an important political language that helps invent our geographical communities. A century ago legal language, as we have seen, helped invent a community that drastically undermined the public sphere and the capacity of government to regulate the excesses of capitalism. As we step back for a final overview of legal reasoning, we shall examine how legal talk indicates both where we have been and where we may be heading.

---

[10]See his *Constructing the Political Spectacle* (Chicago: University of Chicago Press, 1988).

This theme could fill many books, and we can only sample the phenomenon here. However, you should know that much conventional research in cognitive psychology supports this perspective. It seems that all of us need to fit information into some kind of story, narrative, or drama before it makes sense to us.[11] This perspective also rests very much in the mainstream of social and political philosophy at the end of the twentieth century. In fact, this view "harmonizes" a surprisingly large number of perspectives. Starting in the 1970s, critical legal scholars did much to debunk the legal profession's claim to unique insights into truth.[12]

New pragmatists, particularly Richard Rorty and Richard Bernstein, have helped fill the space created by the critical debunking. Pragmatism, as originally developed by William James and John Dewey and elaborated by Rorty and Bernstein, recognizes that for millennia people have killed each other for the sake of a doctrine or ideology that they claim to be absolutely true. In the 1990s, the horrors of "ethnic cleansing" in Bosnia, which pits Muslims and different Christian sects against one another, reminds us powerfully of the evils that pragmatic liberalism tries to overcome. The tragic deaths of the Branch Davidian cult members in Waco, Texas, in 1993 fits the same pattern. In the vein of classical liberal philosophy, pragmatism downplays the importance of ideology; it emphasizes instead that language and experience, not doctrine, should shape our beliefs and actions and that human cooperation depends on continuously learning from experience, rather than applying abstract rules and principles dogmatically.[13] In 1985 and again in 1990 the *Southern California Law Review* published long symposium issues discussing many of the pragmatic elements in legal reasoning.[14]

These developments dovetail nicely with the work of Milner Ball and James Boyd White who discuss the literary qualities of legal analysis. Yet all of these positions in contemporary legal theory may simply elaborate on the conclusion reached earlier by one of the century's most admired legal philosophers, Lon Fuller.

> If I were asked . . . to discern one central indisputable principle of what may be called substantive natural law . . . I would find it in the injunction: Open up, maintain and preserve the integrity of the channels of communication.[15]

Before we examine these upcoming samples of legal language as it invents and reflects communities, I need to anticipate another potential source of confusion.

---

[11]See, for example, Nancy Pennington and Reid Hastie, "A Cognitive Theory of Juror Decision Making: The Story Model," 13 *Cardozo Law Review* 519 (1991) and "Jurors Hear Evidence and Turn It into Stories," *New York Times*, May 12, 1992, p. B5, quoting Professor Pennington: "People don't listen to all the evidence and then weigh it at the end. They process it as they go along, composing a continuing story throughout the trial that makes sense of what they're hearing."

[12]See Rogers Smith, "After Criticism: An Analysis of the Critical Legal Studies Movement," in Michael McCann and Gerald Houseman, eds. *Judging the Constitution* (Chicago: Scott Foresman, 1989), pp. 92–124.

[13]See, for example, Rorty's "Philosophy without Principles," in W. J. T. Mitchell, ed., *Against Theory* (Chicago: University of Chicago Press, 1985) and Bernstein's *Beyond Objectivism and Relativism* (Philadelphia: University of Pennsylvania Press, 1983) and *Philosophical Profiles* (Cambridgeshire: Polity Press, 1986). And see Michael Perry, *Love and Power* (New York and Oxford: Oxford University Press, 1991), especially Chapter 4.

[14]"Symposium on Interpretation," 58 *Southern California Law Review* (1985) and "Symposium on the Renaissance of Pragmatism in American Legal Thought," 63 *Southern California Law Review*, no. 6 (1990).

[15]*The Morality of Law* (New Haven: Yale University Press, 1964), p. 186. See more recently Peter Teachout's superb analysis of Fuller's jurisprudence in "The Soul of the Fugue: An Essay on Reading Fuller," 70 *Minnesota Law Review* 1073 (1986).

Throughout this book, I have emphasized that—even though we cannot demonstrate conclusively that certain legal answers are correct—we can distinguish between better and worse legal arguments, and we can talk about why we take the positions we do. The "harmonized" views in contemporary philosophy that I have just summarized agree with that position, but they also make a more disturbing point. If our rhetoric defines our community, then *all* forms of legal justification are politically potent and significant. The dominant patterns of legal reasoning and rhetoric do not necessarily take us in desirable directions. Hence this final section examines the moralistic legal and political rhetoric of a prior era. It then asks you to contrast that rhetoric with a sample from our own day.

Law and Moralistic Communities:
The Mann Act Revisited

Recall from the last chapter how, in 1893, Justice David Brewer defended the role of the judiciary "to restrain the greedy hand of the many from filching from the few that which they have honestly acquired" (p. 128). This moralistic rhetoric captures not merely one side of a political issue; it describes a common fabric of custom and popular beliefs—one that many today would find racist, sexist, and unacceptably intolerant. I mean that this kind of legal rhetoric transcended liberal or conservative positions. Justice Harlan, dissenting from *Plessy v. Ferguson*'s separate but equal holding in 1896, spoke this way:

> The white race deems itself the dominant race in this country. And so it is, in prestige, in achievements, in education, in wealth and in power. So, I doubt not, it will continue to be for all time, if it remains true to its heritage. . . . But in view of the Constitution, . . . [t]here is no caste here. Our Constitution is color-blind, and neither knows nor tolerates classes among citizens. . . . The humblest is the peer of the most powerful.

Justice Harlan reaches a "liberal" result, but his moralistic belief in the superiority of white culture goes hand in glove with his moral reading of the equal protection clause. In other words, the language of moral certainty itself structures a reality in which racism becomes "real."

But how do we know that moralistic rhetoric pervaded political culture generally? Because we have spent some considerable time on the Mann Act cases, we will return to the political context in which those cases arose. Prepare for a surprise or two—early Mann Act cases were headline-making national moral scandals.

The Mann Act prosecution in 1912–1914 of heavyweight boxing champion Jack Johnson, the first black champion (who had defeated "the Great White Hope" Jim Jeffries in 1910) set the tone. Johnson had paid for a girlfriend to travel from Pittsburgh to Chicago to meet him. She was white, and the appellate court implied that their racial differences converted their sexual relationship into "debauchery."

The prosecutions of Drew Caminetti and his friend, Maury Diggs—which, unlike Johnson's case, made it to the Supreme Court—were even more sensational, for both defendants were the sons of well-known Democratic politicians (Caminetti's father was U.S. Commissioner of Immigration under President Woodrow Wilson) and prosecuted by a Republican U.S. attorney. Attempts were made to postpone the trial of what one Democrat called a "little fornication case from California." But Republicans forced the prosecution with rhetoric like this: "It has long been believed by the masses that there is one kind of law for the rich and the politically powerful in this country and another kind of law for the poor, the friendless, and the weak." Here are the facts.[16]

Maury Diggs and Drew Caminetti, both married men with children, publicly chased Marsha Warrington and Lola Norris, working girls with high-school degrees. The men seemed at the time to use their political connections to flaunt conventional morality.

The girls admittedly engaged in scandalous excursions with full knowledge of Diggs's and Caminetti's marital status and of the potential (and threatening) repercussions. Diggs and Caminetti enjoyed the company of the girls frequently, both publicly and privately. The couples met three or four times a week, sometimes more. They took off on numerous Saturday evening automobile rides and made stops at taverns where Diggs and Caminetti would buy drinks and bring them out to the girls. They also made trips to roadhouses where they danced. And there was a stop in Stockton, where Maury rented a room or a cottage for just a few hours. But in her testimony, Lola said, "Nothing wrong occurred there." On their last excursion before making the trip across state lines to Reno, Marsha informed Diggs that she was pregnant with his child. But it was not until they made the trip to a bungalow in Reno that Lola had intercourse with Caminetti.

Civil suits and criminal prosecution against the four were threatened. The girls faced charges of "alienating their (the wives') husbands' affections" and being named as corespondents in divorce actions. The girls, still minors, feared the juvenile courts and "reform school." As rumors began to flare, Marsha's father went so far as to say if he ever found Diggs with his daughter he would kill them both. Ultimately, a policeman advised Diggs to leave town because their affairs had become common knowledge.

Lola and Marsha finally agreed to leave with Diggs and Caminetti. Diggs and Caminetti both promised to divorce their wives and marry the girls. In their testimony, Lola and Marsha argued they really didn't want to go to Reno, but they had no choice given the situation.

Shortly after the trip to Reno, Diggs was brought under investigation for an incident involving a bad check. It didn't take long for the scandal involving Diggs and Lola to come under investigation as well. Shortly thereafter, charges were brought against Maury Diggs and Drew Caminetti under the Mann Act. A trial date was set for early May. The moralistic rhetoric that constituted the community at the turn of the century was about to convert a local act of adultery into a national scandal.

Commissioner Caminetti sent a recommendation from Washington that the cases be postponed for two weeks and that the trial not be set until May 19th. He wanted to be present at the trial. However, during the interim between May 5th and May 19th, a similar conviction was handed down for Jack Johnson. Commissioner Caminetti also requested a conference with U.S. Attorney John L. McNab.

The Republican McNab was "confident" that the cases fell under federal jurisdiction. McNab had been described as "one of the ablest lawyers and jurists in California."

---

[16]This account follows that of Robert L. Anderson, *The Diggs-Caminetti Case* (Lewiston, N.Y.: E. Mellen Press, 1990).

A local newspaper captioned McNab as: "The fighting and tireless bulldog who will prosecute Diggs and Caminetti." Nevertheless, fear had been expressed by some local citizens that Diggs and Caminetti might "escape justice." But McNab dictated the following response to the local newspaper:

> There will be no delay in the prosecution of this case. The U.S. District Attorney's office has taken charge of this prosecution and will conduct it to a finish. Those who ridicule the prosecution of these men know little or nothing of the precision and effectiveness of the Federal Court. Enough facts are already in my possession to send both of these men to the penitentiary. Under the evidence in my possession, that is where I expect to see them land.

To no one's surprise, the conference requested by Caminetti never took place, lending even more evidence to suspicions of his political motives. After the Johnson decision was handed down, yet another wire was sent to McNab, this time from Attorney General McReynolds. The Democratic Attorney General requested a further delay of the Caminetti trial and asked for information regarding the case. McNab was again forced, against his recommendations, to move the trial date back to July 26th. Coincidentally, the Attorney General sent yet another order to McNab. McNab was instructed to postpone the trial until autumn.

Representative Mann summed up the situation in an address to the House in late June:". . . the present Commissioner General [Caminetti] has used both political and official influence to prevent his son from being brought to a speedy trial under the Mann Act for one of the more horrible of the offenses, the ruination of a young girl." Apparently it was an influence that an idealistic servant of justice, such as McNab, could not stomach, and perhaps rightly so. District Attorney John McNab submitted his letter of resignation shortly thereafter. He was driven from his position "for objecting to corrupt and inexcusable delay." McNab could no longer fulfill his responsibilities in the judicial "system"—a system stagnated in his view by political interference and corruption.

McNab was arguably justified in submitting his letter of resignation to both McReynolds and President Wilson. The district attorney had already informed the Department of Justice that attempts had been made to corrupt the government witnesses. Maury Diggs had made several attempts to influence the testimony of Lola and Marsha. And the friends of the defendants publicly boasted that the wealth and political influence of Caminetti and Diggs would stay McNab's hand through influence at Washington. The friends of the defendants repeatedly stated that they could "easily fix the case" and that they had too much influence at their command to cause them to worry. McNab insisted that McReynolds had postponed the cases until autumn "with absolute indifference to the rights of this office and the honor of the Department of Justice."

McNab also sent a lengthy statement of resignation to the president reflecting his disgust with the situation in graphic detail: "In these cases two girls were taken from cultured homes, bullied and frightened, in the face of their protests, into going into a foreign state, were ruined and debauched by the defendants, who abandoned their wives and infants to commit the crime." McNab insisted Maury Diggs and Drew Caminetti were indicted for a "hideous crime, which had ruined two respectable homes and shocked the moral sense of the people of California." The district attorney reportedly said that Diggs and Caminetti had to be rushed secretly from the train and rushed into Sacramento by automobile "to avoid lynching by enraged citizens."

The scandal of the Caminetti case continued to steal the headlines, but they were no longer focused on lurid romantic interludes. Now the presidential administration and the Department of Justice were commanding the press. Political battles erupted in the House as Representative Mann launched a heated attack on the Democratic Party and President Wilson. Mann called for the removal of Commissioner Caminetti for using both political and official influence to prevent his son from being brought to a speedy trial under the Mann Act. Mann also insisted the president was interfering with upholding of the law. Mann's moral indignation contradicted his prior statement that the bill's purpose was not to interfere with the police power of the states and that it was not an attempt to regulate sexual behavior. Mann now referred to the bill in a speech to the House as "a great moral reform law." Mann also revealed in a speech: ". . . you cannot always divine motives of people. A man might be prosecuted under the law for transporting a woman, when the question of money did not enter in it at all."

You know how the *Caminetti* case came out. The majority opinion by Justice Day insisted that the words of the Mann Act plainly included the immorality involved here. In moralistic tones, Justice Day wrote that it "would shock the common understanding of what constitutes an immoral purpose" to hold that "furnishing transportation in order that a woman may be debauched, or become a mistress or a concubine" did not violate the Mann Act.[17]

Even the dissenters, who insisted that the Mann Act only applied to sexual conduct that men purchased, wrote, "Any measure that protects the purity of women from assault or enticement to degradation finds an instant advocate in our best emotions. . . ." The dissenters suggested that the majority had failed law's internal moral test: Instead of considering and deciding "with poise of mind," the majority had yielded "to emotion. . . ."[18]

This history suggests many fascinating intersections between law and politics. Political loyalties and partisan infighting may influence the decision to prosecute. The personal values of the participants inevitably shape their perceptions of justice and fairness. The process that nominates and appoints judges and public officials generally will shift the direction the law takes, and so on. But the main political message runs broader and deeper. Moralistic rhetoric did at one time dominate American culture. Law both reflected and encouraged moralism. And that trait, while it no longer dominates us, still seems attractive to many people. Robert Bork's *The Tempting of America* and *Slouching Toward Gomorrah,* from their titles forward, speak in an overtly religious and moralistic voice. (See p. 9.) But the next section illustrates more typical contemporary legal rhetoric in a case nested in a morally charged environment. What communities do the contrasting rhetorics of majority and dissent in this next case imply? Do you feel more attracted to one or the other? Why?

Law in Conditions of Diversity: Emerging Issues of Gay Rights

John Dewey pointed out many decades ago that the word *community* comes from the root word for *communication*. That root happens to be the Latin word for *common*. The preceding section suggests that at the turn of the century, people shared a common

[17]242 U.S. 470 at 486.
[18]242 U.S. 470 at 501–502.

moralistic view of social arrangements and that legal and political rhetoric inevitably (and for its time rightly) communicated that way. But law, like politics and life itself, constantly changes.[19]

Today's political world acknowledges and accepts a diversity of interests that the world of the Mann Act did not. Supreme Court decisions interpreting the equal protection clause continue to play a role in defining that newer world. Yet a segment of that diverse world continues to press moralistic claims in the political arena. It has every right to do so. But does this diversity effectively prevent courts from communicating with us in common ways?

To assist grappling with that question, this section closely examines a 1996 case. It arose in a moralistic arena—the emerging issue of gay rights under the due process and equal protection clauses. In this particular case, the Supreme Court struck down an amendment to the constitution of the state of Colorado, passed by 53 percent of those voting in a statewide Colorado referendum in November 1992. The amendment stated

> No Protected Status Based on Homosexual, Lesbian, or Bisexual Orientation. Neither the State of Colorado, through any of its branches or departments, nor any of its agencies, political subdivisions, municipalities or school districts, shall enact, adopt or enforce any statute, regulation, ordinance or policy whereby homosexual, lesbian or bisexual orientation, conduct, practices or relationships shall constitute or otherwise be the basis of or entitle any person or class of persons to have or claim any minority status, quota preference, protected status or claim of discrimination. This section of the Constitution shall be in all respects self-executing.

The text of the amendment was written by Tony Marco and Kevin Tebedo of the organization Colorado for Family Values, based in Colorado Springs.

Colorado Springs's Focus on the Family, which claims 2 million members nationwide and whose head, Dr. James Dobson, reaches about 5 million listeners daily via his radio broadcasts, supported the campaign for Amendment 2, as did Will Perkins, a local automobile dealer, and the Rev. Ted Haggard, the leader of Colorado Springs's 4800-member New Life Church.

Offical pleadings in this case list 11 plaintiffs. Richard Evans, the first-named plaintiff, served as an administrator for the City and County of Denver. Angelo Romero was a Denver police officer. The list also included Denver itself and the cities of Boulder and Aspen. All plaintiffs had actively supported the various ordinances that Amendment 2 struck down. They filed suit very shortly after voters approved Amendment 2 on the Colorado ballot.

On January 14, 1993, Denver District Judge Jeffrey Bayless issued a temporary restraining order prohibiting enforcement of the amendment. The next day he made the order permanent pending review by the Colorado Supreme Court, which affirmed his injunction. In December of 1993, Judge Bayless held the amendment in violation of the Constitution after a lengthy trial involving witnesses from around the United States.

---

[19]For example, the week I began this final section, the news media reported the first conclusive empirical connection between specific chemicals in cigarette smoke and cancerous changes in lung-tissue cells. (See "Direct Link Found Between Smoking and Lung Cancer," *New York Times,* October 18, 1996, p. A1.) This factual finding will impact litigation against tobacco companies, but this litigation, in turn, raises philosophical and social questions that will generate new tort law on the distinctions between personal and corporate responsibility for assuming risks in life. For a recent examination of Dewey's thought and impact, see Alan Ryan, *John Dewey and the High Tide of American Liberalism* (New York: W. W. Norton, 1995).

The Colorado Supreme Court affirmed this decision on October 11, 1994, and Colorado petitioned for certiorari to the U.S. Supreme Court.

Here are more key pieces of background information:

1. In 1986, the Supreme Court, in *Bowers v. Hardwick*, refused to extend the due process clause right of personal privacy (articulated in the birth control and abortion cases in the 1960s and 1970s) to protect against state prosecution those who engaged in acts of sodomy. Sodomy for practical (if not historical) purposes refers to homosexual acts. Hence for purposes of the legal arguments in the Colorado case, homosexual behavior had no more protected civil liberties status than would, say, car-driving behavior.

2. Prior to the passage of this amendment, a number of local jurisdictions, including Denver, Boulder, and Aspen, Colorado, had passed ordinances protecting those of homosexual or bisexual orientation against discrimination in employment and housing.

3. Tony Marco, one of the original drafters of the amendment, split from Colorado for Family Values during this litigation. In an interview with the *Denver Post* several years after the amendment passed, Mr. Marco explained that he had in 1991 believed that a minority of powerful and wealthy people within the gay community, "masquerading as a disadvantaged class," was about to convince the state legislature to pass a statewide antidiscrimination bill. He therefore hurriedly drafted the amendment and got it on the ballot. In the interview he said he wished he and his group had worded the text differently. "You know, we put this together so quickly. . . . I take responsibility for the way the amendment was framed because there was no other way to do it at the time, or so it seemed." He said in the interview that his intent was not to condemn the gay community but to prevent a kind of "civil rights fraud" whereby the rich obtained for themselves protections designed for the poor and powerless.[20]

4. Friend of the Court ("amicus curiae") briefs were filed in support of the Colorado Supreme Court result by, among others, a team of constitutional law scholars led by Laurence Tribe of Harvard Law School and by George Bushnell, Jr., president of the American Bar Association. Robert Bork filed an amicus brief for a group titled "Equal Rights, Not Special Rights," supporting the constitutionality of Amendment 2.

5. Oral argument before the Supreme Court in October of 1995 was intense. Linda Greehouse's lead story for the *New York Times* began, "With the Justices debating one another at least as vigorously as they questioned the lawyers before them. . . ."[21]

At a local forum in Colorado Springs in 1996, the attorneys—Colorado Solicitor General Tim Tymkovich for the state and Jean Dubofsky, former Colorado Supreme Court Justice for the respondents—told me that they counted more than 120 separate questions from the bench in their combined 60 minutes of argument time in the case.

6. Finally, some specific legal details need highlighting. First, Amendment 2 prohibits antidiscrimination laws against those with a homosexual orientation. It does not limit itself to behavior and would effect those who, by age, disease, or preference, are sexually inactive. Second, Amendment 2, read carefully, does more than prevent the passage of antidiscrimination laws. The courts of Colorado are "political subdivisions" of the state. The amendment appears to strip courts of their capacity to grant relief for someone who, for example, lost a lawsuit unrelated to gay issues because the judge in the case was homophobic. Arguably, a litigant who lost because of a homophobic judge

---

[20]"Controversial Law's Final Test," *Denver Post*, September 24, 1995, p. 1A.
[21]"U.S. Justices Hear, and Also Debate, a Gay Rights Case," *New York Times*, October 11, 1995, p. A1.

would have no recourse even if the litigant were straight but the judge mistakenly believed otherwise. Third and finally, consider a hypothetical case. If a state passes a constitutional amendment requiring all motor vehicle drivers regularly to pass a drug test before getting or keeping their licenses, would not all those thereby denied a license automatically lose their capacity to argue for a different law under the ordinary political process? Would they not have to seek a new constitutional amendment to change the result? If losing that political voice would not violate their constitutional right to participate, does it make sense to say that Amendment 2 *does* deprive homosexuals of such a political right to participate, short of advocating a change in the state's constitution?

As you read the following opinions, first by the Colorado Supreme Court and then by the U.S. Supreme Court, keep several levels of questions in mind:

- *The quality of judicial communication:* Does this judicial language communicate to you? That is, do you understand what each judge is saying, quite apart from whether you agree with it?
- *The adequacy of legal reasoning:* How effectively does each of these opinions articulate and harmonize the four elements of legal reasoning? For example, how well do these opinions harmonize the constitutional law of equal protection already covered in this book? See pp. 135–140.
- *The political implications of judical rhetoric:* What would communities look like, broadly speaking, if people talked politically as does Colorado Chief Justice Rovira? Justice Erickson? Justice Kennedy? Justice Scalia? Do you prefer some such communities to others? Can you imagine better ways of talking than any of these four?

Evans v. Romer
Supreme Court of Colorado
882 P.2d 1335 (Colo. 1994)

Chief Justice ROVIRA delivered the opinion of the court.

. . . We reaffirm our holding that the constitutionality of Amendment 2 must be determined with reference to the strict scrutiny standard of review. A legislative enactment which infringes on a fundamental right or which burdens a suspect class is constitutionally permissible only if it is "necessary to promote a compelling state interest," *Dunn v. Blumstein*, 405 U.S. 330 (1972), and does so in the least restrictive manner possible. *Plyler v. Doe*, 457 U.S. 202 (1982). The question of what constitutes a compelling state interest is one of law and thus, we review the trial court's ruling de novo. Defendants argue that Amendment 2 is supported by a number of compelling state interests and is narrowly tailored to serve those interests.

Defendants' first asserted governmental interest is in protecting the sanctity of religious, familial, and personal privacy. Freedom of religion is expressly guaranteed by both the First Amendment to the United States Constitution and article II, section 4 of the Colorado Constitution and stands at the core of our Nation's history and tradition. It is among the highest values of our society. There can be little doubt that ensuring religious freedom is a compelling governmental interest. . . .

Assuming arguendo that ordinances such as that in effect in Boulder, which prohibit discrimination against gay men, lesbians, and bisexuals in housing and employment but which contain no exception for religiously based objections, substantially burden the religious liberty of those who object to renting or employing gay men, lesbians, or bisexuals on religious grounds, the enactment of Amendment 2 clearly is not narrowly tailored to serve the interest of ensuring religious liberty. To the contrary, an equally effective and substantially less onerous way of accomplishing that purpose simply would be to require that antidiscrimination laws which include provisions for sexual orientation also include exceptions for religiously based objections. This is precisely what the Denver antidiscrimination laws provide. Similar exemptions for religious organizations are found in federal antidiscrimination statutes. Defendants do not, and we doubt that they could, argue that the Denver ordinance impairs religious freedom.

It is clear that Amendment 2, which affects the fundamental right of gay men, lesbians, and bisexuals to participate equally in the political process, is not the least restrictive means of ensuring religious liberty, and is not narrowly tailored to serve the compelling governmental interest in ensuring the free exercise of religion. . . .

Defendants contend that the "right of familial privacy" is "severely undermined" by the enactment of antidiscrimination laws protecting gay men, lesbians, and bisexuals because "if a child hears one thing from his parents and the exact opposite message from the government, parental authority will inevitably be undermined." This argument fails because it rests on the assumption that the right of familial privacy engenders an interest in having government endorse certain values as moral or immoral. While it is true that parents have a constitutionally protected interest in inculcating their children with their own values, defendants point to no authority, and we are aware of none, holding that parents have the corresponding right of insuring that government endorse those values. . . .

Defendants next assert that . . . Amendment 2 serves the compelling governmental interest in seeing that limited resources are dedicated to the enforcement of civil rights laws intended to protect suspect classes rather than having a portion of those resources diverted to the enforcement of laws intended to protect gay men, lesbians, and bisexuals.

It is well-settled that the preservation of fiscal resources, administrative convenience, and the reduction of the workload of governmental bodies are not compelling state interests. Consequently, we conclude that defendants' asserted interest in preserving the fiscal resources of state and local governments for the exclusive use of enforcing civil rights laws intended to protect suspect classes does not constitute a compelling state interest. . . .

Defendants next argue that Amendment 2 "promotes the compelling governmental interest of allowing the people themselves to establish public social and moral norms." In support of this proposition, defendants define two related norms which are promoted by Amendment 2: Amendment 2 preserves heterosexual families and heterosexual marriage and, more generally, it sends the societal message condemning gay men, lesbians, and bisexuals as immoral.

The only authority relied on to support the view that the protection of morality constitutes a compelling governmental interest is *Barnes v. Glen Theatre, Inc.*, 501 U.S. 560 (1991). Defendants cite the plurality opinion in *Barnes* for the proposition that "the State's interest in protecting order and morality is compelling; substantial; subordinating; paramount; cogent; strong." *Barnes* does not support defendants' contention that protecting public morality constitutes a compelling governmental interest.

In *Barnes,* four Justices held that "the public indecency statute . . . furthers a substantial government interest in protecting order and morality." Justice Souter provided the fifth vote in *Barnes,* however he did not rely "on the possible sufficiency of society's moral views to justify the limitations at issue." Rather, he was of the opinion that the Indiana law at issue (which prohibited completely nude dancing) was permissible due to the "State's substantial interest in combating the secondary effects of adult entertainment establishments. . . ." None of the justices in *Barnes* concluded that furthering public morality constitutes a compelling state interest.

Consequently, defendants have cited no authority to support the proposition that the promotion of public morality constitutes a compelling governmental interest, and we are aware of none. At the most, this interest is substantial. However, a substantial governmental interest is not sufficient to render constitutional a law which infringes on a fundamental right—the interest must be compelling. . . .

Defendants contend that Amendment 2 "prevents government from supporting the political objectives of a special interest group." The only argument offered to substantiate the contention that this is a compelling state interest is the following observation from *Lyng v. International Union*, 485 U.S. 360 (1988): "At the heart of the First Amendment is the notion that an individual should be free to believe as he will, and that in a free society one's beliefs should be shaped by his mind and his conscience rather than coerced by the State."

Defendants do not claim that the laws which Amendment 2 is intended to prohibit constitute an infringement on the First Amendment liberties identified in *Lyng*. Similarly, they do not take the position that those laws amount to a "coercion by the State" to believe anything. Rather, they assert that the laws which Amendment 2 is intended to prohibit constitute an implicit endorsement of homosexuality and that this somehow vitiates the right of individuals "to make their own judgments on this question. . . ." As explained above, however, we do not believe that antidiscrimination laws constitute an endorsement of the characteristics that are deemed an unlawful basis upon which to discriminate against individuals. . . .

Defendants claim that Amendment 2 "serves to deter factionalism through ensuring that decisions regarding special protections for homosexuals and bisexuals are made at the highest level of government." More specifically, they argue that "Amendment 2 is intended, not to restrain the competition of ideas," but "seeks to ensure that the deeply divisive issue of homosexuality's place in our society does not serve to fragment Colorado's body politic." Amendment 2 accomplishes this end by eliminating "city-by-city and county-by-county battles over this issue."

We reject the argument that the interest in deterring factionalism, as defined by defendants, is compelling. Political debate, even if characterized as "factionalism," is not an evil which the state has a legitimate interest in deterring but rather, constitutes the foundation of democracy. "There is no significant state or public interest in curtailing debate or discussion of a ballot measure." *Citizens Against Rent Control v. City of Berkeley*, 454 U.S. 290 (1981). We fail to see how the state, which is charged with serving the will of the people, can have any legitimate interest in preventing one side of a controversial debate from pressing its case before governmental bodies simply because it would prefer to avoid political controversy or "factionalism." . . .

Last, defendants argue that even if Amendment 2 is in conflict with the Fourteenth Amendment to the United States Constitution, it is nevertheless a constitutionally valid exercise of the people's reserved powers under the Tenth Amendment. In short, the argument is that the power to amend the state constitution is reserved to Colorado's voters under the Tenth Amendment, and even if the voters amend the state constitution in such a way as to violate the federal constitution, such an amendment is per se valid. . . .

States have no compelling interest in amending their constitution in ways that violate fundamental federal rights. *Reitman v. Mulkey*, 387 U.S. 369 (1967) (no reserved power to make right to discriminate a part of the state's basic charter); *Lucas v. Colorado Gen. Assembly*, 377 U.S. 713 (1964) ("A citizen's constitutional rights can hardly be infringed simply because a majority of the people choose that it be."). We reject defendants' argument that Amendment 2 is a constitutionally valid exercise of state power under the Tenth Amendment.

The state has failed to establish that Amendment 2 is necessary to serve any compelling governmental interest in a narrowly tailored way. Amendment 2 is not severable and not a valid exercise of state power under the Tenth Amendment. Accordingly, we affirm the trial court's entry of a permanent injunction barring its enforcement.

Justice ERICKSON dissenting.

I respectfully dissent. In *Evans v. Romer*, 854 P.2d 1270 (Colo. 1993) (*Evans I*), cert. denied, 114 S.Ct. 419 (1993), the majority crafted a new fundamental right that had never been recognized by the United States Supreme Court or by any court other than a federal district court in Ohio that relied on *Evans I*. Ironically, judicial review of Amendment 2 has accomplished exactly what the voters who passed Amendment 2 sought to prevent—the majority has effectively created a heightened protection for homosexuals, lesbians, and bisexuals.

In establishing what is essentially a new substantive due process right disguised as a previously unrecognized "fundamental right," the majority . . . has overlooked a crucial aspect of the case before us: we are not evaluating an act of the legislature or pronouncement of the executive—we are reviewing a constitutional amendment adopted by the people of the State of Colorado. . . .

In my view, the state has a legitimate interest in protecting religious freedoms and Amendment 2 bears a rational relationship to that interest. . . .

[Second, in] my view, the state has a legitimate interest in promoting statewide uniformity in matters of statewide concern and Amendment 2 bears a rational relationship to that interest. . . .

[Third, the] State of Colorado, through entities such as the Colorado Civil Rights Division, has attempted to further the interest in remedying specific instances of sexual and racial discrimination through existing civil rights laws and enforcement programs. However, owing to the fiscal constraints which are inevitably a part of public administration, unlimited funds are not available for this purpose. Therefore, it is incumbent upon the state to set priorities for its enforcement efforts. In this case, the setting of priorities is a legitimate state interest and Amendment 2 is rationally related to that interest. . . .

Therefore, I dissent.

Romer v. Evans
Supreme Court of the United States
116 S.Ct. 1620 (1996)

Justice KENNEDY delivered the opinion of the Court.

One century ago, the first Justice HARLAN admonished this Court that the Constitution "neither knows nor tolerates classes among citizens." *Plessy v. Ferguson,* 163 U.S. 537 (1896) (dissenting opinion). Unheeded then, those words now are understood to state a commitment to the law's neutrality where the rights of persons are at stake. The Equal Protection Clause enforces this principle and today requires us to hold invalid a provision of Colorado's Constitution. . . .

The State's principal argument in defense of Amendment 2 is that it puts gays and lesbians in the same position as all other persons. So, the State says, the measure does no more than deny homosexuals special rights. This reading of the amendment's language is implausible. We rely not upon our own interpretation of the amendment but upon the authoritative construction of Colorado's Supreme Court. The state court, deeming it unnecessary to determine the full extent of the amendment's reach, found it invalid even on a modest reading of its implications. The critical discussion of the amendment, set out in *Evans I,* is as follows: "The immediate objective of Amendment 2 is, at a minimum, to repeal existing statutes, regulations, ordinances, and policies of state and local entities that barred discrimination based on sexual orientation. . . ."

The change that Amendment 2 works in the legal status of gays and lesbians in the private sphere is far-reaching, both on its own terms and when considered in light of the structure and operation of modern anti-discrimination laws. That structure is well illustrated by contemporary statutes and ordinances prohibiting discrimination by providers of public accommodations. "At common law, innkeepers, smiths, and others who 'made profession of a public employment,' were prohibited from refusing, without good reason, to serve a customer." *Hurley v. Irish-American Gay, Lesbian and Bisexual Group of Boston, Inc.* [115 S.Ct. 2338] (1995). The duty was a general one and did not specify protection for particular groups. The common law rules, however, proved insufficient in many instances, and it was settled early that the Fourteenth Amendment did not give Congress a general power to prohibit discrimination in public accommodations, *Civil Rights Cases,* 109 U.S. 3 (1883). In consequence, most States have chosen to counter discrimination by enacting detailed statutory schemes. Colorado's state and municipal laws typify this emerging tradition of statutory protection and follow a consistent pattern. . . .

These statutes and ordinances also depart from the common law by enumerating the groups or persons within their ambit of protection. Enumeration is the essential device used to make the duty not to discriminate concrete and to provide guidance for those who must comply. . . .

Amendment 2 bars homosexuals from securing protection against the injuries that these public-accommodations laws address. That in itself is a severe consequence, but there is more. Amendment 2, in addition, nullifies specific legal protections for this targeted class in all transactions in housing, sale of real estate, insurance, health and welfare services, private education, and employment. . . .

Amendment 2's reach may not be limited to specific laws passed for the benefit of gays and lesbians. It is a fair, if not necessary, inference from the broad language of the amendment that it deprives gays and lesbians even of the protection of general laws and policies that prohibit arbitrary discrimination in governmental and private settings. . . .

The Fourteenth Amendment's promise that no person shall be denied the equal protection of the laws must co-exist with the practical necessity that most legislation classifies for one purpose or another, with resulting disadvantage to various groups or persons. We have attempted to reconcile the principle with the reality by stating that, if a law neither burdens a fundamental right nor targets a suspect class, we will uphold the legislative classification so long as it bears a rational relation to some legitimate end. See, e.g., *Heller v. Doe,* 509 U.S.—(1993).

Amendment 2 fails, indeed defies, even this conventional inquiry. First, the amendment has the peculiar property of imposing a broad and undifferentiated disability on a single named group, an exceptional and, as we shall explain, invalid form of legislation. Second, its sheer breadth is so discontinuous with the reasons offered for it that the amendment seems inexplicable by anything but animus toward the class that it affects; it lacks a rational relationship to legitimate state interests.

Taking the first point, even in the ordinary equal protection case calling for the most deferential of standards, we insist on knowing the relation between the classification adopted and the object to be attained. The search for the link between classification and objective gives substance to the Equal Protection Clause; it provides guidance and discipline for the legislature, which is entitled to know what sorts of laws it can pass; and it marks the limits of our own authority. In the ordinary case, a law will be sustained if it can be said to advance a legitimate government interest, even if the law seems unwise or works to the disadvantage of a particular group, or if the rationale for it seems tenuous. By requiring that the classification bear a rational relationship to an independent and legitimate legislative end, we ensure that classifications are not drawn for the purpose of disadvantaging the group burdened by the law.

Amendment 2 confounds this normal process of judicial review. It is at once too narrow and too broad. It identifies persons by a single trait and then denies them protection across the board. The resulting disqualification of a class of persons from the right to seek specific protection from the law is unprecedented in our jurisprudence.

It is not within our constitutional tradition to enact laws of this sort. Central both to the idea of the rule of law and to our own Constitution's guarantee of equal protection is the principle that government and each of its parts remain open on impartial terms to all who seek its assistance. "'Equal protection of the laws is not achieved through indiscriminate imposition of inequalities.'" *Sweatt v. Painter,* 339 U.S. 629 (1950) (quoting *Shelley v. Kraemer,* 334 U.S. 1 [1948]). Respect for this principle explains why laws singling out a certain class of citizens for disfavored legal status or general hardships are rare. A law declaring that in general it shall be more difficult for one group of citizens than for all others to seek aid from the government is itself a denial of equal protection of the laws in the most literal sense. "The guaranty of 'equal protection of the laws is a pledge of the protection of equal laws.'" *Skinner v. Oklahoma ex rel. Williamson,* 316 U.S. 535 (1942) (quoting *Yick Wo v. Hopkins,* 118 U.S. 356 (1886)).

Davis v. Beason, 133 U.S. 333 (1890), not cited by the parties but relied upon by the dissent, is not evidence that Amendment 2 is within our constitutional tradition, and any reliance upon it as authority for sustaining the amendment is misplaced. In *Davis,* the Court approved an Idaho territorial statute denying Mormons, polygamists, and advocates of polygamy the right to vote and to hold office because, as the Court construed the statute, it "simply excludes from the privilege of voting, or of holding any office of honor, trust or profit, those who have been convicted of certain offences, and those who advocate a practical resistance to the laws of the Territory and justify and approve the commission of crimes forbidden by it." To the extent *Davis* held that persons advocating a certain practice may be denied the right to vote, it is no longer good law. *Brandenburg v. Ohio,* 395 U.S. 444 (1969) (*per curiam*). To the extent it held that the groups designated in the statute may be deprived of the right to vote because of their status, its ruling could not stand without surviving strict scrutiny, a most doubtful outcome. To the extent *Davis* held that a convicted felon may be denied the right to vote, its holding is not implicated by our decision and is unexceptionable.

A second and related point is that laws of the kind now before us raise the inevitable inference that the disadvantage imposed is born of animosity toward the class of persons affected. Even laws enacted for broad and ambitious purposes often can be explained by reference to legitimate public policies which justify the incidental disadvantages they impose on certain persons. Amendment 2, however, in making a general announcement that gays and lesbians shall not have any particular protections from the law, inflicts on them immediate, continuing, and real injuries that outrun and belie any legitimate justifications that may be claimed for it. We conclude that, in addition to the far-reaching deficiencies of Amendment 2 that we have noted, the principles it offends, in another sense, are conventional and venerable; a law must bear a rational relationship to a legitimate government purpose, and Amendment 2 does not.

The primary rationale the State offers for Amendment 2 is respect for other citizens' freedom of association, and in particular the liberties of landlords or employers who have personal or religious objections to homosexuality. Colorado also cites its interest in conserving resources to fight discrimination against other groups. The breadth of the Amendment is so far removed from these particular justifications that we find it impossible to credit them. We cannot say that Amendment 2 is directed to any identifiable legitimate purpose or discrete objective. It is a status-based enactment divorced from any factual context from which we could discern a relationship to legitimate state interests; it is a classification of persons undertaken for its own sake, something the Equal Protection Clause does not permit. "Class legislation . . . [is] obnoxious to the prohibitions of the Fourteenth Amendment. . . ." *Civil Rights Cases.*

We must conclude that Amendment 2 classifies homosexuals not to further a proper legislative end but to make them unequal to everyone else. This Colorado cannot do. A State cannot so deem a class of persons a stranger to its laws. Amendment 2 violates the Equal Protection Clause, and the judgment of the Supreme Court of Colorado is affirmed.

It is so ordered.

Justice SCALIA, with whom the CHIEF JUSTICE and Justice THOMAS join, dissenting.

The Court has mistaken a Kulturkampf ["culture war"] for a fit of spite. The constitutional amendment before us here is not the manifestation of a "'bare . . . desire to harm'" homosexuals, but is rather a modest attempt by seemingly tolerant Coloradans to preserve traditional sexual mores against the efforts of a politically powerful minority to revise those mores through use of the laws. That objective, and the means chosen to achieve it, are not only unimpeachable under any constitutional doctrine hitherto pronounced (hence the opinion's heavy reliance upon principles of righteousness rather than judicial holdings); they have been specifically approved by the Congress of the United States and by this Court.

In holding that homosexuality cannot be singled out for disfavorable treatment, the Court contradicts a decision, unchallenged here, pronounced only 10 years ago, see *Bowers v. Hardwick,*

478 U.S. 186 (1986), and places the prestige of this institution behind the proposition that opposition to homosexuality is as reprehensible as racial or religious bias. Whether it is or not is precisely the cultural debate that gave rise to the Colorado constitutional amendment (and to the preferential laws against which the amendment was directed). Since the Constitution of the United States says nothing about this subject, it is left to be resolved by normal democratic means, including the democratic adoption of provisions in state constitutions. This Court has no business imposing upon all Americans the resolution favored by the elite class from which the Members of this institution are selected, pronouncing that "animosity" toward homosexuality, is evil. I vigorously dissent. . . .

[T]he principle underlying the Court's opinion is that one who is accorded equal treatment under the laws, but cannot as readily as others obtain preferential treatment under the laws, has been denied equal protection of the laws. If merely stating this alleged "equal protection" violation does not suffice to refute it, our constitutional jurisprudence has achieved terminal silliness.

The central thesis of the Court's reasoning is that any group is denied equal protection when, to obtain advantage (or, presumably, to avoid disadvantage), it must have recourse to a more general and hence more difficult level of political decisionmaking than others. The world has never heard of such a principle, which is why the Court's opinion is so long on emotive utterance and so short on relevant legal citation. And it seems to me most unlikely that any multilevel democracy can function under such a principle. For whenever a disadvantage is imposed, or conferral of a benefit is prohibited, at one of the higher levels of democratic decisionmaking (i.e., by the state legislature rather than local government, or by the people at large in the state constitution rather than the legislature), the affected group has (under this theory) been denied equal protection. To take the simplest of examples, for the provision. If it is rational to criminalize the conduct, surely it is rational to deny special favor and protection to those with a self-avowed tendency or desire to engage in the conduct. Indeed, where criminal sanctions are not involved, homosexual "orientation" is an acceptable stand-in for homosexual conduct. . . .

Moreover, even if the provision regarding homosexual "orientation" were invalid, respondents' challenge to Amendment 2–which is a facial challenge–must fail. "A facial challenge to a legislative Act is, of course, the most difficult challenge to mount successfully, since the challenger must establish that no set of circumstances exists under which the Act would be valid." *United States v. Salerno*, 481 U.S. 739 (1987). It would not be enough for respondents to establish (if they could) that Amendment 2 is unconstitutional as applied to those of homosexual "orientation"; since, under *Bowers*, Amendment 2 is unquestionably constitutional as applied to those who engage in homosexual conduct, the facial challenge cannot succeed. Some individuals of homosexual "orientation" who do not engage in homosexual acts might successfully bring an as-applied challenge to Amendment 2, but so far as the record indicates, none of the respondents is such a person.

The foregoing suffices to establish what the Court's failure to cite any case remotely in point would lead one to suspect: No principle set forth in the Constitution, nor even any imagined by this Court in the past 200 years, prohibits what Colorado has done here. But the case for Colorado is much stronger than that. What it has done is not only unprohibited, but eminently reasonable, with close, congressionally approved precedent in earlier constitutional practice.

First, as to its eminent reasonableness. The Court's opinion contains grim, disapproving hints that Coloradans have been guilty of "animus" or "animosity" toward homosexuality, as though that has been established as Unamerican. Of course it is our moral heritage that one should not hate any human being or class of human beings. But I had thought that one could consider certain conduct reprehensible—murder, for example, or polygamy, or cruelty to animals–and could exhibit even "animus" toward such conduct. Surely that is the only sort of "animus" at issue here: moral disapproval of homosexual conduct, the same sort of moral disapproval that produced the centuries-old criminal laws that we held constitutional in *Bowers*. The Colorado amendment does not, to speak entirely precisely, prohibit giving favored status to people who are homosexuals; they can be favored for many reasons—for example, because they are senior citizens or members of racial minorities. But it prohibits giving them favored status because of their homosexual conduct—that is, it prohibits favored status for homosexuality. But though Coloradans are, as I say, entitled to be hostile toward homosexual conduct, the fact is that the degree of hostility reflected by Amendment 2 is the smallest conceivable. The Court's portrayal of Coloradans as a society fallen victim to point-less, hate-filled "gay-bashing" is so false as to be comical. Colorado not only is one of the 25 States that have repealed their antisodomy laws, but was among the first to do so. But the society that elim-inates criminal punishment for homosexual acts does not necessarily abandon the view that homo-sexuality is morally wrong and socially harmful; consider a state law prohibiting the award of municipal contracts to relatives of mayors or city councilmen. Once such a law is passed, the group composed of such relatives must, in order to get the benefit of city contracts, persuade the state legislature—unlike all other citizens, who need only persuade the municipality. It is ridiculous to consider this a denial of equal protection, which is why the Court's theory is unheard of.

The Court might reply that the example I have given is not a denial of equal protection only because the same "rational basis" (avoidance of corruption) which renders constitutional the sub-stantive discrimination against relatives (i.e., the fact that they alone cannot obtain city contracts) also automatically suffices to sustain what might be called the electoral-procedural discrimination against them (i.e., the fact that they must go to the state level to get this changed). This is of course a perfectly reasonable response, and would explain why "electoral-procedural discrimination" has not hitherto been heard of: a law that is valid in its substance is automatically valid in its level of enactment. But the Court cannot afford to make this argument, for as I shall discuss next, there is no doubt of a rational basis for the substance of the prohibition at issue here. The Court's entire novel theory rests upon the proposition that there is something special—something that cannot be justified by normal "rational basis" analysis—in making a disadvantaged group (or a nonpreferred group) resort to a higher decisionmaking level. That proposition finds no support in law or logic.

I turn next to whether there was a legitimate rational basis for the substance of the constitutional amendment—for the prohibition of special protection for homosexuals. It is unsurprising that the Court avoids discussion of this question, since the answer is so obviously yes. The case most relevant to the issue before us today is not even mentioned in the Court's opinion: In *Bowers v. Hardwick*, 478 U.S. 186 (1986), we held that the Constitution does not prohibit what virtually all States had done from the founding of the Republic until very recent years—making homosexual conduct a crime. That holding is unassailable, except by those who think that the Constitution changes to suit current fashions. But in any event it is a given in the present case: Respondents' briefs did not urge overruling *Bowers*, and at oral argument respondents' counsel expressly disavowed any intent to seek such overruling. If it is constitutionally permissible for a State to make homosexual conduct criminal, surely it is constitutionally permissible for a State to enact other laws merely disfavoring homosexual conduct. And *a fortiori* it is constitutionally permissible for a State to adopt a provision not even dis-favoring homosexual conduct, but merely prohibiting all levels of state government from bestowing special protections upon homosexual conduct. Respondents (who, unlike the Court, cannot afford the luxury of ignoring inconvenient precedent) counter *Bowers* with the argument that a greater-includes-the-lesser rationale cannot justify Amendment 2's application to individuals who do not engage in homosexual acts, but are merely of homosexual "orientation." Some courts of appeals have concluded that, with respect to laws of this sort at least, that is a distinction without a difference.

But assuming that, in Amendment 2, a person of homosexual "orientation" is someone who does not engage in homosexual conduct but merely has a tendency or desire to do so, *Bowers* still suffices to establish a rational basis for the provision. If it is rational to criminalize the con-duct, surely it is rational to deny special favor and protection to those with a self-avowed ten-dency or desire to engage in the conduct. Indeed, where criminal sanctions are not involved, homosexual "orientation" is an acceptable stand-in for homosexual conduct....

Moreover, even if the provision regarding homosexual "orientation" were invalid, respondents' challenge to Amendment 2—which is a facial challenge—must fail. "A facial challenge to a legislative

Act is, of course, the most difficult challenge to mount successfully, since the challenger must establish that no set of circumstances exists under which the Act would be valid." *United States v. Salerno*, 481 U.S. 739 (1987). It would not be enough for respondents to establish (if they could) that Amendment 2 is unconstitutional as applied to those of homosexual "orientation"; since, under *Bowers*, Amendment 2 is unquestionably constitutional as applied to those who engage in homosexual conduct, the facial challenge cannot succeed. Some individuals of homosexual "orientation" who do not engage in homosexual acts might successfully bring an as-applied challenge to Amendment 2, but so far as the record indicates, none of the respondents is such a person.

The foregoing suffices to establish what the Court's failure to cite any case remotely in point would lead one to suspect: No principle set forth in the Constitution, nor even any imagined by this Court in the past 200 years, prohibits what Colorado has done here. But the case for Colorado is much stronger than that. What it has done is not only unprohibited, but eminently reasonable, with close, congressionally approved precedent in earlier constitutional practice.

First, as to its eminent resonableness. The Court's opinion contains grim, disapproving hints that Coloradans have been guilty of "animus" or "animosity" toward homosexuality, as though that has been established as Unamerican. Of course it is our moral heritage that one should not hate any human being or class of human beings. But I had thought that one could consider certain conduct reprehensible—murder, for example, or polygamy, or cruelty to animals—and could exhibit even "animus" toward such conduct. Surely that is the only sort of "animus" at issue here: moral disapproval of homosexual conduct, the same sort of moral disapproval that produced the centuries-old criminal laws that we held constitutional in *Bowers*. The Colorado amendment does not, to speak entirely precisely, prohibit giving favored status to people who are homosexuals; they can be favored for many reasons—for example, because they are senior citizens or members of racial minorities. But it prohibits giving them favored status because of their homosexual conduct—that is, it prohibits favored status for homosexuality. But though Coloradans are, as I say, entitled to be hostile toward homosexual conduct, the fact is that the degree of hostilty reflected by Amendment 2 is the smallest conceivable. The Court's portrayal of Coloradans as a society fallen victim to pointless, hate-filled "gay-bashing" is so false as to be comical. Colorado not only is one of the 25 States that have repealed their antisodomy laws, but was among the first to do so. But the society that eliminates criminal punishment for homosexual acts does not necessarily abandon the view that homosexuality is morally wrong and socially harmful; often, abolition simply reflects the view that enforcement of such criminal laws involves unseemly intrusion into the intimate lives of citizens.

There is a problem, however, which arises when criminal sanction of homosexuality is eliminated but moral and social disapprobation of homosexuality is meant to be retained. The Court cannot be unaware of that problem; it is evident in many cities of the country, and occasionally bubbles to the surface of the news, in heated political disputes over such matters as the introduction into local schools of books teaching that homosexuality is an optional and fully acceptable "alternate lifestyle." The problem (a problem, that is, for those who wish to retain social disapprobation of homosexuality) is that, because those who engage in homosexual conduct tend to reside in disproportionate numbers in certain communities, and of course care about homosexual-rights issues much more ardently than the public at large, they possess political power much greater than their numbers, both locally and statewide. Quite understandably, they devote this political power to achieving not merely a grudging social toleration, but full social acceptance, of homosexuality.

By the time Coloradans were asked to vote on Amendment 2, their exposure to homosexuals' quest for social endorsement was not limited to newspaper accounts of happenings in places such as New York, Los Angeles, San Francisco, and Key West. Three Colorado cities—Aspen, Boulder, and Denver—had enacted ordinances that listed "sexual orientation" as an impermissible ground for discrimination, equating the moral disapproval of homosexual conduct with racial and religious bigotry. The phenomenon had even appeared statewide: the Governor of Colorado had signed an executive order pronouncing that "in the State of Colorado we recognize the diversity in our pluralistic society and strive to bring an end to discrimination in any form," and directing state agency-heads to "ensure non-discrimination" in hiring and promotion based on, among other things, "sexual orientation." I do not mean to be critical of these legislative successes; homosexuals are as entitled to use the legal system for reinforcement of their moral sentiments as are the rest of society. But they are subject to being countered by lawful, democratic countermeasures as well.

That is where Amendment 2 came in. It sought to counter both the geographic concentration and the disproportionate political power of homosexuals by (1) resolving the controversy at the statewide level, and (2) making the election a single-issue contest for both sides. It put directly, to all the citizens of the State, the question: Should homosexuality be given special protection? They answered no. The Court today asserts that this most democratic of procedures is unconstitutional. Lacking any cases to establish that facially absurd proposition, it simply asserts that it must be unconstitutional, because it has never happened before. . . .

What the Court says is even demonstrably false at the constitutional level. The Eighteenth Amendment to the Federal Constitution, for example, deprived those who drank alcohol not only of the power to alter the policy of prohibition locally or through state legislation, but even of the power to alter it through state constitutional amendment or federal legislation. The Establishment Clause of the First Amendment prevents theocrats from having their way by converting their fellow citizens at the local, state, or federal statutory level; as does the Republican Form of Government Clause prevent monarchists.

But there is a much closer analogy, one that involves precisely the effort by the majority of citizens to preserve its view of sexual morality statewide, against the efforts of a geographically concentrated and politically powerful minority to undermine it. The constitutions of the States of Arizona, Idaho, New Mexico, Oklahoma, and Utah to this day contain provisions stating that polygamy is "forever prohibited." Polygamists, and those who have a polygamous "orientation," have been "singled out" by these provisions for much more severe treatment than merely denial of favored status; and that treatment can only be changed by achieving amendment of the state constitutions. The Court's disposition today suggests that these provisions are unconstitutional, and that polygamy must be permitted in these States on a state-legislated, or perhaps even local-option, basis—unless, of course, polygamists for some reason have fewer constitutional rights than homosexuals.

The United States Congress, by the way, required the inclusion of these antipolygamy provisions in the constitutions of Arizona, New Mexico, Oklahoma, and Utah, as a condition of their admission to statehood. Thus, this "singling out" of the sexual practices of a single group for statewide, democratic vote—so utterly alien to our constitutional system, the Court would have us believe—has not only happened, but has received the explicit approval of the United States Congress.

I cannot say that this Court has explicitly approved any of these state constitutional provisions; but it has approved a territorial statutory provision that went even further, depriving polygamists of the ability even to achieve a constitutional amendment, by depriving them of the power to vote. *Davis v. Beason,* 133 U.S. 333 (1890). To the extent, if any, that this opinion permits the imposition of adverse consequences upon mere abstract advocacy of polygamy, it has of course been overruled by later cases. See *Brandenburg v. Ohio,* 395 U.S. 444 (1969) (*per curiam*). But the proposition that polygamy can be criminalized, and those engaging in that crime deprived of the vote, remains good law. *Beason* rejected the argument that "such discrimination is a denial of the equal protection of the laws." . . .

This Court cited *Beason* with approval as recently as 1993, in an opinion authored by the same Justice who writes for the Court today. That opinion said: "Adverse impact will not always lead to a finding of impermissible targeting. For example, a social harm may have been a legitimate concern of government for reasons quite apart from discrimination. . . . See, e.g., . . . *Davis v. Beason,* 133 U.S. 333 (1890)." *Church of Lukumi Babalu Aye, Inc. v. Hialeah,* 508 U.S. 520 (1993). It remains to be explained how Section 501 of the Idaho Revised Statutes was not an "impermissible targeting" of polygamists, but (the much more mild) Amendment 2 is an "impermissible targeting" of homosexuals. Has the Court concluded that the perceived social harm of polygamy is a "legiti-mate concern of government," and the perceived social harm of homosexuality is not?

I strongly suspect that the answer to the last question is yes, which leads me to the last point I wish to make: The Court today, announcing that Amendment 2 "defies . . . conventional [constitu-tional] inquiry," and "confounds [the] normal process of judicial review," employs a constitutional theory heretofore unknown to frustrate Colorado's reasonable effort to preserve traditional American moral values. The Court's stern disapproval of "animosity" towards homosexuality might be com-pared with what an earlier Court (including the revered Justices HARLAN and BRADLEY) said in *Murphy v. Ramsey*, 114 U.S. 15 (1885), rejecting a constitutional challenge to a United States statute that denied the franchise in federal territories to those who engaged in polygamous cohabitation:

> "Certainly no legislation can be supposed more wholesome and necessary in the found-ing of a free, self-governing commonwealth, fit to take rank as one of the co-ordinate States of the Union, than that which seeks to establish it on the basis of the idea of the family, as consisting in and springing from the union for life of one man and one woman in the holy estate of matrimony; the sure foundation of all that is stable and noble in our civilization; the best guaranty of that reverent morality which is the source of all benef-icent progress in social and political improvement."

I would not myself indulge in such official praise for heterosexual monogamy, because I think it no business of the courts (as opposed to the political branches) to take sides in this culture war.

But the Court today has done so, not only by inventing a novel and extravagant constitu-tional doctrine to take the victory away from traditional forces, but even by verbally disparaging as bigotry adherence to traditional attitudes. To suggest, for example, that this constitutional amendment springs from nothing more than "'a bare . . . desire to harm a politically unpopular group,'" is nothing short of insulting. (It is also nothing short of preposterous to call "politically unpopular" a group which enjoys enormous influence in American media and politics, and which, as the trial court here noted, though composing no more than 4% of the population had the sup-port of 46% of the voters on Amendment 2.)

When the Court takes sides in the culture wars, it tends to be with the knights rather than the villeins—and more specifically with the Templars, reflecting the views and values of the lawyer class from which the Court's Members are drawn. How that class feels about homosexuality will be evi-dent to anyone who wishes to interview job applicants at virtually any of the Nation's law schools. The interviewer may refuse to offer a job because the applicant is a Republican; because he is an adulterer; because he went to the wrong prep school or belongs to the wrong country club; because he eats snails; because he is a womanizer; because she wears real-animal fur; or even because he hates the Chicago Cubs. But if the interviewer should wish not to be an associate or partner of an applicant because he disapproves of the applicant's homosexuality, then he will have violated the pledge which the Association of American Law Schools requires all its member-schools to exact from job interviewers: "assurance of the employer's willingness" to hire homosexuals. This law-school view of what "prejudices" must be stamped out may be contrasted with the more plebeian attitudes that apparently still prevail in the United States Congress, which has been unresponsive to repeated attempts to extend to homosexuals the protections of federal civil rights laws, and which took the pains to exclude them specifically from the Americans With Disabilities Act of 1990.

Today's opinion has no foundation in American constitutional law, and barely pretends to. The people of Colorado have adopted an entirely reasonable provision which does not even disfavor homo-sexuals in any substantive sense, but merely denies them preferential treatment. Amendment 2 is designed to prevent piecemeal deterioration of the sexual morality favored by a majority of Coloradans, and is not only an appropriate means to that legitimate end, but a means that Americans have employed before. Striking it down is an act, not of judicial judgment, but of political will. I dissent.

CONCLUSION

This book began by reprinting a telling confession by Judge (and later Justice) Benjamin Cardozo, one of this country's most provocative legal thinkers. Cardozo had looked for certainty in the law. When he found that his search was futile, he became depressed until he discovered that at its highest levels legal reasoning doesn't discover something, it creates it. By now I trust you understand this truth: judicial opinions create things. They create more than winners and losers in particular cases. The judicial opinion creates an image of an ethical political life. All four of the opinions in the last section do that. This book has taken the position that legal reasoning, done well, necessarily creates an ethical world we cannot out of hand reject. I believe the differences in the quality of the legal reasoning in these four opinions are clear. Some are better reasoned, and hence politically more constructive, than others. Justice Scalia's opinion misrepresents key legal reasoning elements in the case. Quite apart from our political preferences about gay rights, it is hard to see how this opinion models a political conversation we would, in our time, want to have. It seems a throwback to a moralistic time, a time where a certain conviction that there is "one right way" becomes a kind of partiality, a kind of closed-mindedness that cannot accept the challenges of living in a diverse and conditional world.

Lon Fuller (p. 157) wrote that the morality of law lies in keeping the lines of communication open. Practically speaking, of course, judges render judgments. They are in business to settle disputes, and settling disputes shuts the lines of communication as far as they are concerned. But parties can appeal, and even truly final supreme court opinions in specific cases do not end the chance for further political and legal conversations. The opinions in *Romer v. Evans,* for example, hardly dispose of the question of whether the state may forbid same-sex marriages. But they do give us a sharper vocabulary for debating such a question. Should we apply a strict-scrutiny test to sexual preference discrimination? If so, does it serve a necessary purpose to prohibit people from adopting arrangements that will demand of them commitments to values, like fidelity, that our culture widely shares? There is no single objectively correct answer to this question, but legal reasoning does have a bottom line: Good legal reasoning provokes constructive conversations and spirited debates. Conversations and debates beat shooting at each other to settle differences.

ILLUSTRATIVE CASE

Professor Sanford Levinson of the University of Texas School of Law has presented his students with the following problem at the beginning of their study of constitutional law. It is the concluding piece in the long symposium on interpretation cited in this chapter.[22] How would you answer the questions he poses?

In 1970 a number of concerned citizens, worried about what they regarded as the corruption of American life, met to consider what could be done. During the course of the discussion, one of the speakers electrified the audience with the following comments:

[22]On Interpretation: The Adultery Clause of the Ten Commandments," 58 *Southern California Law Review* 719 (1985).

The cure for our ills is a return to old-time religion, and the best single guide remains the Ten Commandments. Whenever I am perplexed as to what I ought to do, I turn to the Commandments for the answer, and I am never disappointed. Sometimes I don't immediately like what I discover, but then I think more about the problem and realize how limited my perspective is compared to that of the framer of those great words. Indeed, all that is necessary is for everyone to obey the Ten Commandments, and our problems will all be solved.*

Within several hours the following plan was devised: As part of the effort to encourage a return to the "old-time religion" of the Ten Commandments, a number of young people would be asked to take an oath on their eighteenth birthday to "obey, protect, support, and defend the Ten Commandments" in all of their actions. If the person complied with the oath for seventeen years, he or she would receive an award of $10,000 on his or her thirty-fifth birthday.

The Foundation for the Ten Commandments was funded by the members of the 1970 convention, plus the proceeds of a national campaign for contributions. The speaker quoted above contributed $20 million, and an additional $30 million was collected—$15 million from the convention and $15 million from the national campaign. The interest generated by the $50 million is approximately $6 million per year. Each year since 1970, 500 persons have taken the oath. *You are appointed sole trustee of the Foundation, and your most important duty is to determine whether the oath-takers have complied with their vows and are thus entitled to the $10,000.*

It is now 1987, and the first set of claimants comes before you:

(1)   Claimant *A* is a married male. Although freely admitting that he has had sexual intercourse with a number of women other than his wife during their marriage, he brings to your attention the fact that "adultery," at the time of Biblical Israel, referred only to the voluntary intercourse of a married woman with a man other than her husband. He specifically notes the following passage from the article *Adultery,* I JEWISH ENCYCLOPEDIA 314:

> The extramarital intercourse of a married man is not *per se* a crime in biblical or later Jewish law. This distinction stems from the economic aspect of Israelite marriage: The wife as the husband's possession . . . , and adultery constituted a violation of the husband's exclusive right to her; the wife, as the husband's possession, had no such right to him.
>
> *A* has taken great care to make sure that all his sexual partners were unmarried, and thus he claims to have been faithful to the original understanding of the Ten Commandments. However we might define "adultery" today, he argues, is irrelevant. His oath was to comply with the Ten Commandments; he claims to have done so. (It is stipulated that *A*, like all the other claimants, has complied with all the other commandments; the only question involves compliance with the commandment against adultery.)
>
> Upon further questioning, you discover that no line-by-line explication of the Ten Commandments was proffered in 1970 at the time that *A* took the oath. But, says *A*, whenever a question arose in his mind as to what the Ten Commandments required of him, he made conscientious attempts to research the particular issue. He initially shared your (presumed) surprise at the results of his research, but further study indicated that all authorities agreed with the scholars who wrote the *Jewish Encyclopedia* regarding the original understanding of the Commandment.

Cf. Statement of President Ronald Reagan, Press Conference, February 21, 1985, reprinted in the *New York Times,* February 22, 1985, § 1, at 10, col. 3: "I've found that the Bible contains an answer to just about everything and every problem that confronts us, and I wonder sometimes why we won't recognize that one Book could solve a lot of problems for us." [note in original]

(2) Claimant *B* is *A*'s wife, who admits that she has had extramarital relationships with other men. She notes, though, that these affairs were entered into with the consent of her husband. In response to the fact that she undoubtedly violated the ancient understanding of "adultery," she states that that understanding is fatally outdated:

(a) It is unfair to distinguish between the sexual rights of males and females. That the Israelites were outrageously sexist is no warrant for your maintaining the discrimination.

(b) Moreover, the reason for the differentiation, as already noted, was the perception of the wife as property. That notion is a repugnant one that has been properly repudiated by all rational thinkers, including all major branches of the Judeo-Christian religious tradition historically linked to the Ten Commandments.

(c) She further argues that, insofar as the modern prohibition of adultery is defensible, it rests on the ideal of discouraging deceit and the betrayal of promises of sexual fidelity. But these admittedly negative factors are not present in her case because she had scrupulously informed her husband and received his consent, as required by their marriage contract outlining the terms of their "open marriage."

(It turns out, incidentally, that *A* had failed to inform his wife of at least one of his sexual encounters. Though he freely admits that this constitutes a breach of the contract he had made with *B*, he nevertheless returns to his basic argument about original understanding, which makes consent irrelevant.)

(3) *C*, a male (is this relevant?), is the participant in a bigamous marriage. *C* has had no sexual encounters beyond his two wives. (He also points out that bigamy was clearly tolerated in both pre- and post-Sinai Israel and indeed was accepted within the Yemenite community of Jews well into the twentieth century. It is also accepted in a variety of world cultures.)

(4) *D*, a practicing Christian, admits that he has often lusted after women other than his wife. (Indeed, he confesses as well that it was only after much contemplation that he decided not to sexually consummate a relationship with a co-worker whom he thinks he "may love" and with whom he has held hands.) You are familiar with Christ's words, *Matthew* 5:28: "Whosoever looketh on a woman to lust after, he hath committed adultery with her already in his heart." (Would it matter to you if *D* were the wife, who had lusted after other men?)

(5) Finally, claimant *E* has never even lusted after another woman since his marriage on the same day he took his oath. He does admit, however, to occasional lustful fantasies about his wife, *G*, a Catholic, and is shocked when informed of Pope John Paul II's statement that "adultery in your heart is committed not only when you look with concupiscence at a woman who is not your wife, but also if you look in the same manner at your wife." The Pope's rationale apparently is that all lust, even that directed toward a spouse, dehumanizes and reduces the other person "to an erotic object."

Which, if any, of the claimants should get the $10,000? (Remember, *all* can receive the money if you determine that they have fulfilled their oaths.) What is your duty as Trustee in determining your answer to this question?

More particularly, is it your duty to decide what the best *single* understanding of "adultery" is, regarding the Ten Commandments, and then match the behavior against that understanding? If that is your duty, how would you go about arriving at such an understanding? You may object to the emphasis that is being placed on *your* deciding. Instead, you might wish to argue that someone else, whether a discrete person or an authoritative institution, has the capacity to decide, and your role is simply to enforce that understanding. This argument is certainly possible. To whom, though, would you look to for such authoritative resolution?

Is it possible that your duty, rather than seeking the best single definition of adultery, is instead to assess the plausibility of the various claims placed before you? That is, are there several acceptable answers to the question of what constitutes adultery? Is it enough that you find an argument plausible even though you personally reject it as ultimately mistaken? That is, *you* might not have behaved as did a given claimant, considering *your* understanding of "adultery," but does this automatically translate into the legitimate rejection of someone else's claim to have remained faithful to the Commandment?

Is the "sincerity" or "good faith" with which an argument is made relevant? Would it make a difference to you, in *A*'s case, whether he had researched the original understanding of the Commandment *after* he had engaged in his liaisons? What if he had learned about ancient Israel only a week before, after consulting the best lawyer in town who will receive one-fourth of the $10,000 as a contingency fee should you award the money to *A*?

Let us stipulate that you deny the $10,000 award to *A*, *B*, and *D*, who promptly race to the nearest courthouse and sue you in your capacity as Trustee. They claim that you have violated your duty to enforce in good faith the terms of the Foundation's contract with the oath-takers. You may further assume that there are no special contract problems involved: the court determines that an enforceable contract was created by taking the oath and by the oath-takers' detrimental reliance on the Foundation's promise to award the money in return for the expected behavior. *D* testified, for example, that one reason for his painful decision not to consummate the affair was his family's need for the $10,000. The only question before the court, therefore, is who breached the contract, the claimants or you.

What questions should the court ask in reaching its decision? How, if at all, do they differ from the questions you have asked as Trustee? Is it the task of the court to determine whether you "got it right" as to what "adultery" means, or is it sufficient that you attempted to fulfill your duties conscientiously and that your views are plausible, even if the court might disagree with you? If you choose the latter alternative, consider the following (possible) paradox: If *your* position should be upheld because of your good-faith belief in a plausible view, independently of the court's agreement with you, how can you justify not applying a similar test in regard to the claimants? . . .

FOR FURTHER THOUGHT

1. The extent to which the elements of an argument harmonize is rarely a binary, "do or don't" proposition. How well the parts of an argument fit together is a matter of degree and perception; different people will see different qualities in arguments. There is no "right answer" to the adultery problem, which is just the point. However, sometimes situations arise when a particularly striking and obvious misfit takes place. When it does, we know that decisions are based on power, not on reason. In one such example, the Georgia attorney general's office revoked the hiring of a recent law graduate when she announced her plans to wed another woman. The attorney general, Michael Bowers, said his office withdrew the employment offer "to insure public perception" that the office enforced the law. But Georgia's sodomy law, passed in the 1830s, makes criminal sexual behaviors commonly engaged in by heterosexual couples that society today regards as entirely normal. Georgia does *not* enforce this reading of the sodomy laws, so the event of any heterosexual marriage would send exactly the same legal signal that the lesbian marriage did.[23]

[23]See "Judge Affirms Suit by Lesbian in Rights Case." *New York Times*, March 11, 1992. p. A12. However, in an extraordinary Georgia sexual assault case, a trial judge instructed a jury that it could bring in a conviction of sodomy after the defendant described having voluntary oral sex with the complainant, his own wife. The jury acquitted all sexual assault charges, but—even though not originally charged with sodomy—it

2. The U.S. Congress passed (and President Clinton signed on February 8, 1996) the "Communications Decency Act," which provided in part that any person in interstate or foreign commerce who,

> by means of a telecommunications device . . . knowingly . . . makes, creates, or solicits [and] initiates the transmission [of] any comment, request, suggestion, proposal, image, or other communication which is obscene or indecent, knowing that the recipient of the communication is under 18 years of age . . . shall be criminally fined or imprisoned.

The American Civil Liberties Union filed a suit against Attorney General Janet Reno to enjoin enforcing the law the day the president signed the bill. The American Library Association filed suit before the month was out. The federal district court (trial court) for the Eastern District of Pennsylvania held this statute unconstitutional on June 11, 1996. Here is the opening of District Judge Dalzell's opinion. Apply the three questions posed for you about the opinions in *Romer* (pp. 164, above) to this excerpt. I recommend the entire opinion to those concerned with the issue of censorship on the Internet, as well as for those looking for an example of a particularly well-reasoned opinion. On June 26, 1997, the U.S. Supreme Court also struck down this provision of the statute.[24]

> I begin with first principles: As a general rule, the Constitution forbids the Government from silencing speakers because of their particular message. *R.A.V. v. City of Saint Paul*, 505 U.S. 377, 381–82 (1992). "Our political system and cultural life rest upon this ideal." *Turner Broadcasting Sys. v. FCC*, 114 S.Ct. 2445 (1994). This general rule is subject only to "narrow and well-understood exceptions". Id. A law that, as here, regulates speech on the basis of its content, is "presumptively invalid." *R.A.V.*, 505 U.S. at 381–82.

> Two of the exceptions to this general rule deal with obscenity (commonly understood to include so-called hardcore pornography), *Miller v. California*, 413 U.S. 15 (1973), and child pornography, *New York v. Ferber*, 458 U.S. 747 (1982). The Government can and does punish with criminal sanction people who engage in these forms of speech. . . . Indeed, the Government could punish these forms of speech on the Internet even without the CDA. E.g., *United States v. Thomas*, 74 F.3d 701, 704–05 (6th Cir.1995) (affirming obscenity convictions for the operation of a computer bulletin board).

> The Government could also completely ban obscenity and child pornography from the Internet. No Internet speaker has a right to engage in these forms of speech, and no Internet listener has a right to receive them. Child pornography and obscenity have "no constitutional protection, and the government may ban [them] outright in certain media, or in all." *Alliance for Community Media v. FCC*, 56 F. 3d. 105, 112 (D.C.Cir. 1995).

> The cases before us, however, are not about obscenity or child pornography. Plaintiffs in these actions claim no right to engage in these forms of speech in the future, nor does the Government intimate that plaintiffs have engaged in these forms of speech in the past.

---

brought in a sodomy conviction based on his testimony. The trial judge sentenced the defendant to two years imprisonment on the sodomy charge. The trial judge displayed an extremely mechanistic view of law when the explained his decision to interviewers this way: "It's on the law books. It's a criminal offense. I'm sworn to uphold the laws of the state of Georgia." "ACLU Eyes Test Case of Man Convicted of Sodomy with Wife," *Atlanta Journal and Constitution* August 2. 1989, p. A1.

[24]*Reno v. ACLU*, 65 U.S.L.W. 4715 (1997).

This case is about "indecency," as that word has come to be understood since the Supreme Court's decisions in *FCC v. Pacifica Foundation*, 438 U.S. 726 (1978), and *Sable Communications v. FCC*, 492 U.S. 115 (1989). The legal difficulties in these actions arise because of the special place that indecency occupies in the Supreme Court's First Amendment jurisprudence. While adults have a First Amendment right to engage in indecent speech . . . the Supreme Court has also held that the Government may, consistent with the Constitution, regulate indecency on radio and television, and in the "dial-a-porn" context, as long as the regulation does not operate as a complete ban. Thus, any regulation of indecency in these areas must give adults access to indecent speech, which is their right.

The Government may only regulate indecent speech for a compelling reason, and in the least restrictive manner. *Sable*, 492 U.S. at 126. . . . "It is not enough to show that the Government's ends are compelling; the means must be carefully tailored to achieve those ends." Id. This "most exacting scrutiny," *Turner*, 114 S.Ct. at 2459, requires the Government to "demonstrate that the recited harms are real, not merely conjectural, and that the regulation will in fact alleviate these harms in a direct and material way." *United States v. National Treasury Employees Union* . . . 115 S.Ct. 1003, 1017, 130 L.Ed.2d 964 (1995) (citing *Turner* . . . 114 S.Ct. at 1017). Thus, although our analysis here must balance ends and means, the scales tip at the outset in plaintiffs' favor. This is so because "[r]egulations which permit the Government to discriminate on the basis of the content of the message cannot be tolerated under the First Amendment." *Simon & Schuster, Inc. v. Members of the New York State Crime Victims Board*, 502 U.S. 105 (1991). . . .

3. What characterizes a good lawyer? Stewart Macaulay has reviewed some empirical studies showing how lawyers define and differentiate their status and prestige within the profession. See "Law Schools and the World Outside Their Doors."[25] But my question concerns skill, not status. What is the essence of this skill? In addition to the several answers this chapter has already provided, consider the following passage. It is from an essay titled "Thomas More's Skill."

Skill, character and knowledge. This lawyer skill is not a matter of principles. Lawyers use legal principles, but they use them more to garnish their work than to carry it out. Lawyers, when being candid, admit scant regard for legal principles. Nonlawyers may think that lawyers disdain principles, or that we disdain the idea of government under law. But the lawyer thinks of legal principles as something to be taken apart and made to fit the client's needs. The lawyer thinks this work *is* government under law. Principles and facts are the lawyer's raw materials. What is sacred in the law is not legal principles. The sacred thing in the law, to a lawyer, is the fact that those who have power are bound to respect skill and knowledge in the wielding of power—skill and knowledge even among those who merely wield power, who do not have it. This is, at last, we think, the political side of a respect for *character*. With regard to what is *legal*, principles come last. Thomas More understood that. He lived it. It was important to him. Bolt understands that; it is part of the reason he thinks that More's life might stand up as an illustration of the courage to preserve one's soul—one's unbudgeable self—in the modern world.[26]

---

[25]32 *Journal of Legal Education* 506 (1982).

[26]Thomas Shaffer. *On Being a Christian and a Lawyer, supra.* Chapter 18 (written in collaboration with Stanley Hauerwas), p. 195.

Introduction to Legal Procedure and Terminology

Here is a relatively short but complete judicial opinion. This "case of the stolen airplane" made a brief appearance in Chapter 1 and plays a more important analytical role in Chapter 3. At the end of the case, this appendix introduces you to most of the more common terms of judicial organization and procedure, using the case to illustrate each term as it arises.

THE CASE

McBoyle v. United States
Supreme Court of the United States
283 U.S. 25 (1931)

Mr. Justice HOLMES delivered the opinion of the Court.

The petitioner was convicted of transporting from Ottawa, Illinois, to Guymon, Oklahoma, an airplane that he knew to have been stolen, and was sentenced to serve three years' imprisonment and to pay a fine of $2,000. The judgment was affirmed by the Circuit Court of Appeals for the Tenth Circuit. 43 F.(2d) 273. A writ of *certiorari* was granted by this Court on the question whether the National Motor Vehicle Theft Act applies to aircraft. Act of October 29, 1919, c. 89, 41 Stat. 324, U.S. Code, title 18, § 408. That Act provides: "Sec. 2. That when used in this Act: (a) The term 'motor vehicle' shall include an automobile, automobile truck, automobile wagon, motor cycle, or any other self-propelled vehicle not designed for running on rails. . . . Sec. 3. That whoever shall transport or cause to be transported in interstate or foreign commerce a motor vehicle, knowing the same to have been stolen, shall be punished by a fine of not more than $5,000, or by imprisonment of not more than five years, or both."

Section 2 defines the motor vehicles of which the transportation in interstate commerce is punished in Section 3. The question is the meaning of the word "vehicle" in the phrase "any other self-propelled vehicle not designed for running on rails." No doubt etymologically it is possible to use the word to signify a conveyance working on land, water, or air, and sometimes legislation extends the use in that direction, e.g., land and air, water being separately provided for, in the Tariff Act, September 21, 1922, c. 356, § 401 (b), 42 Stat. 858, 948. But in everyday speech "vehicle" calls up the picture of a thing moving on land. Thus in Rev. St. § 4, intended, the Government suggests, rather to enlarge than to restrict the definition, vehicle includes every contrivance capable of being used "as a means of transportation on land." And this is repeated, expressly excluding aircraft, in the Tariff Act, June 17, 1930, c. 497, § 401 (b), 46 Stat. 590, 708. So here, the phrase under discussion calls up the popular picture. For after including automobile truck, automobile wagon, and motor cycle, the words "any other self-propelled vehicle not designed for running on rails" still indicate that a vehicle in the popular sense, that is a vehicle running on land, is the theme. It is a vehicle that runs, not something, not commonly called a vehicle, that flies. Airplanes were well known in 1919 when this statute was passed, but it is admitted that they were not mentioned in the reports or in the debates in Congress. It is impossible to read words that so carefully enumerate the different forms of motor vehicles and have no reference of any kind to aircraft, as including airplanes under a term that usage more and more precisely confines to a different class. The counsel for the petitioner have shown that the phraseology of the statute as to motor vehicles follows that of earlier statutes of Connecticut, Delaware, Ohio, Michigan, and Missouri, not to mention the late Regulations of Traffic for the District of Columbia, title 6, c. 9, § 242, none of which can be supposed to leave the earth.

Although it is not likely that a criminal will carefully consider the text of the law before he murders or steals, it is reasonable that a fair warning should be given to the world in language that the common world will understand, of what the law intends to do if a certain line is passed. To make the warning fair, so far as possible the line should be clear. When a rule of conduct is laid down in words that evoke in the common mind only the picture of vehicles moving on land, the statute should not be extended to aircraft simply because it may seem to us that a similar policy applies, or upon the speculation that if the legislature had thought of it, very likely broader words would have been used. *United States v. Bhagat Singh Thind*, 261 U.S. 204, 209, 43 S.Ct. 338.

Judgment reversed.

LEGAL TERMS

When a person feels disappointed by the result a court reaches in a lawsuit in which they are a **party,** they may (unless the highest court has already heard their case) **appeal** to a higher court. In an appeal the **appellant** (the party taking the appeal up) argues that the lower court judge interpreted and applied the law of the case erroneously. Appeals do not reopen the facts of the case or consider new testimony or evidence. Appeals are limited to questions about whether the lower court reasoned well about the legal issues in the case. In *McBoyle,* the appellant (Mr. McBoyle) argued successfully that the lower courts wrongly interpreted the National Motor Vehicle Theft Act to include airplanes. Thus in this case the **appellee,** the U.S. government, lost in the "court of last resort."

In this and all cases, the initial **plaintiff** (in this case the United States) must prove it has a **cause of action.** That is, the plaintiff must find some official legal text somewhere that says that what the initial **defendant** (McBoyle) did was wrong. A cause of action clearly exists in this case, since McBoyle obviously helped transport something stolen. But not all harms are legal causes of action. If, for example, I wear an offensively ugly necktie to class and a student sues me for the pain he suffers at having to stare at rank ugliness for 50 minutes, he will lose because no legal text makes such an offense **actionable.** Note, however, that the student can sue me. The interesting question in the legal system is never "Can I sue?" (The answer is always *yes*. All it takes to sue is to fill out the appropriate forms and pay the appropriate fees at a courthouse.) The question is whether the court will have some reason to throw the suit out without hearing its merits. If an official legal text made recovery actionable for the tort of having to look at ugly neckties, then the plaintiff might recover money **damages** from me or might win a court **injunction** in which a court would order me never to wear such a tie again.[1]

A cause of action existed in *McBoyle* because the plaintiff, in this case the United States government, could claim that the defendant, Mr. McBoyle, violated a legal rule enacted by Congress: the National Motor Vehicle Theft Act. No statutes, common law cases, or bureaucratic regulations protect against the hurt we call embarrassment, so embarrassment does not constitute a legal cause of action. There are, however, common law rules of negligence. If I wear a combination of pants, jacket, and necktie that causes a student of mine to have a severe seizure, if that student then explains to me the problem and asks me not to wear that combination again, and if I then forget and cause a second seizure requiring medical attention, the rules of negligence would give my student a cause of action against me.

The legal system normally classifies legal actions as either **civil** or **criminal.** As long as we don't think about it too much, we think we know the difference: In a criminal case like McBoyle's a governmental official—**a prosecutor**—has the responsibility for filing complaints for violations of laws that authorize the judge to impose a punishment—usually fine, imprisonment, or both—on behalf of the polity. *McBoyle* is a criminal case, prosecuted by a U.S. Attorney working for the U.S. Department of Justice, because the National Motor Vehicle Theft Act prescribes a punishment for those convicted under it.

In a civil case, on the other hand, the plaintiff seeks a judicial decision that will satisfy him personally. Civil remedies usually consist of a court award of money damages to compensate for harm already done or of a court order commanding the defendant to stop doing (or threatening to do) something injurious.

In practice these distinctions between civil and criminal actions tend to break down. Units of government, acting as civil plaintiffs, may file lawsuits to enforce policies that benefit the entire country. The United States government does so when it files civil antitrust actions. A private citizen may file and win a civil rights complaint in which the judge imposes "punitive damages" on defendants. Then damages awarded can far exceed the harm the plaintiff actually experienced. (See *BMW v. Gore,* p. 143.)

Occasionally in public debate we here talk about "decriminalizing" some form of behavior. To decriminalize something does not automatically legalize it. In 1996 there was considerable discussion about decriminalizing physician-assisted suicide. To do so would prevent prosecutors from seeking criminal convictions of physicians who assist others who are terminally ill to take their own lives. However, civil remedies might remain in place, so that surviving family members might still bring successful civil lawsuits against doctors for the tort of wrongful death, particularly in the event that the deceased may not have made a fully knowing and voluntary decision to end his or her

---

[1]For a thorough (and dramatic) description of the details of litigation at the trial level, see Jonathan Harr, *A Civil Action* (New York: Random House, 1995).

life. When a legal issue is civil rather than criminal, the rules of evidence change significantly. For example, in the civil trial brought against O. J. Simpson for wrongful death by the heirs of Ron Goldman and Nicole Brown, Mr. Simpson could not refuse to testify. Double jeopardy protections apply only to defendants in criminal cases, and Simpson no longer faced criminal prosecution for these deaths.

The kind of rule on which a lawsuit is based very much shapes the **evidence** that the parties introduce in trial. We can, for example, imagine that when the owner of the airplane McBoyle transported got it back, he found that it needed $1000 of repairs. The owner of the plane might file a civil suit against McBoyle seeking to recover damages from McBoyle to pay for the repairs plus the damage the owner suffered by not having use of his vehicle. At this imaginary trial, McBoyle's lawyers might try to introduce evidence that the airplane needed the repairs before McBoyle transported it. In the actual criminal case, however, the facts at issue and the evidence presented are completely different. The evidentiary questions at this trial might wrestle with whether McBoyle knew the plane was stolen. In the actual criminal trial, McBoyle denied any involvement, but the trial court found that he had hired a Mr. Lacey to steal the airplane directly from the manufacturer and fly it to Oklahoma. The jury found that McBoyle paid Lacey over $300 to do so. See *McBoyle v. United States*, 43 F. (2d) 273 (1930).

The four elements of legal reasoning introduced in Chapter 1 include two kinds of facts about which lawyers and judges may reason. One set of facts we may call the facts of the dispute at issue between the parties. These are events and observations that the people in the lawsuit must either prove or disprove through their evidence to prevail at trial. Thus the United States government had to prove that McBoyle knew the plane he transported was indeed stolen. These facts are settled one way or the other by the **trier of fact:** a jury or a judge sitting without a jury. (Jury trials are longer and more costly than "bench trials." The large majority of lawsuits filed are in fact settled by negotiation without any trial, and most trial court proceedings take place without juries.)

A second kind of fact, which I have labeled "social background facts," also influences legal reasoning. In *McBoyle*, the court, including the trial judge, must interpret the word "vehicle" in this statute so as to decide whether it covers airplanes. Social background facts help decide that question: How common were airplanes when Congress passed the statute in 1919? Did congressional debates discuss and reject the idea of including the word "airplanes" in the statute? What social problem prompted busy Congress members to pass the National Motor Vehicle Theft Act? Every state had laws prohibiting theft. Why, historically, was a national law about stealing and transporting motor vehicles necessary in 1919?

Notice that, unlike the facts at issue between the parties, these social background issues have no direct connection with the parties at all. They do not have to be proved at trial. Sometimes lawyers at trial will address them, but just as often these factual issues will arise only on appeal, where the lawyers will argue them orally or in their written briefs. Furthermore, judges are free to research such issues on their own or through their clerks with no help from the parties before them, and base their legal conclusions on them. Often the social background facts appear only implicitly in the opinion. They are the judge's hunches about the way the world works that we can only infer from what the judge does say. Every appellate opinion reviewed in these pages rests on such explicit or implicit hunch assertions.

In addition to the requirement of a cause of action, litigants must meet a number of other procedural requirements before courts will decide their case "on the merits." For our purposes we may divide these procedures into requirements for **jurisdiction** and **justiciability.**

"Jurisdiction" prescribes the legal authority of a court to decide the case at all. More specifically, a court must have (a) **jurisdiction over the subject matter** and (b) **jurisdiction over the person** before it can decide. Neither of these requirements is terribly mysterious. Subject matter jurisdiction refers to the fact that all courts are set up by statutes that authorize the court to decide some kinds of legal issues but not others. A local "traffic court" has jurisdiction to hear only a small subset of cases: criminal traffic violations. State probate courts hear issues about the wills and estates of the deceased. The federal court system has a variety of specialized courts, such as the United States Customs Court and the United States Court of International Trade. In both federal and state judicial systems, some courts have statutory authority to hear a broad scope of cases. These are called courts of "general jurisdiction." The U.S. District Court and (in most states) state "superior courts" serve as the trial courts in which most serious lawsuits begin. The U.S. District Court for the Western District of Oklahoma is such a court, and it therefore had subject matter jurisdiction to try the criminal case against McBoyle.

Jurisdiction over the person refers to the fact that agents of a court must catch the defendant and serve him with the papers notifying him that a suit has been filed against him before the court can enter a judgment against him. The agents who "serve process" on defendants—sheriffs in the states and U.S. marshalls in the federal system—only have authority to find people and serve notice on them within the geographic territory the court governs. A sheriff working for a Superior Court in Georgia cannot serve someone who lives in Alabama unless the sheriff can catch the person (or attach land of his) in Georgia. This jurisdiction over the person is sometimes called "territorial jurisdiction."[2]

McBoyle's case raises an interesting problem of jurisdiction over the person. Federal law requires that defendants be tried in the district where the crime was committed. McBoyle claimed that because he never flew the airplane, or left Illinois for that matter, he could not have committed a crime in the Western District of Oklahoma, Mr. Lacey's destination. The U.S. Court of Appeals for the Tenth Circuit rejected that argument, saying that the crime ran with the airplane, and that the crime was committed in Oklahoma, even if McBoyle wasn't in Oklahoma at the time. See 43 F. (2d) 273 at 275 (1930).

Most courts in the United States possess authority to decide what the U.S. Constitution (in Article III) calls "cases" and "controversies." Over the years this phrase has become synonymous with a genuinely adversarial contest in which plaintiff and defendant desire truly different outcomes. Judges cannot initiate lawsuits. They respond to the initiatives taken by the litigants.

Rules of **justiciability** ensure that judges decide true adversary contests. These rules serve three functions: (a) To avoid wasting judicial time and resources on minor matters; (b) to improve the quality of information that reaches them by hearing different points

---

[2]Courts are just beginning to wrestle with the problems of jurisdiction presented by legal conflicts that arise in cyberspace. See "Trying to Resolve Jurisdictional Rules on the Internet" *New York Times,* April 14, 1997, p. B1.

of view; (c) to justify refusing to decide politically delicate cases that might damage the courts' political popularity.

Thus courts generally refuse to hear **moot** cases, cases in which the harm the plaintiff tried to prevent never happened or, for whatever reasons, cannot happen in the future. Plaintiffs must have **standing,** which means that the plaintiff must be among those directly injured (or directly threatened) by the defendant's actions. To illustrate, in 1996 federal courts held that the city seal of Edmond, Oklahoma, violated the Constitution because it contained a Christian cross. The plaintiffs in that case, Unitarian and Jewish residents of Edmond, argued successfully that their very membership in a community with a religious symbol directly injured them enough to have standing to sue. **Exhaustion** requires that plaintiffs exploit their primary opportunities for settling a case, especially through bureaucratic channels, before going to court, and **ripeness** requires that the defendant actually threaten what the plaintiff fears. Thus, partly to avoid getting itself in hot political water, the U.S. Supreme Court at first refused to consider the constitutionality of Connecticut's laws against distribution and use of birth control devices. It insisted that Connecticut wasn't bothering to enforce these laws and that therefore the case wasn't ripe. No justiciability problems arose in *McBoyle.*

McBoyle's case reached the U.S. Supreme Court in this fashion: The trial court found McBoyle guilty. (In criminal cases the trial court expresses its **disposition** in terms of guilt and innocence. Civil dispositions find defendant "liable" or "not liable.") McBoyle appealed, and the Court of Appeals, ruling on both the jurisdictional claim and the statutory interpretation claim, **affirmed** (upheld) the trial court's decisions on these two matters of law. McBoyle appealed again, and the U.S. Supreme Court **reversed.**

CREDITS

The author gratefully acknowledges permission to quote material from the following sources.

INDEX

INDEX OF CASES

Boldface page numbers indicate pages on which a significant excerpt from an opinion in the case begins. All other page numbers denote in-text case references. This index excludes cases of minor significance—cases, for example, cited only within other quoted cases and secondary citations, particularly in footnotes.